LF

EXPLORATIONS IN
Time-Limited Counseling
and Psychotherapy

GUIDANCE AND COUNSELING SERIES

Roger A. Myers, Consulting Editor

CHARLES J. GELSO AND DEBORAH HAZEL JOHNSON

Explorations in Time-Limited
Counseling and Psychotherapy

CONTRIBUTORS

Diane M. Adelstein

Janet Lynn Cornfeld

Christine A. Courtois

Fay H. Dworkin

James R. Haws

Marilyn V. Keilson

Daniel S. McKitrick

Jacque Moss Miller

David H. Mills

Judy P. Pelham

Kathryn G. Reed

Phyliss Elayne Riddle

Sharon Baron Spiegel

Daniel Wasserman

Jean P. Whittaker

EXPLORATIONS IN
Time-Limited
Counseling and
Psychotherapy

**Charles J. Gelso
and
Deborah Hazel Johnson**

Teachers College, Columbia University
NEW YORK AND LONDON   1983

Published by Teachers College Press, 1234 Amsterdam Avenue,
New York, New York 10027

Library of Congress Cataloging in Publication Data

Main entry under title:

Explorations in time-limited counseling and psychotherapy.

(Guidance and counseling series)
Includes bibliographical references and index.
Contents: The effectiveness of time-limited therapy in a university counseling center / by Marilyn V. Keilson, Fay H. Dworkin & Charles J. Gelso —
Clients' and counselors' reactions to time-limited and time-unlimited counseling / by Charles J. Gelso, Sharon Baron Spiegel & David H. Mills — The
change process following time-limited therapy / by Diane M. Adelstein . . . et
al. — [etc.]

1. Psychotherapy, Brief—Addresses, essays, lectures. I. Gelso, Charles
J., 1941-   II. Johnson, Deborah Hazel, 1951-   III. Series.
[DNLM: 1. Counseling. 2. Psychotherapy, Brief. WM 420 E96]
RC480.55.E95 1982   616.89'14   82-6032
ISBN 0-8077-2726-1

Manufactured in the United States of America
87 86 85 84 83   1 2 3 4 5 6

Dedication

To Jean and Ted, our respective spouses,
who provided us with time-unlimited
patience, love, and intellectual stimulation
throughout this project.

Contents

PART ONE
The Outcomes of Time-Limited Counseling and Psychotherapy

PART TWO

Client and Therapist Factors Influencing the Outcomes of Time-Limited Therapy

PART THREE

Expectancies and Process of Time-Limited Therapy

PART FOUR

Conclusion

Tables

Figure

Foreword

In the early 1950s, Horace B. English was fond of saying in class that "The psychology of learning is the psychology of rats and college students—treated as if they were rats." Prof. English was, we all inferred, inveighing against the dominance of Clark Hull's notions and research strategies which, at that time, seemed to be overshadowing more cognitively oriented ways of trying to understand learning. No doubt he was also making his wry joke about the legions of subjects in Psych. 101 who were eager to "volunteer" to face the memory drum in order to avoid failing the course.

So sensitized, my (now hoary) classmates and I have frequently marveled at the paradoxical fact that structured observation of the student-subject has been such an important part of psychological inquiry in the psychology of learning, in experimental social psychology, in differential psychology, and so on, but has been so perversely ignored in the research and scholarship about counseling and psychotherapy. Specifically, the work issuing from university counseling centers has been consistently undervalued, when it has been regarded at all, by investigators of the talking cure.

For example: Williamson and Darley's early work on diagnosis and Bordin and Pepinsky's elegant refinement thereof never found their way into the mainstream literature on diagnosis. Robinson's decades of research on content analysis of counseling center interviews—which, some say, led the way for Rogers's Chicago era research—is scarcely mentioned when naturalistic observation of therapy process is the issue. When therapy outcome is the issue, the pioneering contributions of Williamson and Bordin are seldom recognized; the ambition and success of Campbell's 25-year follow-up of counseled college students is hardly known; the impressive success of Volsky, Magoon, Norman, and Hoyt in conquering the difficulties of agency cooperation and management problems in outcome research go largely unnoticed. Kell and Mueller's insights about the change process and about the difficulties of supervision are similarly neglected.

Is it that counseling and psychotherapy in the college setting is so unique that what we learn by skillfully observing such an enterprise is of no value to the clinic, the hospital, and the private consulting room? It seems unlikely, and especially so when the problems of interest are problems of inquiry. What seems more likely is that scholars and researchers who sincerely assert that "the differences between counseling and psychotherapy will be disregarded for the purposes of this review," usually excuse themselves from surveying both zones of literature with equal vigor.

Gelso, Johnson, and their colleagues do not seem likely to be ignored, despite the fact that their observations took place in a university counseling service. Time-limited treatment is a timely issue and one that has not been addressed frequently or recently. Especially rare is their dogged investigation of the phenomenon that will serve as a model for inquiry about counseling and psychotherapy, be it time limited or not. Despite the rigor of the studies and the caution of the investigators, a discernible set of prescriptions for using a time-limited treatment strategy has emerged. Better yet, the links between the findings and the prescriptions are carefully identified.

In addition there are other prescriptions to be found in this book, some so subtle that readers might benefit from being forewarned. Carefully stitched into the fabric of the book is a delicate thread that connects agency policy (try to reduce the waiting time), therapist's prerogative (what kind of treatment for which client?), and persuasion (on what kind of evidence are the decisions made?). Equally implicit is the strategy for a collaborative and integrated research program, the impossible dream of so many inquiring practitioners. Thinly veiled is a deep concern for the unintended consequences of successful time-limited treatment on the counselors and therapists, that is, concern about what might happen to the helper if he or she stimulates the process of facilitative change but is not permitted the psychic pay of seeing that process evolve.

These issues and many more are identified and illuminated in this volume. All deserve the attention and careful consideration of incumbents of and aspirants to the helping professions.

—Roger A. Myers

Acknowledgments

Writing an acknowledgment section for a book such as this is unusually difficult. The research we describe spanned several years, and so many people made important and helpful contributions. There is a fear of forgetting someone, or perhaps even worse, of not making clear just how much we appreciate the contributions of others.

Above all, we would like to thank colleagues at the University Counseling Center, University of Maryland, College Park. These colleagues provided the kind of intellectual climate that facilitated the conduct of research and writing, in addition to engendering thoughtful clinical practice. We have the clear impression that the level of intellectual and clinical stimulation, particularly when combined with a high degree of respect for empirical research, was rather extraordinary at the Center during the time of this research. The tone was probably set by Drs. Thomas Magoon and David Mills, the Director and Assistant Director, Counseling Division, respectively. Both these individuals showed that they valued our work, and perhaps as important and unusual, followed through with such practical necessities as release time from clinical duties, clerical aid, and other assistance. Tom Magoon, in our view, represents the rare administrator who places a premium on empirical data as a means of answering clinical and agency questions. Dave Mills, in particular, was a supportive boss, a research collaborator, and a friend, all in one package.

We do not want to make it appear that the Center was composed of an encouraging and dominant administration who supported our research and a staff that simply followed. Few things could be further from the truth. Indeed, the professional staff, surely very high on autonomy needs, contributed greatly and enthusiastically to the various research studies. There were points at which staff members who were not directly involved in the research made contributions to questions of methodology and practical implementation, for example, how to accommodate the research demands in such areas as random assignment of clients to treatments. At the most elementary level, the staff helped enormously (with only a little prodding from the researchers) by completing our many questionnaires, performing time-limited therapy (for example) when that was called for by the research, and so on. Our deep appreciation goes to Drs. Janice Birk, Vivian Boyd, Stanley Hunt, Jessy Leonard, James McKenzie, Yvonne McMullan, Arnold Medvene, Stanley Pavey, Shirley Pumroy, Philip Ray, Brenda Sigall, Mary Faith Tanney, and Franklin Westbrook. Former interns who served as counselors for the project reported in Chapters 2 and 4 are Drs. Susan Bennett, Margaret Bonz, Martha Kazlo, Howard Silverman, and Bruce Wine.

We would also like to acknowledge the monumental typing job of Diane Lewis, Amina Adam, and Deloris Holmes. Deloris Holmes's affection and friendly abuse while typing and retyping the chapters made the drudgery of this stage of the work, thankfully, a bit lighter. Nona Kuhlman deserves a special vote of thanks for her great patience and wisdom. She, with only the most modest complaint, was responsible for the keypunching and data analysis of the bulk of the research. Her personal qualities were invaluable (and a great relief to us) when the entire data for the study reported in Chapters 2 and 4 had to be fully and meticulously re-analyzed. The computing time and facilities were generously provided by the University of Maryland Computer Science Center.

The real *sine qua non* of the book, however, was our population of clients. Although they must remain nameless, their participation in the various stages of the research cannot be forgotten. We are most grateful for their willingness to assist us in the research at the very time that they were seeking assistance.

During the writing stage of the book, one of us (DHJ) moved to the Baltimore County campus of the University of Maryland. There, the psychological support and release time given by Dr. Scott Rickard, Vice Chancellor for Student Affairs, and Dr. Warwick Troy, Counseling Center Director, were of great help in the completion of the book.

Drs. Jean Carter, Bruce Fretz, Clara Hill, and Sharon Spiegel all read our final chapter and provided extremely helpful comments and suggestions. Jean Carter deserves special thanks for doing likewise for four additional chapters.

We also are most appreciative of the help from the Teachers College Press staff. Dr. Roger Myers, Series Editor, deserves much thanks for his enthusiasm about the manuscript, beginning with our initial contact with the Press. Carol Napier, Executive Editor, and Esther Luckett, Editor, have provided us with extremely competent assistance in preparing the manuscript and have been most responsive to our questions. One could not have asked for a more pleasant group of publishing professionals.

Finally, for those of us who are fortunate, there are people who are available during certain critical times in our lives to provide the kinds of human nourishment that allow later accomplishments, viz., the thinking, researching, and writing in this book. One of us (CJG) would like to acknowledge, with warmth and appreciation, Carolyn Marianacci, Joseph Osticco, and Dr. J. Alfred McCauslin, who, each in his or her own way, made the current work possible. Similarly, for the other of us (DHJ), the foundations for this work were laid over the years by Irene M. Johnson, James H. Johnson, Elmer Horsky, and Dr. Robert Warehime. We are indebted to these people for their important and personal contributions.

Introduction

This book presents a series of field and laboratory investigations aimed at examining the effects of brief, time-limited counseling and psychotherapy in a university counseling center. Additionally, the researches discussed in the book seek to uncover some of the therapist, client, and situational factors underlying or influencing the outcomes of time-limited therapy (TLT), and delineate, at least in a beginning way, the process of TLT.

From its inception in 1973 the research program has been coordinated by the first author, Charles J. Gelso. It originated from two related sets of concerns. First, from an agency viewpoint, the Counseling Center of the University of Maryland was plagued, it seemed like forever, with disturbingly large waiting lists. At the time when the research reported here was getting under way the waiting list, which had gradually expanded over the years, was hovering around the 200 mark. During peak times clients had to wait two months or more to be seen beyond the initial intake interview. Viewed from another perspective, one student out of every 200 in this large multiversity might be found on our waiting list at any given time. While eclectic generally, the staff seemed to hold to a psychoanalytic/psychodynamic position that viewed long-term treatment as the therapeutic ideal. In fact, informal data gathered at the Center indicated that when senior staff members (i.e., vs. practicum students and interns) were the treatment providers, the mean number of sessions for personal counseling or psychotherapy on an individual basis approached 25. While a series of 25 sessions is by no means long-term therapy by private practice standards or, of course, psychoanalytic institute standards, it is very long term indeed for a mental health agency such as a university counseling center that was spawned from a counseling psychology tradition emphasizing health versus pathology and placing a premium on briefer interventions.

Thus, the first concern underlying the development of our research program on brief, time-limited therapy was an agency issue. We wanted to find out if we could begin to tackle this frustrating waiting list problem, while at the same time continuing to provide high-quality clinical services. In keeping with the empirical orientation of the Center under the wise leadership of Dr. Thomas M. Magoon, the director, and Dr. David H. Mills, the assistant director in charge of the Counseling Division of the Center, we decided that a sensible first step would be to institute a large-scale agency study aimed at comparing clients' and counselors' reactions to time-limited procedures of different durations, as against their evaluations of open-ended treatment. We also hoped to assess a host of client and counselor variables that might influence outcome measures across the different treatments.

The aspect of that study dealing with questions of outcome and effectiveness is presented in Chapter 2, entitled "Clients' and Counselors' Reactions to Time-Limited and Time-Unlimited Counseling." We should note that, prior to the formulation of that field experiment, Keilson, Dworkin, and Gelso's outcome study (Chapter 1, "The Effectiveness of Time-Limited Therapy in a University Counseling Center") had been completed, and provided some optimistic results vis-à-vis the viability of brief, time-limited treatment. Yet too many questions remained after that experiment to allow anything like a major agency reorientation, for example, away from longer-term work and toward brief, time-limited counseling. So a more comprehensive investigation seemed warranted.

Why was so much empirical support needed in order to permit a change in agency policy? Maryland's Counseling Center is data oriented, and possesses an unusual amount of respect for scientific methods of answering clinical questions. So it was not unusual for the agency to seek to assess the viability of a new procedure before deciding whether to institute it. Probably a more potent reason for this call for empirical data, however, has to do with the general uneasiness among practitioners concerning the use of time limits. Counselors and psychotherapists are involved in the business of nurturing and helping troubled individuals, and we suggest that such an involvement is and should be at the heart of the clinical activities of even the most psychoanalytically abstinent or behavioristically mechanical of us. To most of us, setting a time limit on the work we do with our clients *seems* inimical to what we are and want to be about. This is especially so when a limit is established that is going to matter from an agency viewpoint, that is, when the time limit is appreciably less than the typical duration of treatment at the agency. For example, if 25 sessions were the typical duration and we decided to establish a time limit of, let us say, 40 sessions, that would not be a source of discomfort to practitioners—but neither would the limit matter from a viewpoint of agency time-savings.

So the establishment of a practically meaningful time limit makes the therapist uneasy and violates in perhaps a basic way some of the central needs underlying his or her clinical activity. In a certain way, it also violates the therapist's clinical experiences. If my personal experience is that clients I work with in a university agency will typically continue for 20–40 sessions before some "satisfactory resolution" of their issues is reached, then it seems and "feels" like setting a 10-session limit with such clients would have to be ineffectual, even harmful. Much more than the fragmentary data on the efficacy of time-limited therapy that existed prior to our program and after our first experiment was needed if our staff was to feel comfortable enough with the procedures to employ them on a wide scale—and employ them without a sense of resentment that might sabotage the potential effectiveness of the treatment.

We have been examining practical agency issues that served as an impetus for our program of research and helped shape that program. A second set of issues was at once more scientific and personal than practical. Personally, the authors as well as most of the practitioners at Maryland's Counseling Center experienced puzzling and vexing contradictions in their postdoctorate experiences and training as compared to their doctoral education. Most of us received our graduate training in counseling psychology programs. The specialty of counseling psychology has historically focused on brief interventions emphasizing individuals' strengths, even when the individuals manifest severe or pervasive psychopathology. At the same time, we were practicing our trade in an area of the country that is a haven of psychoanalytic and psychodynamic thought that seems to dictate long-term interventions emphasizing individuals' pathological processes, even when the individuals exhibit a great deal of psychological strength. (Parenthetically, the prototype of this paradigm of human functioning and its psychological treatment is classical analysis, a procedure that is tailored to persons with the greatest psychological resources.)

Given the wide range of client problems with which we worked (being the central mental health agency in a huge, complex university), it was probably inevitable that most of us felt caught in the conflict between the above two traditions. This conflict created more than the usual amount of interest in learning how temporal factors affect the process of personal counseling or psychotherapy. So, as often occurs when personal and scientific issues become melded, we decided to investigate scientifically those phenomena that both tickled our curiosity and clinically vexed us. We sought to assess empirically how time affects treatment.

General Background Underlying the Research

The discussion thus far has focused on the background of our research program from the vantage point of local issues—practical, personal, and scientific ones. It is important to note, however, that the research presented in this book was also spawned from more general issues and themes in counseling and psychotherapy. Let us note some of the more salient ones.

As we have discussed in a recent paper (Johnson and Gelso, 1980), the zeitgeist in counseling and psychotherapy has reflected a serious concern about limiting the traditionally long duration of psychological treatment. A number of factors have influenced this development. Probably first and foremost, increased demands for service have left mental health agencies overtaxed. Long waiting lists and the resulting delays in service have become common. Also, generally heightened public awareness of the role of psychological factors in human functioning and dysfunctioning has caused different types of people to seek treatment. Psychologically healthier people and/or those experiencing less than overwhelming crises have goals far less extensive than the traditional analysis and reconstruction of personality. Third, the extension of mental health services to populations other than the verbal middle class has suggested the unsuitability of more traditional interventions for many clients. Finally, demands on health insurance policies to pay for mental health treatment have involved insurance companies in investigations of the efficacy of brief treatments.

Theorizing about the use of time limits goes back many years, for example, to the work of Ferenzi and Rank (1923/1956), to the seminal work of Rank (1945), and indeed to Freud himself (1937/1963). Until the past decade or so, however, writing on the topic has been quite infrequent and sketchy. Recently there has been a virtual explosion of such literature. The use of time-limited approaches has been recommended by writers of just about every theoretical persuasion. At the same time, and perhaps ironically, much of the recent theoretical work on brief and time-limited treatment has come from psychoanalysis (e.g., Malan, 1976; Mann, 1973; Sifneos, 1972; Lewin, 1970). Parenthetically, it probably makes a great deal of sense that a treatment ideology (i.e., psychoanalysis) entailing treatment of the longest duration would be most involved in speculations about limiting treatment duration. This occurs when such practitioners become concerned with making a treatment accessible to clientele other than just the wealthy and/or generously insured.

Empirical Background of the Research

We have noted that recent years have witnessed a dramatic increase in writing about and acceptance of the use of time limits in therapy. There has been no such increase, however, in scientific attempts to assess this treatment modality. The dearth of research is especially notable when one scans the literature for studies that contain at least a minimum of quantification and methodological control. Thus, the little work that has been done leaves a great deal to be desired from the viewpoint of methodology (and thus from the viewpoint of what may safely be concluded about the results).

We think it is safe to say that at the time when the Maryland research program was getting under way very little was known about the outcome of time-limited therapy including basic questions revolving around its general efficacy. While little was known about outcome, next to nothing was known (at least from scientific as opposed to clinical evidence) about critical issues such as what client and therapist factors influence the outcome of time-limited treatment, what is the process of time-limited therapy like, how does that process differ from that of open-ended treatment, what are clients' and counselors' initial expectancies like in time-limited versus open-ended treatment and in what ways do these expectancies then play into the process and outcome of counseling. These are critical questions indeed, and prior to our project it was difficult to locate even beginning efforts to tackle them.

So, although reviewers of the research scene such as Meltzoff and Kornreich (1970) labeled this area a "natural" for research, scientific efforts seemed to trail well behind popular thinking and prescription. As so often is the case in counseling and psychotherapy, clinical testimony seems to precede sound, well-designed research.

But what was empirically known about time-limited therapy as we began our efforts? The exhaustive review of literature by Luborsky, Chandler, Auerbach, Cohen, and Bachrach (1971) suggested that, while duration of treatment was positively related to quality of outcome, brief time-limited treatment seemed at least as effective as open-ended therapy. Thus, an apparent contradiction existed. In therapy that was not time-limited the old axiom seemed to hold up when put to the empirical test, that is, the more therapy the better. Yet, when time limits were established, the briefer, time-limited treatment seemed to show quite well; the axiom was not supported. At the same time, the research on time-limited therapy was fraught with methodological and conceptual problems, to the point that not much faith could be placed in the results.

The preceding treatment deals with the most global questions about time-limited therapy—does it work, and how does its effectiveness compare to treatment without a time limit. As one of the authors has explored in detail elsewhere (Gelso, 1979), questions of this degree of generality are important first steps in scientific activity. And yet they must be accompanied or at least followed by more specific who, what, when, and where questions. In short, we must examine the question of who time-limited therapy is profitable for, when the treatment is dispensed, by what kinds of therapists, under which treatment conditions, and given what sets of goals. While there existed a paucity of controlled research on the global question of the general efficacy of time-limited therapy when we began our program, questions of who, what, when, and where (as well as how) had hardly begun to be tackled. Of these questions, probably the most basic pertains to the characteristics of clients who do and do not profit from this modality. As Lambert's (1979) review indicates, our knowledge in this area is primitive; we have some knowledge of the characteristics of clients who profit from therapy in general, but not of how those characteristics coincide with or are different from those of clients who succeed and fail in time-limited treatment.

The Plan of the Book

This book presents the results of seven different studies on the process and outcome of TLT. Part One treats the findings of three field studies on the effects of this treatment. We examine the effects in comparison to open-ended treatment as well as a waiting-list control group in Chapter 1; and in Chapter 2 we present the results of a large-scale, agency-based study examining clients' and therapists' reactions to two different time limits, as compared to open-ended counseling. Chapter 3 investigates a particular hypothesis about TLT, the "change in motion" hypothesis; we examine whether TLT is effective in beginning or setting in motion a change process that continues or accelerates after counseling terminates.

Part Two does not present results of any additional data gatherings. Rather, it organizes the parts of the data gatherings presented in Chapters 2 and 3 that pertain to therapist and client factors influencing outcome. Chapter 4 presents the relationships of a host of client and therapist variables related to therapists' outcome judgments and to clients' evaluations of outcome 1 month and 18 months after termination. Chapter 5 examines therapist-rated client factors predictive of change following counseling, that is, between termination and a 1-year follow-up study.

Part Three of the book presents the results of four different investigations of expectations and processes in TLT. Two of the studies are laboratory analogues of counseling (McKitrick & Gelso, Chapter 6; Johnson, Chapter 7), and two are field studies (Cornfeld, Johnson, Spiegel, Whittaker and Wasserman, Gelso, Chapter 8; and Miller, Courtois, Pelham, Riddle, Spiegel, Gelso and Johnson, Chapter 9). The first three chapters in Part Three study client and/or therapist expectancies in and for TLT, while the last chapter looks at the process of TLT, especially in terms of James Mann's theory of this treatment format.

The final chapter of the book integrates the results of the entire program of research, and examines how our findings fit into the existing literature on time-limited treatment. There we examine both what we have learned and some salient islands of ignorance that remain in our understanding of the phenomena of interest.

We would like to note that only two of the seven data gatherings have been published prior to this book. We have chosen to include those two papers in this book because of their connection to the other studies.

Finally, regarding the organization of the book, we have attempted to fit the studies under coherent headings. Each section introduces the studies it then describes; and each chapter and section builds on the prior ones, although the chapters may be read nonsequentially.

Throughout the book, the reader will notice that terms such as *counseling* and *therapy* (as well as *counselor* and *therapist*) are used interchangeably. Drawing distinctions between counseling and psychotherapy is usually very difficult business, and indeed many would suggest that counseling and therapy really reflect the same process. Whether or not (and in what ways) counseling is generally different from therapy, we offer that it is not useful to attempt differentiating them in the kind of activity being studied and written about in this book.

REFERENCES

FERENCZI, S., & RANK, O. *The development of psychoanalysis* (C. Newton, trans.). New York: Dover, 1956. (Originally published, 1923.)

FREUD, S. Analysis, terminable and interminal. In I. Freud, *Therapy and technique*. New York: Crowell-Collier, 1963. (Originally published, 1937.)

GELSO, C. J. Research in counseling: Methodological and professional issues. *The Counseling Psychologist,* 1979, *8,* 7–36.

JOHNSON, D. H., & GELSO, C. J. The effectiveness of time limits in counseling and psychotherapy: a critical review. *The Counseling Psychologist,* 1980, *9,* 70–83.

LAMBERT, M. J. Characteristics of patients and their relationship to outcome in brief psychotherapy. *Psychiatric Clinics of North America,* 1979, *2,* 111–123.

LEWIN, K. *Brief Psychotherapy.* New York: International Universities Press, 1970.

LUBORSKY, L., CHANDLER, M., AUERBACH, A. H., COHEN, J., & BACHRACH, H. Factors influencing the outcome of psychotherapy: A review of quantative literature. *Psychological Bulletin,* 1971, *75,* 145–185.

MALAN, D. H. *The frontier of brief psychotherapy.* New York: Plenum, 1976.

MANN, J. *Time-limited psychotherapy.* Cambridge, Mass.: Harvard University Press, 1973.

MELTZOFF, J., & KORNREICH, M. *Research in psychotherapy.* Chicago: Aldine, 1970.

RANK, O. *Will therapy and truth and reality.* New York: Knopf, 1945.

SIFNEOS, P. E. *Short-term psychotherapy and emotional crisis.* Cambridge: Harvard University Press, 1972.

EXPLORATIONS IN
Time-Limited Counseling
and Psychotherapy

PART ONE

The Outcomes of Time-Limited Counseling and Psychotherapy

Introduction to Part One

Part One of this book presents the results of the three field investigations on the effects or outcomes of time-limited therapy in our research program. The studies were done in a natural setting, the University of Maryland's Counseling Center, and were aimed both at attacking practical agency problems (e.g., excessively long waiting lists) and acquiring theoretical and empirical understanding of the effects of time-limited therapy from several vantage points.

Chapter 1 presents an outcome study by Marilyn V. Keilson, Fay H. Dworkin, and Charles J. Gelso. This was the first investigation of our program, and it sought to assess the effectiveness of 8-session TLT, as against both open-ended counseling and a control group.

The results of that study were instrumental in the development of our second investigation, the study by Charles J. Gelso, Sharon Baron Spiegel, and David H. Mills reported in Chapter 2, which represents the major field study of the program. It was a large-scale agency study employing nearly all the Counseling Center's senior counseling staff and interns over a 2-year period. The investigation sought to compare TLT with two different time limits, 8 and 16 sessions, as against open-ended therapy in terms of both clients' and counselors' judgments of treatment effectiveness. This outcome portion of the study is presented in Chapter 2. In addition to outcome, the study aimed at examining a host of client and counselor variables that might influence the outcomes of time-limited and time-unlimited treatments. With the exception of one such moderator variable, a measure of initial adjustment, the findings on client and counselor influences on outcome are presented in Part Two, where we integrate such research as it emerged from the projects reported in Chapters 2 and 3.

Chapter 3 presents the results of a 1-year follow-up study that assessed the extent to which changes that occur during time-limited therapy are sustained or magnified following termination. This investigation, reported by Diane M. Adelstein, Charles J. Gelso, James R. Haws, Kathryn G. Reed, and Sharon Baron Spiegel, examines what we have labeled the "change in motion" hypothesis. That is, we hypothesized that TLT is effective in setting in motion a change process that continues or possibly increases after the counseling terminates. As in Chapter 2, the investigation reported in Chapter 3 included an assessment of therapist-rated client variables that influence change. The findings on client factors influencing change are reported in Part Two of this book.

1

The Effectiveness of Time-Limited Therapy in a University Counseling Center

Marilyn V. Keilson, Fay H. Dworkin,
and Charles J. Gelso

The establishment of time limits in counseling and psychotherapy is one obvious method of dealing with the perennial problem of long waiting lists, and preliminary evidence suggested that TLT, at least with certain types of clients, may be at least as effective as open-ended treatment (Munro & Bach, 1975; Shlien, Mosak, & Dreikurs, 1962). Thus, the present study seemed to be useful from both the vantage point of agency problems as discussed in the Introduction, and the potential contribution it could make toward extending the literature on time limits in counseling/therapy.

While the existing literature on time limits prior to this study was largely positive regarding the efficacy of TLT, the research had not adhered to certain important ingredients of outcome assessment in time-limited treatment. None of the existing research had *at once* (a) compared the outcomes of TLT with those of open-ended therapy and a control group; (b) randomly assigned clients to these

This paper is a slightly revised version of an article by the same authors, The effectiveness of time-limited psychotherapy in a university counseling center, *Journal of Clinical Psychology*, 1979, *35*, 631–636. Copyright © 1979 by the Clinical Psychology Publishing Co., Inc. Adapted by permission of the author.

three conditions; (c) employed a time limit that would be practically useful to an essentially short-term treatment agency such as a counseling center;* (d) post-tested all treated clients at the end of therapy, for example, Munro and Bach posttested clients who received open-ended counseling at the end of their 8 sessions, when the time-limited clients terminated; and (e) employed anything like a long-term follow-up procedure.

The present experiment aimed at assessing the outcomes of time-limited therapy, taking into account each of the above five points. It compared changes in self-concept among clients receiving TLT with an 8-session time limit, those receiving open-ended therapy, and those in a no-treatment control group. All subjects were posttested immediately following counseling, and an attempt was made to follow up subjects 2½ years later. The experiment was the first in a series of laboratory and field studies at Maryland on the process and outcomes of TLT.

In designing this study, we struggled with the question of what would constitute an appropriate time limit. We settled on an 8-session limit because it was consistent with the limits used in a number of studies and approaches (see Meltzoff & Kornreich, 1970; Munro & Bach, 1975), because based on agency data such a time limit would be expected to result in considerable agency time-savings, and, finally, because from a clinical point of view, the 8-session limit appeared to allow enough time to facilitate important client growth.

Method

Subjects

Seventy-nine students who sought personal counseling or psychotherapy at the University of Maryland's Counseling Center during an approximate 6-week period of the 1973 spring semester comprised the potential pool from which subjects for the current experiment were drawn. To be included in the study, students met the following criteria: (a) they were identified by their intake interviewer as having a personal-social problem, appropriately treated by individual counseling or therapy at the Center; (b) they were identified by the intaker as not needing immediate crisis help; (c) they completed the Minnesota Multiphasic Personality Inventory (MMPI) and the Index of Adjustment and Values (IAV) (Bills, Vance, & McLean, 1951); and (d) their scores on 6–7–8 (paranoia, psychasthenia, schizophrenia) of the MMPI neither dominated scores on 1–2–3, the "neurotic triad" (hypochondriasis, depression, hysteria), nor exceeded a t score of 70. These MMPI criteria were employed because of the researchers'

---

*In order to be practically useful, the time limit would need to save agency time, i.e., staff hours. Shlien et al., for example, used a 20-session time limit, and that is much beyond the average number of sessions at typical short-term agencies. Thus, few if any staff hours would be saved by such a limit.

concerns about the use of brief, time-limited procedures with more severely disturbed clients, and because some data suggest that persons with such MMPI profiles may not accurately respond to perceived–ideal–self items (Friedman, 1958; Chase, 1957), the kinds of items used in our criterion measure.

Of the 79 potential subjects, 22 (28%) were screened out by our MMPI selection, and 15 (19%) for a variety of other reasons—for example, no-showed for the first session, terminated via phone call before the first session, did not take the MMPI or the IAV ($n = 2$) or, not more were experiencing an immediate crisis ($n = 1$). Thus, the final example consisted of 42 noncrisis clients who were seeking counseling for personal-social problems but were probably within the normal, moderately neurotic, range of adjustment.

Therapists

Therapists for the study were 19 of the 21 full-time and part-time staff of the Counseling Center. There were 13 senior staff members, 12 with doctorates in clinical or counseling psychology and 1 with an MSW; 6 were counseling interns at the Center. While time-limited counseling per se had not been conducted at the Center prior to this investigation, the staff did have experience with time limits because of the natural time limits in university settings (e.g., semester breaks, graduation) and because the Center did provide brief time-limited treatments for specific problems (e.g., 4-session assertiveness training groups).

Instrumentation

The MMPI was employed as a selection device in the study. The IAV (Bills, Vance, & McLean, 1951) was our criterion measure. The IAV consists of 50 adjectives; subjects rate themselves on each adjective, and then rate how they would ideally like to be on each. The discrepancy between perceived and ideal self on the IAV forms the measure of adjustment-maladjustment. Reliability and validity data in the Index are quite supportive (Wylie, 1974), and recent research supports its sensitivity to the effects of brief treatments as well as long-term counseling (Berman, Gelso, Greenfeig, & Hirsch, 1977). Reliability estimates on the IAV have been obtained on heterogeneous college populations. Since the present study was concerned with a particularly defined subpopulation, it was desirable to obtain our own estimate. The use of Schafer's (1972) method, which combined two types of split-half coefficients and a cross validation technique, yielded a corrected split-half reliability index of .91 for the composite scale.

Procedure

During an approximate 6-week period of the 1973 spring semester, all students who came to the Counseling Center were given a letter requesting their cooperation in "an important research project concerned with the type of counseling most effective for a student population." Students who agreed to participate and met the criteria for inclusion in the study were asked to come to the Center to fill out a counseling questionnaire before their first appointment. At that time they completed the IAV, the pretherapy measure for the study.

Assignment to time-limited, time-unlimited, and control conditions was random. Therapy for clients in the two experimental conditions was begun according to normal Center practice. As soon as a participating therapist became available, with an open hour that fit a particular client's available times, assignment was made to that therapist, and the therapist was informed by the first author whether the client was time limited or not. Clients assigned to the time-limited condition were informed of the limit during their first session. Therapists were asked to present this to the client in their own manner, but (a) to avoid telling clients that they were setting a limit because of the experiment, and (b) to identify with the efficacy of time-limited therapy if possible, for example, "We will meet for a limit of eight sessions because it is an effective way to work." Time-unlimited clients were serviced by the Center in the usual manner, leaving the termination date open ended. Control group subjects were placed on the waiting list for 8 weeks, a wait period only slightly longer than the typical wait at peak periods at the Center (Collins, Gelso, Kimball, & Sedlacek, 1973).

Clients in time-limited and time-unlimited treatments were posttested after their last session. Therapists gave the IAV to clients during the last session and asked them to mail the completed form to the Center in a self-addressed envelope. Therapists made clear that responses would be confidential, that they would in no way affect the therapist, and that the purpose was to study clients' postcounseling status. This procedure along with a follow-up phone call from the first author to nonresponders brought returns from all 42 clients. Subjects in the control group were tested for the second time after their 8-week wait and immediately before they began their counseling.

An attempt was made to follow-up all 42 clients approximately 2½ years after the beginning of the experiment. Mailing procedures allowed the researchers to reach only 18 (43%) former clients; all 18 completed the IAV and a specially devised questionnaire evaluating their therapy and any additional counseling. It should be kept in mind that while we were only able to reach 43% of the original sample, we did obtain results from all of those we did reach. Thus, while the small sample size makes for cautious generalizations, external validity is not impeded by self-selection factors, that is, in terms of which clients chose to respond.

Statistical Design

A 2×3 repeated measures analysis of variance (Lindquist I) was used to analyze immediate follow-up results. Here time of testing (pre and post) and treatment (time limited, unlimited, control) were the independent variables. The sample sizes per group were: time limited, 15; time unlimited, 14; control, 13. This same design was employed for the long-term follow-up, only this time a 3 × 3 was performed (3 times of testing for the follow-up). Cell sizes were: time limited, 8; time unlimited, 5; control, 5.

Results

Table 1–1 presents the results of the immediate follow-up. It may be seen that clients in both time-limited and unlimited conditions manifested lower discrepancy scores (better adjustment) after treatment than before. The control group, however, evidenced minimal change.

The analysis of variance indicated a main effect for time of testing, as indicated in Table 1–2. Since this main effect includes the control group in the repeated measures design, however, evidence of a treatment effect is not found here. Rather, it is apparent in the interaction effect, which indicates the differential improvement from pre to post among the three groups. Table 1–2 indicates that this interaction attained significance. Newman-Keuls post hoc tests indicated that pre- to post differences were significant ($p < .05$) for both experimental groups but not for the controls.

A 3 × 3 analysis of variance on the 18 clients who completed the 2½ year follow-up again revealed a main effect for time of testing ($df = 2/30$, $F = 10.52$, $p < .01$); all three groups improved over time. Here, however, no significant treatment by time-of-testing interaction emerged ($df = 4/30$, $F = .81$, $p > .05$). All five control subjects, it must be noted, had received open-ended counseling after their 8-week period. Thus, in effect, we no longer have a control group for

Table 1–1. Means and Standard Deviations of Clients' IAV Discrepancy Scores Before and After Counseling

Condition	Pretest*		End of counseling	
	$\bar{X}$	SD	$\bar{X}$	SD
Time limited ($n = 15$)	48.13	15.06	34.40	14.72
Time unlimited ($n = 14$)	59.86	20.52	39.14	16.02
Control ($n = 13$)	46.31	13.61	44.15	15.48

Note. Lower discrepancy scores indicate better adjustment.
*An analysis of variance on the pretest scores indicated that these initial between-group differences did not approach statistical significance ($p > .20$).

this comparison, and are actually comparing the durability of change across 2½ years for three treated groups. This follow-up does indicate high stability of change from post testing to follow-up, as indicated by the main effect of time of testing given above. Table 1–3 presents the means and standard deviations (*SD*'s) on each testing for those subjects who completed the follow-up.

The lack of a significant treatment by time-of-testing interaction in the long-term follow-up also indicates that clients treated by time-limited therapy maintained their therapeutic gains as well as those receiving open-ended therapy (the time-unlimited group and the controls, who by then received open-ended counseling). This conclusion is supported by data from our follow-up questionnaire indicating that three of the 10 clients in the open-ended conditions (time unlimited and controls) sought treatment again after termination, while approximately the same proportion of time-limited clients did so (two of eight). Finally, in response to an open-ended question, only two clients (one time limited and one time unlimited) expressed negative feelings about the counseling they received at the Center.

Discussion

The results of this investigation suggest that 8-session TLT is a viable treatment, at least for clients who are not severely disturbed. Time-limited therapy seems to produce as much change as open-ended treatment in a university counseling center setting, and the change it does stimulate appears to be durable. This conclusion is consistent with the bulk of evidence heretofore accumulated on the efficacy of time-limited procedures. (Johnson & Gelso, 1980; Meltzoff & Kornreich, 1970.)

Table 1–2. Analysis of Variance Summary Table for the Effects of Time-Limited Counseling

Source	df	SS	MS	F
Among subjects				
Group	2	981.76	490.88	1.28
Subjects	39	14,924.49	382.68	
Within Subjects				
Time of testing	1	3,268.76	3,268.76	18.92**
Time by group	2	1,179.50	589.75	3.41*
Time by subjects	39	6,736.73	172.74	
TOTAL	83	27,091.24		

** = $p < .01$
 * = $p < .05$

It is important to remember that the present study employed only one criterion measure, a paper-and-pencil inventory assessing the discrepancy between real and ideal self. Although this fact reduces the confidence we can place in the results, as indicated the findings are consistent with those of earlier field experiments in counseling centers and other agencies, studies that used similar time limits but widely different criteria (Johnson & Gelso, 1980; Meltzoff & Kornreich, 1970). Following the line of reasoning advanced by Gelso (1979), we chose to employ the single criterion rather than several criteria because in a natural setting the use of additional measures would have attenuated return rates, disrupted agency procedures, and so forth. Thus, the price of using multiple measures, the methodological ideal, was more than the researchers thought useful to pay. Now, the interpretability and certitude of results gathered in single-criterion studies are a function of how those results fit into the pattern of existing findings in a domain, that is, findings based on different criteria and measurement methods. Again, the present findings do serve to corroborate existing research on the subject of brief time-limited counseling or therapy.

Since at least one rationale for all time-limited procedures is that they save agency time and permit more clients to be treated sooner, a crucial question pertains to whether in fact time-limited clients in the present study were seen for fewer sessions than those in open-ended work. The data we gathered on this question revealed that for time-limited and unlimited clients respectively the mean numbers of sessions were 7.5 $(SD = 1.2)$ and 11.6 $(SD = 6.4)$, $t = 2.29$, $p < .05$. Thus, while the mean for open-ended treatment in this study was considerably lower than earlier data we had gathered (indicating some sample bias), the time-limited procedures still took on the average 4.1 fewer sessions, a net agency savings of 35%. Since time savings is a function of the actual time limits in relation to the typical number of sessions clients receive at an agency, not all time-limited

Table 1–3. Means and Standard Deviations of Clients' IAV Discrepancy Scores at Each Testing for Those Clients Participating in the Two and One-Half Year Follow-Up

Condition	Pretest		End of counseling		Follow-Up	
	$\overline{X}$	SD	$\overline{X}$	SD	$\overline{X}$	SD
Time limited ($n = 8$)	54.38	9.38	40.62	7.40	39.88	14.79
Time unlimited ($n = 5$)	66.40	25.49	37.60	13.08	47.20	21.02
Control ($n = 5$)	49.60	14.97	38.20	16.75	38.00	9.57

Note. Lower discrepancy scores indicate better adjustment.

work will result in agency savings, for example, had we established a limit of 30 sessions, no agency time would have been saved. Many studies, in fact, fail to report on such data (Johnson & Gelso, 1980), and in light of the reasoning discussed above, we recommend that all future research present data on average numbers of sessions and so forth in time-limited and unlimited conditions.

Future research should aim at isolating an optimum range of sessions, from the joint vantage points of client gain and agency time-savings. (Note that the latter is itself related to client gain, since it results in being seen sooner, not languishing on waiting lists, and so forth). It seems likely that this range will vary, to some extent, as a function of the type of agency and, correspondingly, the type of clients seeking treatment at a given agency. For example, a time limit of 8 sessions may be insufficient at an agency specializing in longer-term, uncovering therapy, that is, especially in light of the likelihood that such an agency will thus attract clients who are suitable and motivated for such treatment. Such an agency, if considering setting time limits with certain clients, might more profitably consider limits, for example, ranging from 25 sessions (e.g., parallel to 6-month therapy) to 50 sessions. In light of this sort of thinking, our findings are probably most generalizable to agencies, such as the Counseling Center at Maryland, that specialize in briefer therapies to begin with, for example, community mental health centers. At the same time, since much personal counseling and psychotherapy is of a fairly brief nature (see Garfield, 1971, 1978), the present results, based on an 8-session time limit, would seem to have wide applicability.

A final qualifier should be added. The most severely disturbed students in our potential pool were not included in the present investigation. Thus, generalizations to the most disturbed of our clients must be made only with great caution. Researchers could profitably devote energies to determining whether in fact time-limited procedures should be used with the most disturbed clients, and to devising time-limited treatment methods that might be effective with such clients. The following chapter considers whether initial client-adjustment level influences outcome in time-limited and unlimited treatment. This question is also addressed in several later chapters.

REFERENCES

BERMAN, M., GELSO, C., GREENFEIG, B., & HIRSCH, R. The efficacy of supportive learning environments for returning women: An empirical evaluation. *Journal of Counseling Psychology*, 1977, *24*, 324–331.

BILLS, R., VANCE, E., & McLEAN, O. An index of adjustment and values. *Journal of Consulting Psychology*, 1951, *15*, 257–261.

CHASE, P. Self-concepts in adjusted and maladjusted hospital patients. *Journal of Consulting Psychology*, 1957, *21*, 495–497.

COLLINS, A., GELSO, C., KIMBALL, R., & SEDLACEK, W. An evaluation of a counseling center innovation. *Journal of College Student Personnel*, 1973, *14*, 144–148.

FRIEDMAN, I. Phenomenal, ideal and projected conception of self. *Journal of Abnormal and Social Psychology*, 1958, *45*, 207–211.

GARFIELD, S. L. Research on client variables in psychotherapy. In A. E. Bergin and S. L. Garfield (Eds.), *Handbook of psychotherapy and behavior change*. New York: Wiley, 1971.

GARFIELD, S. L. Research on client variables in psychotherapy. In S. L. Garfield and A. E. Bergin (Eds.), *Handbook of psychotherapy and behavior change* (2nd ed.). New York: Wiley, 1978.

GELSO, C. J. Research in counseling: Methodological and professional issues. *The Counseling Psychologist*, 1979, *8*, 7–36.

JOHNSON, D. H., & GELSO, C. J. The effectiveness of time limits in counseling and psychotherapy: A critical review. *The Counseling Psychologist*, 1980, *9*, 70–83.

MELTZOFF, J., & KORNREICH, M. *Research in psychotherapy*. New York: Atherton, 1970.

McKITRICK, D., & GELSO, C. Initial client expectancies in time-limited counseling. *Journal of Counseling Psychology*, 1978, *25*, 246–249.

MUNRO, J., & BACH, T. Effect of time-limited counseling on client change. *Journal of Counseling Psychology*, 1975, *22*, 395–398.

SCHAFER, W. A computer program to generate reliability indices for composite tests including a cross-validation technique. *Educational and Psychological Measurement*, 1972, *32*, 793–794.

SHLIEN, J., MOSAK, H., & DREIKURS, R. Effect of time limits: A comparison of two psychotherapies. *Journal of Counseling Psychology*, 1962, *9*, 31–34.

WYLIE, R. *The self-concept: A review of methodological considerations and measuring instruments*. (Rev. ed.) Lincoln: University of Nebraska Press, 1974.

2

Clients' and Counselors' Reactions to Time-Limited and Time-Unlimited Counseling

**Charles J. Gelso, Sharon Baron Spiegel,
and David H. Mills**

As scientific investigations should, the study presented in the last chapter generated at least as many questions as it answered. For example, while TLT appeared to hold up quite well and as well as open-ended work in terms of one measure of adjustment, how effective is it in terms of clients' and therapists' evaluations? Little evidence exists on this question, as few researchers have investigated the participants' feelings and thoughts about the TLT process.

A second set of questions raised by the Keilson, Dworkin, and Gelso paper pertains to the interaction of client characteristics and treatment modalities. It will be recalled that the most severely disturbed clients (28% of the potential pool of clients) were not included in that study. Thus, the design did not allow for an analysis of the influence of client factors such as initial adjustment, severity of disturbance, and the like, on their responsiveness to TLT and time-unlimited therapy (TUT). Specifically, is the initial level of client disturbance a factor in their response to the different modalities? Prior to the current study, there has been almost nothing but clinical lore aimed at addressing this question (Lambert, 1979), which is obviously critical and deserving of our best empirical efforts.

A third question stimulated by Keilson et al. is whether different time limits produce different outcomes. This question is of both theoretical and practical interest. Theoretically, it would be illuminating to identify the range of number of sessions as well as treatment duration that would produce optimal outcome. From a practical agency point of view, more evidence is needed than is provided by the Keilson et al. study to allow confident use of time limits. For example, while they report that self- ideal–self discrepancies appeared to lessen equally in 8-session TLT and open-ended counseling, it may well be that clients and/or therapists themselves negatively evaluate such brief work (an 8-session time limit) and value positively open-ended work or therapy with a more extended time limit. Thus, if only on the basis of agency reputation and staff morale, the use of an 8-session time limit may be questionable. With this thought in mind, the present study compared therapists' and clients' reactions to three different therapy structures: 8-session TLT, 16-session TLT, and TUT. The 16-session limit was employed because such a limit might avoid some negative reactions that could occur toward very brief therapy (8-session TLT), but still save agency hours. It will be recalled that students in open-ended therapy or personal counseling with senior staff at the Center, on the average, received 20–25 sessions. Thus, a 16-session limit should save considerable agency time.

In addition to the questions raised by the Keilson study, that investigation contained the following problems: the small number of individuals contacted for the long-term follow-up, the relatively small sample size to begin with, and exclusion of the most maladjusted clients from the study, thus precluding an analysis of the effects of initial adjustment on the outcomes of TLT and TUT. The present study sought to build on that of Keilson et al. by addressing the questions raised above and by attempting to avoid some of the problems with the earlier study.

In summary then, the investigation reported in Chapter 2 is the major field study of our research program. Its primary purposes were to (a) compare clients' and counselors' reactions to TLT (with an 8-session limit and a 16-session limit) to therapy with no time limit; (b) determine if clients' initial level of adjustment was a factor in their differential responsiveness to the three treatments; and (c) examine whether the treatment differences and the gains 1 month after termination were maintained 18 months later. Along with these primary objectives, the study sought to answer several important but secondary questions. For example, do people in TLT return for treatment more frequently than those in open-ended counseling? This question raises the ubiquitous recidivism issue in therapy research. It is an especially pressing one when we are dealing with time-abbreviated therapy. While such therapies may demonstrate high degrees of efficacy and efficiency on our usual criterion measures, they remain suspect until we can demonstrate that clients who recieve brief TLT do not simply seek treatment elsewhere after termination.

The data reported in this chapter are based mostly on the outcome aspect of our study. In addition, we gathered a wide variety of counselor and client data that might moderate therapy outcome. Our general research question in that "moderator" aspect of the study was "What client and counselor characteristics influence treatment outcome, both generally and differentially across the three treatments?" Only one such factor, initial client adjustment level, is examined in this chapter because we view that factor as central to the basic design of the study. Data from the "moderator" aspect of the study are examined in Chapter 4, which focuses on the role of client and therapist factors in outcome.

Method

Subjects

The subjects were 78 students from the University of Maryland, College Park, who sought psychotherapy or personal counseling at the University's Counseling Center during a 28-month period beginning November 1973. To be eligible for the study, students had to be (a) assigned only to individual personal counseling following a routine initial screening interview, (b) assigned to a staff member who had agreed to participate in the project, and (c) planning to enroll in the University for at least one semester following the beginning of treatment. This latter criterion was used to insure a fair comparison of the treatments. Thus, for example, if a client planned to graduate during the semester in which treatment began and would only have a small number of sessions before termination, a valid assessment of the effects of brief TLT, as against open-ended therapy, would be precluded. No additional client restrictions were imposed, as such restrictions would impede the examination of client factors moderating outcome.

Forty-four (56%) of the clients were female, and 34 (44%) were male. The male-female breakdown by treatment groups was equivalent, although there were slightly more females in TUT and relatively more males in the 8-session TLT group. Chi-square analysis of sex differences among groups revealed that such differences did not approach statistical significance ($\chi^2 = 2.11$; with 2 df's, $p <$ .30).

The Therapists

Outcome studies in counseling and psychotherapy often fail to recognize that generalizations from sample to population are based as much on the therapist sample as the client sample. Thus, we need to know who are the treaters in the sample at least as much as who are the treated (*at least* as much because the usually small therapist sample, along with the relatively wide variability in treatment approaches among therapists, is less likely to insure representativeness).

Therapists in the present study were 10 of the 14 senior staff members of the Counseling Service branch of the University of Maryland's Counseling Center. Also participating were 5 of the 12 interns during the 1973–1974 and 1974–1975 academic years. Of the therapists, 7 were female, and 8 were male. Participation was voluntary. The fact that this study was viewed by the staff as a major agency undertaking probably accounts for the very high participation rate among senior staff. Additionally, the staff's participation in the formulation of the study's basic design, for example, the decision to establish limits of 8 and 16 sessions, probably enhanced their cooperation considerably. Interns' participation (5 of 12 interns) was lower, probably because of their interest in having the opportunity to continue in treatment with appropriate clients throughout the internship year.

All senior staff had obtained doctoral degrees in clinical or counseling psychology, and interns were in their final year of doctoral training. This was a relatively experienced senior staff, with years of postdoctoral counseling experience ranging from 2 to 16 ($\overline{X} = 7.2$).

Therapist questionnaire data were gathered immediately following the termination of their last client in the project. The essential results of this survey are presented in Appendix A. In this chapter we shall attempt to summarize some of the central results as they pertain to the kinds of practitioners doing the therapy in our study.

Most of the therapists had experience with structured short-term work prior to this project (8 of the 10 senior staff and 3 of the 5 interns), although fewer had had experience with TLT (6 of 10 senior staff and 3 of 5 interns). The typical senior staff counselor viewed himself or herself as having about an average amount of experience, relative to other therapists he or she knew, in TLT and structured short-term work. While the therapists personally felt most comfortable doing "moderately long-term therapy" (6 months to a year in duration), they possessed a "somewhat positive" attitude toward the efficacy of brief TLT prior to the project. The typical intern was, as expected, less experienced in TLT and structured short-term therapy, but felt more comfortable with short-term interventions (as compared to senior staff). Like the senior staff, interns had a "somewhat positive" attitude toward the efficacy of brief TLT.

In terms of theoretical orientation, this was a staff that prided itself in its diversity. Thus, most therapists clearly viewed themselves as eclectic, with theoretical leanings in one direction or another. When asked to "partial out the following influences on your theoretical orientation to counseling" by indicating a percentage adjacent to each label, these means emerged: Behavioral, 18.3%; gestalt, 18.3%; phenomenological/existential/Rogerian, 31.5%; psychoanalytic, 25.1%; other, 5.3%.

In sum, the 15 therapists who participated in the study represented a wide range of experience. While they had only a modest amount of experience with TLT prior to the project (about average for therapists in general), they did have more experience with structured, short-term therapy. The therapists were theoretically eclectic and, especially among the senior staff, there was a clear personal preference for doing moderately long-term therapy, as opposed to brief work. At the same time, it is probably most accurate to say that at the beginning of the project the staff possessed a guarded but positive view of the potential of brief TLT.

Instrumentation

CLIENT-COMPLETED FORMS.   The initial research plan was to use two client-completed outcome measures, the Bills Index of Adjustment and Values (IAV, as discussed in Keilson et al.) before and after treatment, and a modification of the University of Maryland Counseling Center Follow-up Questionnaire (CCFQ) after treatment only. Pilot study of six clients, however, suggested that getting former clients to complete these two forms 1 month after ending treatment, to say nothing of 18 months, would be difficult; return rates would be much lower than we were willing to accept. Thus, we opted for a single client-completed form to assess outcomes from the client's perspective, and chose the CCFQ over the Bills IAV for several reasons. Most notably, the CCFQ would provide more incremental evidence, since Keilson et al. had already used the IAV (see Chapter 1). Also, the CCFQ would yield more useful agency data, since, although brief, it samples a rather wide range of client reactions.

The CCFQ, as we employed it, was a slight modification of a follow-up device employed at the Counseling Center for over a decade. It contains 50 items eliciting clients' global and specific reactions to diverse aspects of their counseling. Clients rate their growth since beginning counseling, between the end of counseling and the time of follow-up, the quality of the treatment they received, its effects, and their satisfaction. An item was added to assess whether clients feel counseling lasted long enough to meet their needs (Item IV), and Items VIIIb and IX were used in only the 18-month postcounseling assessment. The CCFQ is presented in Figure 2–1.

Evidence on the reliability of the CCFQ items, along with similar types of items, comes from an independent study. Wood (1979) found retest reliability for periods ranging from 1 to 5 months was quite acceptable for the seven items she studied (Items IIa, IIb, IIc, IId, IIe ranged from .57 to .68; Items III = .82; VIa = .87; VIb = .85). Further evidence of retest reliability of CCFQ items is presented in Appendix B.

Figure 2–1. The Counseling Center Follow-Up Questionnaire

Name _____

FOLLOW-UP QUESTIONNAIRE

I. Total change: How do you feel *now* compared with when you first came to the Center?

    a. I feel: ___ Better   ___ No change ___ Worse

    b. I relate with people: ___ Better   ___ No change ___ Worse

    c. I accomplish things   More   Less
        I need to do: ___ effectively ___ No change ___ effectively

    d. I think: More
                               ___ clearly   ___ No change ___ Less clearly

Figure 2–1. (continued)

e. Others act as though I have   For the   For the
changed: ___ better   ___ No change ___ worse

II. Change due to counseling: What amount of change do you feel was a result of your counseling? (As opposed to other things that can cause change.)

a. I feel: ___ Better   ___ No change ___ Worse

b. I relate with people: ___ Better   ___ No change ___ Worse

c. I accomplish things I need More ef-   Less ef-
to do: ___ fectively   ___ No change ___ fectively

d. I think: More   Less
___ clearly   ___ No change ___ clearly

e. Others act as though I   For the   For the
have changed: ___ better   ___ No change ___ worse

III. How satisfied were you with the results of your counseling? (circle)

1	2	3	4	5
very satisfied	satisfied	neutral	dissatisfied	very dissatisfied

IV. Do you feel your counseling lasted long enough to help you in the way you wanted or need to be helped?   ___ yes   ___ no   ___ not sure

V. Overall, rate the extent to which you and/or your life have changed as a result of your counseling experience. (circle)

1	2	3	4	5
no change for the better		some change for the better		much change for the better

VI. Rate your counselor in terms of how well he/she did in helping you:

	Very Well	Well	Fairly Well	Slight-ly	Not at all
a. helping you understand your concerns	___	___	___	___	___
b. helping you resolve your concerns	___	___	___	___	___
c. creating an atmosphere in which you felt safe in talking about your problems	___	___	___	___	___

(continued)

Figure 2–1.   (continued)

VII. When you came to the Counseling Center, you came with the feeling that something was not going well with you in some areas of your life. Note that you are asked to make two ratings on the lines below—one for any changes at the end of your counseling—one for any changes since then (that is, as of now). Rate only those items which apply to you. Select your ratings from among the following:

1.   Much change for the better
2.   Some change for the better
3.   No change
4.   Some change for the worse
5.   Much change for the worse

MAKE RATINGS IN BOTH COLUMNS

		At the end of counseling	Now
a.	Feelings of loneliness, alienation		
b.	Feeling worried, tense, anxious		
c.	Depression, despondency		
d.	Low self-esteem		
e.	Family problems		
f.	Difficulties with inter-personal relationships		
g.	Difficulties with the opposite sex		
h.	Marital or premarital problems		
i.	Homosexuality		
j.	Other sexual concerns		
k.	Problems with drugs		
l.	Problems with drinking		
m.	Difficulty in concentration		
n.	Efficiency in study methods		
o.	Plan for major field of study to follow		
p.	Plan for occupation to pursue		
q.	Grades earned		

Figure 2–1. (continued)

VIII. a. What is the most noticeable change (if any) you see in yourself since coming to the Counseling Center?

b. Can you make any additional comments that help clarify what this counseling experience meant to you, how you felt about it, etc.? (On 18-month Follow-up only; clients in one-month follow-up were only asked for "additional comments")

IX. Have you received additional counseling or therapy during the past year (since seeing Dr.)? If so, please specify (how long? weekly? has it helped?) (On 18-month Follow-up only)

Along with the CCFQ, clients were given the Bills IAV before their first counseling session to determine pretreatment adjustment level. (Reliability and validity data on the IAV were noted in Chapter 1.)

COUNSELOR-COMPLETED FORMS. Following their first interview with each client, therapists completed the *Pre-Counseling Assessment Blank* (Appendix C). This five-item questionnaire asks counselors to rate on 7-point Likert scales (a) degree of disturbance or psychopathology, (b) motivation for counseling, (c) willingness to change, (d) the therapist's confidence that the client will profit from the treatment that will be offered, and (e) the predicted therapist enjoyment in working with the client. This questionnaire aimed at determining if clients were initially comparable among the three treatment groups, whether the five factors predict client and therapist outcome evaluations, and if their correlations with outcome differ in 8-session TLT, 16-session TLT, and TUT.

Upon completion of counseling, therapists responded to the *Post-Counseling Assessment Blank* (Appendix D), a questionnaire containing seven items, each rated on a 7-point Likert scale. Items 1, 2, and 3 assessed therapists' self-ratings on activity level, structure, and the use of historical material in each therapy sequence. These items were aimed at examining therapists' self-perceptions on three factors often viewed in the TLT literature as distinguishing TLT from TUT.

The remaining four items asked therapists to rate (a) clients' overall personality change as a result of treatment, (b) the extent to which clients were behaving more effectively due to counseling, (c) the extent to which clients were feeling better due to treatment, and (d) therapists' confidence in the persistence of client change. Both the pre- and postcounseling assessment devices were constructed specifically for the present study. While reliability data were not gathered on the pretreatment measure, numerous data exist in the literature indicating that such counselor estimates obtain sound reliability. Reliability on the postcounseling assessments of personality, behavior, and feeling is provided in Chapter 3, where similar or identical items obtained highly acceptable retest reliability over 2–3 week intervals.

The therapists completed two additional instruments aimed at both describing the therapist sample and assessing how therapist factors might contribute to outcome. The *Time-Limited Therapy Questionnaire* (Appendix A) is a 17-item self-rating scale devised specifically for the study. It asks questions ranging from theoretical orientation to therapists' reactions to the TLT they conducted as part of the current study. Finally, the most recent revision of the *Therapist Orientation Questionnaire* (Sundland, 1972; Appendix E) was completed by all therapists. This is a 104-item questionnaire designed to measure theoretical orientation. Each item is answered on a 5-point scale in terms of agreement-disagreement (5 = strongly agree, 1 = strongly disagree). Reliability and validity data on the *Questionnaire* have been studied rather extensively and are generally quite supportive of its utility (e.g., Howard, Orlinsky & Trattner, 1970; Sundland, 1972; Sundland & Barker, 1962).

Procedure

All clients at the Center received a 30–50-minute intake interview, usually with a senior staff member or intern. Following the intake interview, clients at the time of the study were almost always placed on a waiting list containing anywhere from 50 to 200 or more students (depending on the time of the semester). Although some leeway existed for priority assignments based on the urgency of clients' difficulties, most clients were assigned a regular therapist when it was the client's turn on the waiting list. They were then assigned to a therapist who had an open hour compatible with the list of open times obtained from clients during intake.

Clients in this study followed this same intake-waiting list-assignment procedure. When a client met the criteria for inclusion and was assigned to a participating therapist (by a staff member in charge of such assignments), the researcher (first author) was notified of the assignment. It was then determined, using essentially random assignment procedures, whether the client was to be seen in 8-session TLT, 16-session TLT, or TUT. Specifically, the order in which each therapist was to see clients in the three conditions was determined for that therapist by a coin-tossing procedure. For example, Therapist X's order might be 16-session client first, 8-session client second, and TUT client third; thus, when the first opening for the study became available, a 16-session TLT client was assigned to that therapist, and so forth. Therapists were notified by the researcher of each client's treatment condition at the same time they received notice of the client assignment.

The Bills IAV was mailed to clients along with their first appointment time and their counselors' names. A written request to complete the IAV prior to the first session was followed up by a telephone reminder by one of the researchers. All but 4 of the 78 clients consented and actually completed the IAV. They returned the IAV either through the mail prior to the first session or by dropping it off at the reception desk upon arrival for the first session. Clients were divided into high and low initial adjustment groups on the basis of a median split on their IAV scores. Two clients obtained scores at the median. For these clients as well as the four who did not complete the instrument, their placement into high or low initial adjustment categories was determined by clinical judgment. Two members of the research team studied the clients' diagnostic intake evaluations as well as therapists' ratings after the first counseling session. Following discussion and agreement by the two members (senior staff psychologists), clients were placed into appropriate categories.

Clients in the two time-limit conditions were informed by their therapists of the time limits during the first session. Immediately prior to the implementation of the project, the researchers discussed with therapists the manner in which limits should be presented to clients. In discussion followed by a written reminder, it was suggested to therapists that while they should present the time limit in a way that was comfortable to them, the following points should guide the presentation: (a) time limits must be presented in the first session, and probably early in the session; (b) it is crucial to communicate that the therapist believes TLT works; (c) while the waiting list problem might be used as a partial rationale for the time limit, it should not be the sole rationale; (d) avoid conveying to the client that he or she is a subject in a research project; (e) the counselor must set a time *limit,* not make a contract for a certain number of sessions. Therapists were asked and agreed to violate the time limits only if it was clinically imperative to do so. In such cases, they agreed to end the work "as soon after the expiration of the time limit as possible."

Clients in the TUT condition received counseling as clients ordinarily do at the Center. Their therapists were told simply to provide their customary treatment, without any note of time limits.

Following the first session, therapists completed the Pre-Counseling Assessment Blank. Immediately after termination, therapists notified the researchers of the termination date, and completed the Post-counseling Assessment Blank.

Client Follow-Up Procedures

Clients were followed up both approximately 1 month and 18 months after termination, and were asked at both times to complete the CCFQ. Procedures for both efforts are described below.

The CCFQ was mailed to clients 2–3 weeks after termination. This mailing also included a cover letter from the researchers requesting cooperation, underscoring the usefulness of follow-ups to the Center and thus its clients, and noting the confidentiality of clients' responses. Of the potential pool of 87 clients, 41 (47%) responded to this first effort. Two weeks after the mailing, phone calls were placed to the nonresponders. If clients refused to cooperate no further contact was made. For those who agreed, however, telephone calls were used as reminders at 2-week intervals. The usable CCFQ returns were obtained from 78 of the 87 possible respondents, a return rate of 90%. (Three former clients were not locatable, four refused to participate, and one questionnaire was misplaced by the researchers.) When only locatable clients are included in these figures, the return rate increases to 94% (78 returns from 83 locatable clients.) It should also be noted that 21 client applicants were assigned to therapists but failed to attend any sessions, and are not included in any of the analyses. These students either no-showed for first appointments, or notified the Center prior to the appointment that they decided against counseling.

THE 18-MONTH FOLLOW-UP.   An attempt was made to reach all 78 clients by telephone approximately 1½ years after their termination dates. Given the long delay between termination and follow-up, we reasoned that simply sending a cover letter would yield a low return rate. Our exhaustive and exhausting tracking procedures (telephone calls to all parts of the country) enabled us to reach 71 of the 78 clients. All but 4 clients agreed to complete the CCFQ. If returns were not received 1 month after the initial phone contact, clients were again called as a reminder, and such reminders were given at 1-month intervals for nonrespondents. (For some clients, four or even five contacts were required, although we did not sense that the clients felt "put off" or harrassed.) Thus, we were able to obtain usable results from 67 of the original 78 clients (87%), and from 67 of the 71 locatable clients (94%).[1]

Basic Design of the Study

The initial plan of the study called for a sample size of 90, with 30 clients being counseled under each of three conditions. Further, we had hoped to achieve a crossed and balanced design in which each therapist counseled 6 clients, 2 under each of the three treatment conditions. Although 13 of the 15 therapists actually counseled 2 clients under each condition, lack of follow-up data on some clients allowed this therapist-by-treatment design to accrue fully for only 6 therapists. While the effort to completely cross and balance the design was not successful, the attempt to accomplish it did preclude any gross imbalances regarding therapist by treatment combinations, for example, Therapist X seeing all of his or her clients in the TUT condition and Therapist Y seeing all of his or her clients under the 8-session TLT conditions.[1]

Statistically, this phase of the study (i.e., the outcome phase) basically entailed a series of 2×3 analyses of variance (high vs. low initial adjustment by three treatment groups). The methodological/statistical ideal would have required clients *within* each of the two initial adjustment levels to be assigned randomly to the three treatment conditions. This was not logistically manageable, however, and we had to settle for a posteriori blocking. Clients were randomly assigned to the three treatment conditions according to the procedures discussed earlier. *Then* it was determined whether clients were high versus low on initial adjustment among clients in all three treatment conditions.

Table 2–1 presents the number of clients in each treatment group and for each level of adjustment within the three treatments. It can be seen that while the *n* 's are not equal in each treatment by initial adjustment combination cell, they are approximately so.

While analyses of variance were computed for most dependent measures (items), other analyses, for example, chi square, were computed when the data warranted.

The Findings

Probably the first questions to be asked about the results pertain to whether the time limits were *effective* and *realistic*. The effectiveness of the limits could be determined by the extent to which therapists adhered to them. Results indicated that the time limits were violated in only four instances, two in each of the 8- and 16-session TLT conditions. In no instance did clients receive more than 3 sessions over the limit. Thus, it appears that the limit setting was highly effective.

The extent to which the limits were realistic was assessed by comparing the mean number of sessions received by clients under the three conditions. If, for example, clients in the TUT and TLT conditions receive an approximately equal number of sessions, the time (session) limit that was set may have been quite unrealistic, that is, too high. Data on numbers of sessions per treatment for clients who were above and below the median on initial adjustment are presented in Table 2–2. It can be seen that clients in TUT had more than three times as many sessions as those in 8-session TLT, and more than twice as many as clients in 16-session TLT. Additionally, this pattern holds for both initial adjustment groups.

Table 2–1. Frequency Data on Clients in Each Treatment Group for Both Levels of Initial Adjustment and for Both the 1-Month and 18-Month Follow-Ups

| | | Treatment group | | |
| | | 8-session TLT | 16-session TLT | TUT | Combined treatments |
Time of follow-up	Initial adjustment category				
1 month	High adjustment	13	13	11	37
1 month	Low adjustment	14	15	12	41
1 month	Both	27	28	23	78
18 months	High adjustment	10	12	11	33
18 months	Low adjustment	11	12	11	34
18 months	Both	21	24	22	67

A 2 × 3 analysis of variance (ANOVA, initial adjustment by treatment group) indicated that the main effect for treatment group was highly significant ($F = 10.74$, $p < .001$). Newman-Keuls post hoc tests revealed that the TUT group differed from both TLT groups, while the two TLT groups did not differ from each other. Surprisingly, the main effect for initial adjustment and the interaction effect of initial adjustment with treatment group did not approach statistical significance. (We might and, indeed, did expect the less adjusted clients to receive more sessions than the better adjusted ones, and, furthermore, we expected that this difference would be greatest for the TUT group.)

In sum, it appeared that the limit setting implemented in this study was both effective and realistic. Therapists adhered to the limits to an overwhelming extent, and the limitations did result in the predicted differences in numbers of sessions. At the same time, clients in the 8- and 16-session TLT conditions did not differ significantly in terms of number of sessions. Thus, although the difference between these treatments may be practically significant (essentially they received 6 vs. 9 sessions in 8- and 16-session TLT), we cannot be sure statistically that these are nonchance differences.

Clients' Initial Status on Relevant Variables

A second issue the data must address pertains to this client group's pretreatment characteristics on certain therapy-relevant variables. Relatedly, it is important to determine if the three treatment groups differed initially on such variables.

Five 2 × 3 ANOVA's were conducted on counselor responses to the five items on the *Pre-Counseling Assessment Blank*.

While data on client characteristics prior to therapy were unavailable, Table 2–3 presents therapists' ratings of clients after the first session. It can be seen that therapists' ratings are near the scale midpoint (labeled "moderately" for each item) for each of the five characteristics rated. On the whole, clients were rated slightly

Table 2–2. Means and Standard Deviations for Number of Sessions by Treatment Group and Initial Adjustment Level

| | Treatment group | | | | | |
| | 8 sessions ($n = 27$) | | 16 sessions ($n = 28$) | | Unlimited ($n = 23$) | |
Initial adjustment	$\bar{X}$	SD	$\bar{X}$	SD	$\bar{X}$	SD
High adjustment	7.15	3.65	7.62	5.39	18.82	20.32
Low adjustment	4.93	4.00	9.47	5.93	21.17	18.75
Both high and low	6.00	3.45	8.61	5.66	20.04	19.09

Note. Main effect for treatment group = 10.74, $p < .001$

less than moderately disturbed (i.e., less disturbed), and above the midpoint on the remaining four characteristics—motivation for counseling, willingness to change, counselor confidence that the client would profit from the treatment, and therapist-predicted enjoyment in working with the client.

Probably most important, the data in Table 2–3 indicate that differences among the three treatment groups do not approach statistical significance. Thus, it seems clear that the three groups were very similar on treatment-relevant characteristics in the beginning stages of the work.

Regarding the role of initial adjustment in therapists' ratings after the first session, severity of disturbance ratings were related to initial adjustment, as expected. While mean differences occurred (high adjusted group had a mean severity rating of 3.39, while the low group's mean was 4.28; $F = 11.02, p <$ .01), it should be noted that both initial adjustment groups were well within the moderate range on severity ratings. Along with severity ratings, initial adjustment did influence therapists' predictions of the extent to which they would enjoy working with the client; therapists expected to enjoy working with the better adjusted clients more than the less adjusted ones ($\bar{X}$'s respectively = 5.42 vs. 4.50, $F = 7.03, p < .01$). On the other hand, therapists did not rate initially high versus low adjusted clients differently on motivation, willingness to change, or ability to profit from treatment. While initial adjustment and treatment group did not interact significantly in the ANOVA's on any of the five items, a notable pattern emerged in that counselors exhibited the least confidence in the treatment they had to offer when the clients were more poorly adjusted and in the 8-session TLT group ($\bar{X} = 3.79$) as compared to the remaining five combinations of treatment group by initial adjustment ($\bar{X}$'s in those groups ranged from 4.46 to 4.79, combined $\bar{X} =$ 4.55; t of 3.79 vs. 4.55 = 1.97, $p = .05$). Thus, while we could not safely generalize this finding, it appeared that therapists felt least confident in the efficacy of the treatment when that treatment was 8-session TLT, and when the client was in the low initial adjustment group. This finding should be kept in mind when we discuss outcomes of the three time-duration treatments.

Therapists' Ratings of Their Own Behavior and of Outcome

Immediately following the termination, the therapists completed the *Post-Counseling Assessment Blank*. This measure contained three items eliciting therapists' assessment of their own behavior, and four items pertaining to clients' degree of change.

THERAPIST SELF-RATINGS. Therapists rated themselves in terms of three variables that appear repeatedly in the time-limited therapy literature as distinguishing therapist behavior in TLT versus TUT. Thus, therapists were asked to compare their behavior in therapy in general with their behavior in the particular experience being evaluated in terms of therapist *activity level,* the degree to which the therapist *structured* the therapy, and the extent to which the therapist dealt with

Table 2–3. Counselor Ratings After First Session

Item	Treatment group							
	8 sessions		16 sessions		Unlimited			
	$\bar{X}$	SD	$\bar{X}$	SD	$\bar{X}$	SD	F ratio
1. Severity of client disturbance (1 = mildly, 4 = moderately, 7 = severely)	4.19	1.11	3.71	1.21	3.65	1.40	1.64
2. Client's motivation for counseling (1 = poorly, 4 = moderately, 7 = highly)	5.11	1.48	4.79	1.40	5.09	1.35	.45
3. Client's willingness to change (1 = low, 4 = moderately, 7 = high)	4.26	1.46	4.32	1.36	4.35	1.34	.03
4. Counselor's confidence that client will profit from treatment offered (1 = little, 4 = moderate, 7 = much)	4.11	1.40	4.61	1.29	4.61	1.34	1.10
5. Counselor's prediction of enjoyment working with client (1 = no, 4 = moderate, 7 = much)	4.85	1.63	4.96	1.62	5.04	1.46	.10

Note. None of the F ratios approached the .05 level of confidence.

historical material. The first three items in Table 2–4 show therapists' responses to these variables within each of the three treatment conditions. As expected, therapists' self-ratings of activity level and structuring are higher in the two TLT conditions than in TUT. Regarding the use of historical material, however, the differences are miniscule and in the opposite direction.

Three 2 × 3 ANOVA's revealed significant main effects for treatment group on activity level and structuring (see Table 2–4). Newman-Keuls a posteriori tests indicated that therapists were equally active in 8- and 16-session TLT, while they were more active in both than in TUT. Additionally, counselors imposed more structure, following their self-reports, in 8-session TLT than in TUT. The degree of structure in 16-session TLT was intermediate, but did not differ significantly from that in either 8-session TLT or TUT.

Further analyses revealed that initial client adjustment did not affect therapist behavior on either of these three variables, activity level, structure, and the use of historical material. Finally, no interaction effects between treatment group and initial adjustment emerged.

THERAPISTS' RATINGS OF OUTCOME.   Therapists rated the effects of treatment in terms of four variables: overall personality change, behavior change, feeling change, and confidence that the changes exhibited by the client would persist. As indicated by the means in Table 2–4, therapists evaluated overall personality change to be less than "moderate" (the midpoint of the scale) in all treatment groups. On the other hand, they judged their clients to be behaving more effectively and feeling better after treatment; and therapists felt "moderately" confident that changes occurring during treatment would persist. Table 2–4 also reveals that differences among the three treatment groups do not reach statistical significance on any of these variables. While inspection of the means shows a clear tendency for ratings in the TUT condition to be more positive than those in the two TLT conditions, these differences among the treatment means are minor in relation to the large standard deviations for each item. Thus, great individual differences exist among clients in terms of therapists' outcome ratings, and these within-group variations were not notably diminished by our blocking variable, initial client adjustment.

Along with the lack of significant main effects for treatment, our 2 × 3 ANOVA's indicated nonsignificance both for main effects of initial client adjustment and for interaction effects for initial adjustment by treatment group. Thus, therapists' ratings of the influence of therapy on personality, behavior, feelings, and the expected persistence of change were not affected by treatment group, initial client adjustment, or the interaction of the two (Note, however, trends in the initial adjustment by treatment interactions as displayed in Table 2–6.). Finally, the trend toward TUT being rated more positively than the two TLT conditions should be kept in mind as we examine the clients' evaluations in the following sections.

Table 2-4. Counselor Ratings After Termination

Item	Treatment group						F ratio
	8 sessions		16 sessions		Unlimited		
	$\bar{X}$	SD	$\bar{X}$	SD	$\bar{X}$	SD	
1. Counselor activity level in this therapy compared to usual (1 = much less, 4 = equal, 7 = much more)	4.70	1.14	4.68	1.16	4.00	.74	3.56*
2. Extent counselor structured this therapy vs. structuring in general (1 = much less, 4 = as much, 7 = much more)	4.85	1.03	4.39	1.03	4.04	.83	4.18**
3. Extent counselor dealt with history in this therapy vs. in general (1 = much less, 4 = same, 7 = much more)	3.44	1.01	3.39	1.17	3.65	1.27	.35
4. Overall personality change due to treatment (1 = no change, 4 = moderate, 7 = much)	2.70	1.46	3.25	1.71	3.43	1.62	1.46
5. Client behaving more effectively (1 = no more, 4 = somewhat more, 7 = much more)	3.82	2.06	4.18	2.06	4.57	1.90	.86
6. Client feeling better (1 = no better, 4 = better, 7 = much better)	4.19	2.20	4.36	2.06	4.65	1.85	.34
7. Counselor confidence that change will persist (1 = much doubt, 4 = moderate confidence, 7 = much confidence)	4.00	2.09	3.89	2.04	4.22	1.70	.18

$* = p < .05$ $** = p < .01$

Shortly After Counseling—Clients' Evaluations of Themselves and Their Counseling

Approximately 2–3 weeks after counseling ended, clients were mailed the *Counseling Center Follow-up Questionnaire* (CCFQ). Table 2–5 presents means and standard deviations for clients' (N = 78) responses to 26 items of the CCFQ according to treatment group. Inspection of the table reveals that for 24 of the 26 possible comparisons, clients in the TUT condition obtained more positive means than those in the 8-session TLT condition. In 21 of the 26 comparisons, means in the TUT condition are more positive than those in the 16-session TLT condition. Finally, the 16-session condition exhibited more positive means for 16 of the 26 comparisons than did the 8-session condition.

For each of the 26 items in Table 2–5, the 2 × 3 ANOVA was computed.[2] As indicated by the F ratios in Table 2–5, statistically significant differences ($p < .05$) among the three treatment groups occurred for only three items, although differences approached significance ($p < .10$) on three additional items. Two of the items yielding significance related to clients' ratings of others' perceptions of whether they changed. One item asked this question in terms of *total change* (now as compared to when first coming to the Center) and another asked it in terms of *change due to counseling*. Newman-Keuls a posteriori testing indicated that clients in TUT more often than in 8- or 16-session TLT felt that others acted as though they had changed for the better (in terms of total change, i.e., since coming to the Center), while the two TLT groups did not differ from each other. When rating this same item in terms of change due to counseling, TUT ratings were more positive than those of 8-session TLT. Ratings of 16-session TLT were intermediate, but did not differ significantly from either TUT or 8-session TLT. Finally, between the end of counseling and follow-up, clients in 16-session TLT felt they experienced more "change for the better" than those in 8-session TLT in terms of "difficulties with interpersonal relations." Three additional items exhibited a trend ($p > .05, < .10$), and these items were not analyzed through post hoc testing.

The above analyses seem to reveal a clear and consistent trend toward TUT being rated more positively than TLT, in terms of changes on the whole, changes due to counseling, satisfaction with the experience, counselor helpfulness, and so forth. This trend is itself statistically significant, as revealed by the Sign Test (Siegel, 1956). That is, the number of times TUT means are more positive than either 8-session TLT means and 16-session TLT means (24 and 21 of 26, respectively) is statistically significant ($p < .01$). Yet, in only a few cases are the individual differences among the three treatments of sufficient magnitude to attain statistical significance.

INTERACTIONS. A major expectation was that the relative efficacy of the three treatments would to an important extent depend upon clients' initial adjustment levels. In essence, we expected TLT to be relatively effective with the better adjusted clients, and relatively ineffective with the more poorly adjusted ones.

(continued on page 36)

Table 2–5. Clients' Ratings of Self and Counseling After One Month

Item and subscale	Treatment group (n = 78)						F ratio
	8 sessions (n = 27)		16 sessions (n = 28)		Unlimited (n = 23)		
	$\bar{X}$	SD	$\bar{X}$	SD	$\bar{X}$	SD	
I. *Total Change*—now compared to when first came to Center.							
a. *I feel:* (1 = better, 2 = no change, 3 = worse)	1.26	.53	1.11	.32	1.17	.49	.74
b. *I relate to people:* (1 = better, 2 = no change, 3 = worse)	1.37	.57	1.41	.50	1.26	.54	.48
c. *I accomplish things I need to do:* (1 = more effectively, 2 = no change, 3 = less effectively)	1.63	.63	1.56	.58	1.35	.57	1.43
d. *I think:* (1 = more clearly, 2 = no change, 3 = less clearly)	1.41	.57	1.58	.50	1.30	.56	1.60
e. *Others act as though I have changed:* (1 = for the better, 2 = no change, 3 = for the worse)	1.67	.56	1.65	.49	1.26	.45	5.17***
II. *Change due to counseling*—amount of change resulting from counseling.							
a. *I feel:* (Note: same scale as above)	1.44	.58	1.29	.46	1.26	.54	.93
b. *I relate to people:*	1.56	.58	1.54	.51	1.35	.49	1.16
c. *I accomplish things I need to do:*	1.67	.56	1.68	.48	1.55	.60	.45
d. *I think:*	1.60	.57	1.54	.51	1.26	.45	2.93*
e. *Others act as though I have changed:*	1.77	.59	1.71	.46	1.39	.50	3.68**

Table 2–5. (Continued)

III. Satisfaction with results of counseling: (1 = very satisfied, 2 = satisfied, 3 = neutral, 4 = dissatisfied, 5 = very dissatisfied)	2.33	1.27	2.00	.77	2.04	.83	.93
IV. Did counseling last long enough to help in the way you wanted or needed: (1 = yes, 2 = not sure, 3 = no)	1.85	.91	1.89	.74	1.78	.90	.11
V. Overall change in you and/or your life as a result of counseling: (1 = no change for the better, 3 = some change, 5 = much change for the better)	3.00	1.24	3.00	1.09	3.39	1.12	.95
VI. Ratings of counselor helpfulness in:							
a. Helping you understand your problems:	2.22	1.34	2.21	1.07	1.74	1.10	1.50
b. Helping you resolve your problems:	2.89	1.53	2.56	1.19	2.39	1.27	.94
c. Creating atmosphere where you felt safe to talk about problems: (1 = very well, 2 = well, 3 = fairly well, 4 = slightly, 5 = not at all)	1.93	1.52	1.96	1.00	1.70	1.02	.38

(continued)

Table 2–5. (Continued)

VII. Part 1—*Changes from when came to Center and end of counseling.* Clients only rate items that apply to them. Data presented only for items to which ⅔ or more (n = 51) of clients responded. Scale: 1 = much change for the better, 2 = some, 3 = no change, 4 = some change for worse, 5 = much change for worse)

a. Feelings of loneliness, alienation (n = 59)	2.32	.67	2.10	.70	2.16	.77	.51
b. Feeling worried, tense, anxious (n = 73)	1.92	.81	2.12	.71	1.91	.81	.55
c. Depression, despondency (n = 66)	2.18	.66	2.08	.65	1.85	.81	1.18
d. Low self-esteem (n = 56)	2.32	.95	2.24	.66	1.71	.85	2.95*
e. Family problems (n = 49)	– –	– –	– –	– –	– –	– –	– –
f. Difficulties with interpersonal relations	2.37	.60	2.04	.64	2.05	.78	1.44
g. Difficulties with opposite sex (n = 49)	– –	– –	– –	– –	– –	– –	– –
h. Marital or premarital problems (n = 32)	– –	– –	– –	– –	– –	– –	– –
i. Homosexuality (n = 21)	– –	– –	– –	– –	– –	– –	– –
j. Other sexual concerns (n = 26)	– –	– –	– –	– –	– –	– –	– –
k. Problems with drugs (n = 19)	– –	– –	– –	– –	– –	– –	– –
l. Problems with drinking (n = 19)	– –	– –	– –	– –	– –	– –	– –
m. Difficulty in concentration (n = 42)	– –	– –	– –	– –	– –	– –	– –
n. Efficiency in study methods (n = 36)	– –	– –	– –	– –	– –	– –	– –
o. Plan for major field of study (n = 36)	– –	– –	– –	– –	– –	– –	– –
p. Plan for occupation to pursue (n = 37)	– –	– –	– –	– –	– –	– –	– –
q. Grades earned (n = 34)	– –	– –	– –	– –	– –	– –	– –

Table 2–5. (Continued)

VII. Part 2—*Changes since the end of counseling* (same scale as above)

a. Feelings of loneliness, alienation (n = 51)	2.28	1.07	2.42	.90	1.94	1.00	1.08
b. Feeling worried, tense, anxious (n = 69)	2.17	1.24	2.00	.96	2.30	.98	.43
c. Depression, despondency (n = 61)	1.95	.95	2.22	1.13	2.05	1.05	.36
f. Difficulties with interpersonal relations (n = 53)	2.52	.80	1.82	.59	2.12	.70	4.80***

Note: None of the other 17 items was rated by ⅔ or more of clients.

VIII. *Clients Comments*[a]

a. Most noticeable change since coming to center (n = 70) (1 = positive, 2 = ambivalent, 3 = negative)	1.32	.72	1.50	.81	1.14	.47	1.72
b. Free comments (n = 47) (1 = positive, 2 = ambivalent, 3 = negative)	2.06	.90	1.93	.96	1.36	.74	2.69*

* = $p < .10$
** = $p < .05$
*** = $p < .01$

[a]Two Counseling Center interns not involved in the study in any other way rated Ss' responses independently on Items VIIIa and VIIIb. Interjudge agreement on these items was 67 of 70 and 45 of 47, respectively. The few instances that raters disagreed on were discussed following the rating, and agreement was reached.

Thus, we expected to find a number of significant initial adjustment by treatment group interactions. In fact, only one of the 27 items yielded a statistically significant ($p < .05$) interaction effect. For exploratory purposes, we decided to inspect the pattern of mean differences when a more liberal definition of alpha was used—.25 rather than the conventional .05 level. The rationale for this strategy is based on the view that alpha should be set according to the relative costs of Type I and Type II errors, rather than strict adherence to convention. In this case, we felt that the cost of overlooking real treatment outcome differences based on client adjustment warranted the more liberal alpha. We recognize the more tentative nature of significant findings obtained in this manner. Table 2–6 presents all interaction effects for both counselor- and client-rated items where p was less than .25. The table shows the pattern of means that occurred for the initially high and low adjusted clients separately.

When examined in this way, a rather striking pattern emerged. For clients who were initially more *poorly adjusted*, 8-session TLT received the least favorable rating on all 13 items. (See the column on the far right side of Table 2–6.) Furthermore, TUT obtained the most favorable ratings on 12 of the 13 items for this client group, and was tied with 16-session TLT on the 13th. On the other hand, a very different pattern appears for the initially better adjusted clients, although this pattern was not as consistent. For the *better adjusted* group, 8- or 16-session TLT was more favorably evaluated than TUT on 11 of the 13 items, while TUT received the least positive rating on 5 of the items.

Thus, while caution must be exercized in generalizing from these data, this exploratory analysis suggests that *TUT is more favorably evaluated than TLT, and 16-session TLT more positively evaluated than 8-session TLT when the clients are poorly adjusted. When the clients are better adjusted, however, TLT, if anything, yields more favorable reactions than open-ended counseling.* Does this rather striking pattern hold up well after therapy has ended? This question is explored in the next section, where we examine the results of our 18-month follow-up investigation.

Before moving to the next section, we have further data to clarify the pattern of interactions discussed above. Table 2–7 contains means and *SD*'s for the initially better and more poorly adjusted clients within each treatment group on the three items where interaction effects were most notable ($p < .10$). The first item pertains to the counselor's rating of how treatment affected clients' feelings; the latter two items reflect clients' evaluations of their therapists. A pattern emerges on these items, such that *the most positive ratings occur with the better adjusted clients in 8-session TLT and the most poorly adjusted client in TUT. Thus, the evaluations are in opposite directions for the two adjustment groups, with the briefest TLT being most favorable for the better adjusted clients and TUT being clearly most favorable for the more poorly adjusted clients* (at least in terms of these three items).

Table 2-6. Items on Which Treatment by Initial Adjustment Interaction Approached Significance ($p < .25$)

Item	P-value	Direction of treatment differences	
		Initially better adjusted	Initially more poorly adjusted
1. Overall client personality change due to counseling (counselor rated)	.21	UL < 8 = 16	8 < 16 < UL
2. Client feeling better due to counseling (counselor rated)	.08	UL < 16 < 8	8 < 16 < UL
3. Client thinking more clearly (client rated, as are all below) (Item Id on CCFQ)	.13	16 < UL < 8	8 < 16 < UL
4. Others act as though client has changed for the better (Item X)	.22	8 = 16 < UL	8 < 16 < UL
5. Client relating to people better, due to counseling (Item IIa)	.19	16 < UL < 8	8 < 16 < UL
6. Client accomplishing necessary things	.16	16 < UL < 8	8 < 16 < UL
7. Overall client change due to counseling (Item V)	.13	UL < 16 < 8	8 < 16 < UL
8. Counselor helpfulness in understanding problems (Item VIa)	.02	UL = 16 < 8	8 < 16 < UL
9. Counselor helpfulness in solving problems (Item IIb)	.23	UL < 8 < 16	8 < 16 < UL
10. Counselor's creation of safe atmosphere (Item VIc)	.06	16 < UL < 8	8 < 16 < UL
11. Feelings of alienation, loneliness at end of counseling (Item VIIa)	.12	UL < 16 < 8	8 < 16 = UL
12. Low self-esteem at end of counseling (Item VIId)	.20	16 < 8 < UL	8 < 16 < UL
13. Most noticeable change since coming to center (Item VIIIa)	.12	16 < UL < 8	8 < 16 < UL

*Items 1–2 are counselor rated; 3–13 are client rated.

Table 2–7. Means and SD's for Items on Which Treatment by Initial Adjustment Interaction Was $p < .10$

| Item | Initial adjust-ment category | Treatment group | | | | | |
| | | 8 session | | 16 session | | TUT | |
		$\bar{X}$	SD	$\bar{X}$	SD	$\bar{X}$	SD
1. Degree to which client is feeling better as a consequence of treatment (#6 of *Post-Counseling Assessment Block*; 1 = no better, 4 = better, 7 = much better; counselor rated)	High	5.00	1.63	4.38	2.21	4.18	1.77
	Low	3.42	2.44	4.33	1.98	5.08	3.53
2. How well counselor did on helping client understand his/her concerns (#6a of *CCFQ*; 1 = very well, 2 = well, 3 = fairly well, 4 = slightly, 5 = not at all; client rated)	High	1.53	.78	2.00	.91	2.00	1.41
	Low	2.85	1.46	2.40	1.18	1.50	.67
3. How well counselor did in creating safe atmosphere (#6c of *CCFQ*; same scale as #6a; client rated)	High	1.23	.60	1.92	1.04	1.72	1.27
	Low	2.57	1.83	2.00	1.00	1.67	.78

Finally, across treatment groups, clients' evaluations of themselves and their counseling one month after termination were generally positive. On the whole, clients felt counseling had helped them in a variety of ways, they felt satisfied with the experience, and they felt their therapists did well with them. As implied, however, this general characterization must be somewhat modified by specific treatment groups and by the interaction of type of treatment with clients' initial adjustment level. While statistical significance emerged on few specific items, the overall pattern was for clients in TUT to yield the most positive reactions and, furthermore, for differential reactions to the three treatments to be consistently if not powerfully moderated by initial adjustment level.

Eighteen Months Later—Clients' Reactions to the Extended Follow-Up

Just as with the 1-month follow-up, when former clients ($n = 67$) were surveyed 18 months after termination, they exhibited a consistent tendency to make more favorable evaluations under the TUT condition than either of the TLT conditions. Thus, those in TUT made more favorable evaluations than clients in 8-session TLT on 26 of 32 comparisons (1 tie), and than clients in 16-session TLT on 28 of 32 comparisons. Again, however, 8- and 16-session TLT did not differ in terms of such a pattern, that is, 16-session TLT was more positively evaluated than 8-session TLT on 12 of 29 comparisons, with three ties.

Whereas statistical significance was found on only four items in the 1-month follow-up (in terms of both main effects and interactions), such significance emerged on nine items in the 18-month survey; and the analyses approached significance ($p < .10$) on four more items. Main effects of group existed on seven items. Table 2–8 presents means and SD's for each item that was analyzed on the 18-month follow-up. These are presented for each of the three treatment groups; and the F ratios for the significance of the treatment main effects (for our usual 2 × 3 ANOVA's) are also given in Table 2–8.

Table 2–8 reveals that when the former clients rated *Total Change* on general items assessing their feelings, thinking, relating, and so forth (Category I) *without regard to the effects of counseling,* the aforementioned pattern did not emerge. Thus, regardless of treatment condition, most clients felt better, related better, accomplished necessary things more effectively, thought more clearly, and were perceived by others as having changed for the better 18 months after completing counseling (as compared to when they began counseling).

When clients evaluate *how counseling has affected them* (Categories II, V, and VIIIa), *their feelings about counseling and their therapists* (categories III, VI, and VIIIb), or *their changes in more specific problem areas* (Category VII), the pattern of clients in TUT making more favorable evaluations than those in either of the TLT conditions clearly appears. Regarding statistically significant differences (significant F ratios followed by Newman-Keuls tests), clients in TUT, 18 months

(continued on page 44)

Table 2–8. Clients' Ratings of Self and Counseling After 18 Months

| | Treatment group (n = 67) | | | | | | |
| | 8 sessions (n = 21) | | 16 sessions (n = 24) | | Unlimited (n = 22) | | |
Item and subscale	$\bar{X}$	SD	$\bar{X}$	SD	$\bar{X}$	SD	F ratio
I. Total Change—now compared to when first came to Center.							
a. I feel: (1 = better, 2 = no change, 3 = worse)	1.05	.22	1.04	.20	1.00	.00	.50
b. I relate to people: (1 = better, 2 = no change, 3 = worse)	1.29	.46	1.29	.46	1.33	.48	.07
c. I accomplish things I need to do: (1 = more effectively, 2 = no change, 3 = less effectively)	1.33	.48	1.33	.48	1.27	.46	.12
d. I think: (1 = more clearly, 2 = no change, 3 = less clearly)	1.24	.44	1.38	.50	1.23	.43	.75
e. Others act as though I have changed: (1 = for the better, 2 = no change, 3 = for the worse)	1.43	.60	1.52	.51	1.50	.51	.20
II. Change due to counseling—amount of change resulting from counseling.							
a. I feel: (Note: same scale as above)	1.52	.51	1.46	.51	1.19	.40	2.80*
b. I relate to people:	1.71	.46	1.75	.44	1.43	.51	2.98**
c. I accomplish things I need to do:	1.62	.50	1.78	.42	1.48	.51	2.27
d. I think:	1.52	.51	1.83	.39	1.52	.51	3.01***
e. Others act as though I have changed:	1.76	.54	1.83	.38	1.48	.51	3.41**

Table 2–8. (Continued)

III. *Satisfaction with results of counseling:* (1 = very satisfied,
2 = satisfied, 3 = neutral, 4 = dissatisfied,
5 = very dissatisfied)

2.57	1.12	2.50	1.02	2.09	.92	1.48

IV. *Did counseling last long enough to help in the way you
wanted or needed:* (1 = yes, 2 = not sure, 3 = no)

2.00	.95	2.09	.85	2.05	1.13	.04

V. *Overall change in you and/or your life as a result of
counseling:* (1 = no change for the better, 3 = some
change, 5 = much change for the better)

2.67	1.20	2.58	1.18	3.05	1.21	.96

VI. *Ratings of counselor helpfulness in:*

a. *Helping you understand your problems:*

b. *Helping you resolve your problems:*

c. *Creating atmospheres where you felt safe to talk about
problems:* (1 = very well, 2 = well, 3 = fairly well,
4 = slightly, 5 = not at all)

2.48	1.50	2.70	1.19	2.23	1.31	.74
3.19	1.54	3.21	1.18	2.77	1.27	.76
2.29	1.59	2.29	1.08	2.05	1.40	.22

(continued)

Table 2–8. (Continued)

VII. Part 1—*Changes from when came to Center and end of counseling.* Clients only rate items that apply to them. Data presented only for items to which ⅔ or more (*n* = 44) of clients responded. Scale: 1 = much change for the better, 2 = some, 3 = no change, 4 = some change for worse, 5 = much change for worse)

a. Feelings of loneliness, alienation (*n* = 53)	2.56	.63	2.56	.62	1.95	.71	5.16***
b. Feeling worried, tense, anxious (*n* = 58)	2.21	.86	2.29	.78	2.06	.73	.42
c. Depression, despondency (*n* = 55)	2.39	.85	2.17	.79	1.84	.69	2.20
d. Low self-esteem (*n* = 51)	2.53	.64	2.44	.81	1.85	.67	4.68***
e. Family problems (*n* = 44)	2.67	.62	2.39	.65	2.19	.83	1.69
f. Difficulties with interpersonal relations (*n* = 50)	2.57	.65	2.47	.62	2.00	.67	3.82**
g. Difficulties with opposite sex (*n* = 44)	2.57	.65	2.62	.51	2.35	.79	.65
h. Marital or premarital problems (*n* = 28)	— —		— —		— —		— —
i. Homosexuality (*n* = 15)	— —		— —		— —		— —
j. Other sexual concerns (*n* = 22)	— —		— —		— —		— —
k. Problems with drugs (*n* = 16)	— —		— —		— —		— —
l. Problems with drinking (*n* = 15)	— —		— —		— —		— —
m. Difficulty in concentration (*n* = 32)	— —		— —		— —		— —
n. Efficiency in study methods (*n* = 29)	— —		— —		— —		— —
o. Plan for major field of study (*n* = 28)	— —		— —		— —		— —
p. Plan for occupation to pursue (*n* = 31)	— —		— —		— —		— —
q. Grades earned (*n* = 25)	— —		— —		— —		— —

Table 2-8. (Continued)

VII. Part 2—*Changes since the end of counseling* (same scale as above)

a. *Feelings of loneliness, alienation* ($n = 51$)	2.06	.77	2.24	1.03	1.56	.62	3.02**
b. *Feeling worried, tense, anxious* ($n = 58$)	1.79	.92	1.90	1.02	2.05	.97	.38
c. *Depression, despondency* ($n = 53$)	1.67	.59	1.82	.95	1.89	1.13	.33
d. *Low self-esteem* ($n = 50$)	1.77	.92	1.80	.86	1.55	.76	.71
e. *Family problems* ($n = 44$)	2.20	.94	1.69	.75	1.88	.81	1.40
f. *Difficulties with interpersonal relations* ($n = 50$)	1.71	.91	1.94	.86	1.90	.77	.27

Note: None of the other 17 items were rated by ⅔ or more of clients.

VIII. *Items requiring written responses by client* (#8, 9, 10 on CCFQ)[a]

a. *Most noticeable change since coming* (1 = positive, 2 = ambivalent, 3 = negative)($n = 61$)	1.61	.92	1.50	.80	1.18	.50	1.82
b. *What counseling experience meant to client* (1 = positive, 2 = mostly positive, 3 = mostly negative, 4 = negative) ($n = 62$)	2.62	1.36	2.29	1.23	2.00	1.21	1.26
c. *Mention of dissatisfaction with duration of counseling* (1 = no mention, 2 = mention)	1.24	.44	1.13	.34	1.09	.29	.99

* = $p < .10$
** = $p < .05$
*** = $p < .01$

[a]Subjects' responses to Items VIIIa, b, and c were rated independently by an intern-level doctoral student in counseling psychology and the first author. One hundred percent agreement was obtained on VIIIa and c; on VIIIb the agreement rate was 56 of 62 (90%). Agreement was attained following discussion in these six cases.

later, were more likely than those in TLT to feel that counseling helped them relate to people better and resulted in others acting as though they have changed for the better. Clients in both TUT and 8-session TLT more often than 16-session TLT clients felt that counseling resulted in their thinking more clearly.

When estimating change from beginning to end of counseling, the TUT clients as compared to those in either TLT treatments indicated that significantly more positive change had occurred regarding feelings of loneliness and alienation, self-esteem, and difficulties with interpersonal relationships. Finally, between the end of counseling and the 18-month follow-up, clients in TUT reported significantly further gains than those in 16-session TLT in terms of overcoming feelings of loneliness and alienation.

While the pattern for TUT to receive more positive evaluations than TLT emerged clearly in the data, it ironically did not occur for items dealing specifically with duration of treatment, either in the 1-month or 18-month follow-up. Thus, when asked if counseling lasted long enough to help them in the ways they wanted or needed to be helped (Category IV), clients in the three treatments in both follow-ups did not respond differently. Additionally, no differences appeared among the treatments in terms of the extent to which clients mentioned dissatisfaction with the treatment duration after 18 months (Category VIIIc). Few clients in any condition made such negative allusions to this free-response item. This surprising bit of apparent incongruence is explored further in our final section.

What about the interaction of treatment and initial adjustment? As with the one-month follow-up, we expected TLT to be more positive for the better adjusted clients, and more negative for the more poorly adjusted clients (i.e., relative to their reactions to TUT). As with the one-month follow-up, few of the interaction effects approached the conventional significance level. Table 2–9 presents the interaction patterns that emerged when we again employed the more lenient alpha of .25.

The most prominent interaction pattern in the 1-month follow-up does not appear in this long-term follow-up. That is, a consistent tendency *does not appear* for the more poorly adjusted clients to make the most favorable ratings of TUT, and the least favorable ratings of the 8-session TLT. Close inspection of Table 2–9, however, reveals a most interesting pattern. That is, *the pattern identified after one month does appear, and clearly so, on all five items where clients are asked to evaluate their counseling or their therapists* (These items are underlined in the table for ease of identification.) *For the seven remaining items, on the other hand (those assessing clients' evaluations of themselves and their progress without reference to counseling), an opposite pattern emerges.* For all such items, the more poorly adjusted clients appear to give the most favorable evaluations when they were in the briefest treatments, whereas the better adjusted clients uniformly give the least positive evaluations of themselves and their progress following the briefest treatment, that is, 8-session TLT. This complex and unexpected finding is explored further in our discussion section.

Table 2–9. Items on Which Treatment by Initial Adjustment Interaction Approached Statistical Significance ($p < .25$) on the 18-Month Follow-Up

Item	p-value	Direction of treatment differences	
		Initially better adjusted	Initially more poorly adjusted
1. Client feeling better (Item Ia)	.21	8 < 16 = UL	16 < 8 = UL
2. Client relating to people better (Item Ib)	.06	8 < UL < 16	16 < UL < 8
3. Others act as though client has changed for the better (Item Ie)	.17	8 < 16 < UL	UL < 16 < 8
4. Client satisfaction with result of counseling (Item III)	.12	16 < UL < 8	8 < 16 < UL
5. Overall change in client's life as result of counseling (Item V)	.19	UL < 16 < 8	8 < 16 < UL
6. Counselor helpfulness in understanding problems (Item VIa)	.03	16 < UL < 8	8 < 16 < UL
7. Counselor's creation of safe atmosphere (Item VIb)	.08	UL < 16 < 8	8 < 16 < UL
8. Feeling worried, tense, anxious—between end of counseling and now (Item VII, Part 2, b)	.08	8 < 16 < UL	UL < 16 < 8
9. Depression, despondency—between end of counseling and now (Item VII, Part 2, c)	.08	8 < 16 < UL	UL < 16 < 8
10. Family problems—between end of counseling and now (Item VII, Part 2, e)	.11	8 < UL < 16	UL < 16 < 8
11. Difficulties with interpersonal relationships—between end of counseling and now (Item VII, Part 2, f)	.01	8 < 16 < UL	UL < 16 < 8
12. What counseling experience meant to client (Item VIIIb)	.21	16 < 8 = UL	8 < 16 < UL

Changes in Clients' Reactions Across Time—From One to Eighteen Months

One way of assessing changes in clients' reactions from the 1-month to the 18-month follow-up is to compare data on Tables 2–5 and 2–8 for the main effects of our treatment variable and Tables 2–6 and 2–9 for the interactions of treatment and initial adjustment. A less awkward and more statistically appropriate technique would be to place time of testing into our statistical analysis and only study the 67 clients who completed the CCFQ on both occasions. This section reports the results from such a comparison. We computed a $2 \times 2 \times 3$ analysis of variance (time of testing, 1 month vs. 18 months, by initial adjustment level by treatment) for each item on the CCFQ. For the sake of clarity, these results are summarized under each main section of the CCFQ.

TOTAL CHANGE.   Clients rated their overall change in feelings, relating to people, accomplishing necessary things, thinking, and their perceptions of others' views of their change. These items come from Section I (a, b, c, d, and e) of the CCFQ. Again, the ratings were made 1 month and 18 months after termination.

Clients exhibited more positive ratings of feelings (Item a), accomplishing necessary things (Item c), and thinking clearly (Item d) on the 18-month versus the 1-month follow-up. Furthermore, it will be recalled that one month after treatment ended, clients in TUT felt moreso than did those in 8- or 16-session TLT that others acted as though they had changed for the better. This difference did not appear 18 months later. Thus, as expected, our current analysis yielded a significant time of testing by treatment interaction ($F = 3.82$, $p < .05$); the two TLT groups improved on this variable while the TUT group decreased in their ratings. Surprisingly, however, we also uncovered a significant three-way interaction effect ($F = 3.68$, $p < .05$). Further analysis (with the Newman-Keuls) indicated that the source of this complex interaction was the low initial adjustment group in the TUT condition, that is, their ratings lowered substantially while all others' ratings increased slightly.

CHANGE DUE TO COUNSELING.   The CCFQ asks subjects to, in effect, partial out the amount of total change that is due to the counseling experience on the above five variables (Item II, a through e). When the 1-month and 18-month results are combined, clients in TUT, as compared to either of the TLT conditions, indicated that they related to people more effectively, were able to think more clearly, and that others acted as though they had changed for the better more often. Thus, on three of the five items in this section, TUT clearly received more favorable evaluations than either TLT condition. At the same time, significant time of testing by treatment group interactions on the latter two variables (thinking, and others act as though . . .; both p's $< .01$) revealed that the superiority of the TUT condition diminished slightly with time. Additionally, ratings of the 8-session TLT group increased slightly over time on these variables.

SATISFACTION WITH COUNSELING, WITH DURATION OF COUNSELING, AND THE OVERALL CHANGE DUE TO COUNSELING.   Items III, IV, and V asked clients to make global ratings of (a) their satisfaction with the results of counseling, (b) their perceptions of whether counseling lasted long enough, and (c) the overall change in them and/or their lives due to counseling. The only effects that emerged from our analysis were for time of testing. Clients felt slightly but significantly less satisfied with the results of their counseling 18 months as compared to 1 month afterwards ($F = 9.07$, $p < .01$). They also perceived themselves as evidencing less overall change due to counseling 18 months later ($F = 10.97$, $p < .01$).

EVALUATIONS OF THEIR THERAPISTS.   Two striking patterns emerged in our analysis of the three items asking clients to evaluate their therapists (Items VIa, b, and c). First, clients evaluated their therapists less positively 18 months after counseling than 1 month later. Clients on the whole felt less positively about their therapists' helpfulness in getting them to understand their problems ($\bar{X}$'s = 2.02 at 1 month and 2.47 at 18 months, where 1 = very well, 2 = well, 3 = fairly well, etc., $F = 9.76$, $p < .01$); they felt therapists were less helpful in the resolution of the clients' concerns (respective means = 2.61 vs. 3.03 using the same scale as above; $F = 11.73$, $p < .01$); and they viewed therapists as less helpful in creating an atmosphere where clients felt safe to talk about their problems (respective means = 1.95 vs. 2.47; $F = 3.80$, $p < .05$). Thus, while the means indicated that clients felt their counselors did fairly well to well on three important dimensions of counselor helpfulness, on the whole the ratings were less positive after the 18-month interval.

The second notable pattern in clients' ratings of their therapists was actually an accentuation of a pattern that occurred when the 1- and 18-month data were analyzed separately. That is, when the two times of measurement were combined in the current analysis, the interaction of initial adjustment and treatment group on evaluations of counselors became magnified. Thus, this interaction attained statistical significance on two of the three therapists' evaluation items: therapists' helpfulness in getting the client to understand his or her problems (F for the interaction effect = 5.21, $p < .01$) and therapists creation of an atmosphere where the client felt safe to talk about his or her problems ($F = 3.81$, $p < .05$). The means from this analysis are presented in tabular form in Appendix F. Suffice it to say here that the central elements of the interactions on both items were for the highest ratings to be given by the better adjusted clients in the 8-session TLT condition and the more poorly adjusted clients in TUT. The lowest ratings, on the other hand, were given by the more poorly adjusted clients in 8-session TLT. Thus, our briefest treatment elicited the poorest evaluations of therapists when the client was more poorly adjusted initially, but very positive evaluations when the client was better adjusted. At the same time, open-ended treatment stimulated highly positive evaluations of therapists from initially poorly adjusted clients.

CHANGES IN PROBLEM AREAS FROM THE BEGINNING TO THE END OF COUNSELING.   It will be recalled that when clients rated their pre- to postcounseling changes in particular problem areas one month after counseling ended, statistically nonsignificant trends emerged for TUT to receive more favorable ratings than either of the TLT treatments (see Table 2–5). It will be further recalled that this trend increased on the 18-month follow-up such that differences attained significance on three of seven items, for example, feelings of loneliness and alienation, low self-esteem, and difficulties with interpersonal relations. Our current analysis reflected this difference between clients' responses 1 month and 18 months after treatment. Thus, the interaction of time and treatment attained significance in our current analysis for the item "feelings of loneliness, alienation" ($F = 3.70$, $p < .05$), with the major feature of this interaction being that the two TLT conditions showed a decrement in ratings and the TUT condition received an increment as time passed. Thus, clients in TUT felt more positive change occurred in "feelings of loneliness and alienation" as a function of counseling when they made the rating 18 months after termination than when they made it one month later. The converse was true for clients in the two TLT conditions.

As expected from the data on Tables 2–5 and 2–8, when the two times of testing, 1 month and 18 months, were combined, the main effects for treatment were highly significant on the problem area "low self-esteem" ($F = 8.11$, $p < .001$). The TUT condition was clearly superior in clients' ratings of this item to either of the TLT conditions ($\overline{X}$'s $= 1.68$ for TUT versus 2.34 and 2.53 for 16- and 8-session TLT, respectively). This same trend emerged for the item "difficulties with interpersonal relationships," although the differences did not quite attain statistical significance ($F = 2.85$, $p = .07$).

CHANGES FROM THE END OF COUNSELING TO THE PRESENT.   Students rated changes that occurred in the same problem areas as above "between the end of counseling and now." They made these ratings 1 month and 18 months after termination. Here we found main effects for time on five items: "feelings of loneliness and alienation," "feeling worried, anxious, tense," "depression, despondency," "low self-esteem," and "family problems." In each of these items, greater positive change was noted after 18 months than after 1 month. Thus, it appears that in problem areas such as the above, former clients see themselves improving during at least an 18-month postcounseling period more than during the 1-month period, and this improvement does not seem to be influenced by particular treatment they receive (or we would have uncovered significant time by treatment group interactions).

Additional Questions Addressed by the Data

In this section we examine two questions that were not central to our outcome questions but may be of help in attempting to understand the findings reported thus far.

DO CLIENTS RETURN FOR COUNSELING AFTER TERMINATION, AND IS THIS RETURN RATE DIFFERENT FOR CLIENTS WHO RECEIVE TIME-LIMITED COUNSELING AS OPPOSED TO OPEN-ENDED COUNSELING?   Assessments of the efficacy of time-limited procedures must be made in light of the frequency with which clients return for more counseling. Thus, if we find TLT to be as effective as TUT, but we also find that clients in TLT return for counseling at a much greater rate than TUT clients, our conclusions about the utility of TLT would have to be substantially modified. In the present study we asked former clients in the 18-month follow-up if they had received additional counseling since termination (Item IX of the CCFQ). Nearly one-third (31.3%, 21 of 67) of them had done so, and this return rate was especially prominent in the 8-session TLT group. Table 2–10 presents the number and percentage of clients who sought further counseling within each adjustment level by treatment group combination. As can be seen in the table, nearly half (48%) of the clients in the 8-session treatment sought further counseling, while only 25% and 23% of those in the 16-session group and TUT did so. Although the difference between the 8-session and the combined 16-session and TUT groups did not quite attain significance ($\chi^2 = 3.74$, $p = .054$), this is a rather striking difference that warrants attention.

Table 2–10 also shows the return rates according to our breakdown on initial adjustment. Again, while no statistically significant differences occur according to this breakdown, at least in this sample those clients in the initially less adjusted group receiving open-ended treatment seem to return for counseling *less* than any other group.

Two additional findings regarding return rate appear notable. First, we were able to assess whether clients returned to our agency or went elsewhere for further

Table 2–10.   Frequency of Help Seeking During 18-Month Period Between Termination and Follow-Up

Initial adjustment level	Further counseling	Treatment group		
		8-session TLT ($n = 21$)	16-session TLT ($n = 24$)	TUT ($n = 22$)
High adjustment	Yes	5 (50)	3 (25)	4 (36)
	No	5 (50)	9 (75)	7 (64)
Low adjustment	Yes	5 (45)	3 (25)	1 (9)
	No	6 (55)	9 (75)	10 (91)
High and low combined	Yes	10 (48)	6 (25)	5 (23)
	No	11 (52)	18 (75)	17 (77)

Note: Percentages are in parenthesis adjacent to frequency.

counseling in 16 cases. Eight of those cases sought counseling elsewhere. Thus, if one studied return rates in only the agency where the initial counseling was done, such return rates would be erroneously low. Second, we asked former clients to specify how much additional counseling they received. Codable responses were obtained from 15 of the 21 clients who did so (n's = 7 in 8-session TLT, 4 in 16-session TLT, and 4 in TUT). The results indicate that, if anything, clients in the briefest TLT seek the least amount of continued counseling. Thus, the mean number of additional weeks in counseling for the 8-session group was 6.0 (range from 1 to 12), while the respective means for weeks of continued counseling in the 16-session and TUT groups were 20.5 (range from 1 to 56) and 24.3 (range from 3 to 62). If we combine the admittedly very sketchy data in this section, it appears that clients in the briefest treatment are more likely to seek additional help after termination, but when they do seek more counseling it is usually of a brief nature. On the other hand, clients in TUT tend not to seek more counseling, but when they do it tends to be of a more extended nature.

Is DURATION OF TREATMENT RELATED TO THERAPISTS' AND CLIENTS' EVALUA-TIONS OF COUNSELING, AND IS THIS RELATIONSHIP DIFFERENT FOR CLIENTS IN TIME-LIMITED VERSUS UNLIMITED COUNSELING?   As indicated in the Introduction, prior research has identified a modest relationship between duration of treatment and outcome. Such a finding suggests that the more counseling a client receives, the better. To determine if this finding was confirmed in the current study, we correlated number of sessions with therapists' ratings of personality, feeling, and behavior change, and with their confidence that the changes that occurred would persist. Also, we correlated number of sessions with clients' responses to the CCFQ, both 1 month and 18 months after treatment. These data are shown in Appendix G. To summarize here, modest relationships did occur between thera-pists' evaluations and duration for the entire group of clients; they also occurred for clients in each of the three treatment groups. In fact, if anything, the rela-tionship of duration to outcome according to therapists' ratings appeared strongest in 8-session TLT, for example, note that the correlation of .61 between duration and therapists' ratings of overall personality change for clients in 8-session TLT was the highest correlation for therapist-rated items.

Findings from the client ratings were similar to those already noted. That is, for clients as a whole there exists a modest tendency for duration to be correlated positively with outcome. Note also, however, that this tendency is greater at the 18-month period than the 1-month period. Thus, if anything, the influence of duration on outcome, in clients' eyes anyway, increases as time after treatment passes. Finally, as was the case with the therapists' ratings, the relationship of duration to client-rated outcome occurs in TLT as well as TUT, and this seems especially true for our briefest treatment. Thus, the correlations between duration and client-rated outcome appear highest on the 18-month follow-up for clients in 8-session TLT. These results are examined further in our next section.

Summary, Discussion, and Conclusions

We begin this discussion with several caveats regarding the study and its results in an effort to place the findings into a proper context. First, in attempting to understand the results and to integrate them with existing literature, it must be remembered that we have examined only therapist and client reports. As Bergin and Lambert (1978) have noted, therapy outcome criteria may be categorized according to source of measurement, for example, therapist, client, observer, test data. Since these sources seem to be relatively independent of one another, it is important to refrain from applying findings obtained from one source (e.g., client self-report) to another (e.g., test data). At the same time, outcome assessments by therapists and clients are two obviously crucial sources of measurement (see, for example, Strupp & Hadley's [1977] analysis). The point here is that client and therapist evaluations must be interpreted as just that, and bridges to other criterion sources need to be based on research rather than on inferential leaps.

A second caveat pertains to the therapists' previous experience in and attitudes toward TLT. It will be recalled that, on the whole, our therapists felt most comfortable conducting moderately long-term counseling (6 months to 1 year) and possessed what we labeled a "guarded optimism" about the value of TLT when the project got under way. Furthermore, although the therapists typically reported being as experienced in TLT as most therapists, they were certainly not as experienced in this mode as in therapy without a time limit. Thus, as is the case in nearly all TLT studies, we were comparing treatment providers who were highly experienced in one mode and modestly experienced in the other. This observation must be taken into account in interpreting our findings, even though the therapists became more seasoned in TLT as the study progressed through staff seminars, readings, and so forth.

Therapists' differential experience levels in TLT and TUT make for a conservative test of the efficacy of TLT. This experience differential does not allow an assessment of the *potential* effectiveness of the treatment form; that would require therapists who were experienced experts in the approach. What it does allow, however, is an assessment of current reality, since the overwhelming majority of practicing therapists are probably appreciably more experienced in TUT than TLT.

A third point is not so much a caveat as a statement about our findings that warrants further research attention. We were surprised to find that the differences between the numbers of sessions attended by clients in the 8-session and 16-session treatment groups was only 2.61 ($\bar{X}$'s = 6.0 and 8.61, respectively). More specifically, it was unexpected that those in the 16-session treatment averaged only 8.61 sessions, especially in light of previous agency data indicating that means for open-ended counseling were in the vicinity of 20 sessions. In attempting to explain this finding, it might be useful to consider that therapists who are inexperienced with the use of limits may well treat clients in these two conditions alike. That is, they may not have been able to gauge the difference between what could be done and accomplished in 8 as opposed to 16 sessions, and thus may have treated clients in the longer TLT as if there were actually fewer sessions available—which would have the effect of abbreviating the 16-session TLT experience. While such a hypothesis is not directly testable from the data, there is some indirect support. Therapists reported being equally active with their 8- and 16-session cases, and significantly more active with those cases than with their TUT clients. Further, there was no difference between therapists' treatment of 8- and 16-session clients in terms of degree of structure. Finally, subsequent data from 12-session TLT cases treated by therapists who are highly experienced in TLT indicates that the mean number of sessions for such cases at the Center is approximately 10 (e.g., 2 sessions less than the time limit, as was the case with 8-session TLT in the current study). Whatever the explanation, the difference of only 2.61 sessions between the two TLT treatments should be kept in mind as we explore the meanings of our findings further.

A final caution relates to the meaning of TUT in the current study. While the mean of 20 sessions for TUT clients clearly distinguishes that treatment from both TLT conditions, it is not typical long-term therapy. Thus, straight-forward generalizations to long-term treatment are inappropriate. At the same time, we suggest that our duration means allow for wide applicability since most psychological treatment called counseling or psychotherapy is not long-term and in fact continues for much less than 20 sessions (e.g., Garfield, 1971, 1978).

Summary of the Primary Findings

When queried shortly after the completion of their counseling, clients by and large felt helped by the experience, satisfied with the help they received, positive about their therapists, and improved in a variety of problem areas. As time after termination passed, however, clients exhibited a somewhat different pattern, independent of the treatment group they were in. That is, clients felt more positively about their own growth, but, while still on the positive side, less favorable toward the counseling they received and toward their therapists. Thus, what seems to emerge is a shift in former clients' attributions. Improvement after counseling continues, in the eyes of the clients, yet satisfaction with and the effects of counseling are evaluated less favorably. Perhaps this is an inevitable occurrence. As time after treatment passes, the impact of a few hours of counseling dwindles in clients' minds. The causal attributions to other experiences that occur during the time between termination and follow-up probably increase proportionately.

Those observations are for clients as a whole, as evidenced statistically by the main effects of time of testing, that is, 1 month versus 18 months after termination. Let us now look at the variables with which we are centrally concerned—the effects of TLT in the eyes of clients and therapists, the interactive effects of clients' initial level of adjustment and the treatment they receive, and the interactive effect of time of testing and treatment.

One month after counseling had terminated, our clients exhibited a consistent, if weak, tendency to make more favorable ratings of themselves and their therapy when they received TUT as opposed to either 8- or 16-session TLT. Therapists exhibited the same pattern, although to an extent even greater than with client ratings the counselor ratings contained individual differences so great that they clearly overshadowed possible treatment effects.

The pattern of clients' ratings, if anything, seemed to increase 18 months after termination. Thus, while clients in all three treatments viewed *themselves* as improving, clients in TUT, to a greater extent than those in TLT, saw the improvement as due to counseling, and as in fact occurring during the time of counseling. In attempting to understand this discrepancy, let us first note that, simply from a cognitive dissonance viewpoint, it is not surprising that people who invest more effort and energy in a therapeutic activity, for example, attend more sessions, will evaluate that activity more favorably than will those who invest less. Yet such an explanation should apply as well to both the 1-month and 18-month follow-ups, so it cannot as it stands explain the shift in our findings from one period to the next. A second explanation pertains to the posttreatment help-seeking of former clients. Thus, it appears that clients who receive very brief TLT (8 sessions) are appreciably more likely to seek further counseling than those who received TUT. This phenomenon might help explain why at the 18-month follow-up the TLT clients evaluated their own growth as positively as did the TUT clients, while at the same time feeling less positive about the initial treatment. That is, TLT clients may experience growth equal to that of TUT clients, because if the TLT does not last long enough they simply seek additional help, at the same agency or elsewhere.

Our finding that clients tend to evaluate individual counseling with a time-limited format less positively than TUT, especially some time after termination, is contrary to existing literature, as revealed by an exhaustive review of studies comparing the effects of TLT and TUT (Johnson & Gelso, 1980). In attempting to understand this discrepancy, it is important to note that only five comparative studies utilizing client and/or therapist ratings could be found. None of those studies employed anything like a long-term follow-up. (In fact, two of the studies, Lorr, 1967, and Munro & Bach, 1975, compared TLT clients at termination with TUT clients at the point of TLT termination, that is, before many of the TUT clients must have terminated their counseling!) Thus, the discrepancy between the present study and others may be accounted for by the fact that in clients' eyes the comparatively more positive effects of time-unlimited work may require an extended time after termination to become evident, and only the present investigation contains a long time period between termination and follow-up.

It should also be noted that much of the existing research on clients' reactions to TLT has not employed comparison groups of clients in TUT, especially randomly assigned groups. Had we not used such a group, we might well have concluded loosely that TLT is reacted to as favorably as TUT. That is so because (a) clients and their therapists did respond positively to TLT, especially at short-term follow-up, and (b) the reactions look about as favorable as those that appear in the literature on TUT. In nearly all research employing client and therapist reactions to treatment, such reactions tend to be positive. If between-treatment differences exist, we must utilize appropriate designs to detect them, for example, large enough samples, random or nearly random assignment, quantifiable measures, follow-up procedures.

The Role of Clients' Initial Adjustment Level

Upon termination and shortly after it clients' initial adjustment level appears to influence clients' and therapists' relative assessments of the three treatments. Thus, we find a consistent pattern of therapists and their clients whose pretreatment adjustment scores were below the median making the most favorable evaluations when counseling was not time-limited and least favorable when counseling had an 8-session time limit. We found no such pattern, however, for clients who were above the midpoint in adjustment. If anything, an opposite pattern emerged.

Eighteen months after termination a notable change occurs in the interaction pattern. The trend is sustained only when clients evaluate their counseling and their therapists. When clients rate their own growth rather than counseling and therapists, however, the pattern reverses itself! Thus, we have a highly complex interaction involving, not only initial adjustment and treatment group, but type of item as well.

In thinking about these complexities, it is worth noting that few of the interactions we have been discussing attained conventional significance levels, even though the patterns occurred beyond chance levels. Thus, caution must be exercised in generalizing these findings, and perhaps the results are best viewed as hypotheses awaiting future research. Probably the clearest interaction findings are (a) *the less adjusted clients tend to have lower evaluations of their counseling when it is brief TLT, especially after much time has elapsed since termination,* and (b) *this occurs especially when the low adjusted group rate their therapists in terms of the therapists' helpfulness in generating self-understanding and in creating a safe psychological atmosphere.*

It will be recalled that the therapists, at the time of the study, were not highly experienced in brief TLT and, according to their ratings after the initial session, exhibited the *least amount of confidence* that the treatment would help when the client was in the less adjusted group and the treatment was 8-session TLT. It may be that these expectations played a role in how the counselors behaved with the less adjusted clients in brief TLT. Now, as McKitrick and Gelso note in Chapter 6, evidence suggests that more chronically (vs. acutely) disturbed clients exhibit the least positive outcome expectancies in TLT. Thus, it seems likely that the more disturbed, less adjusted client enters brief TLT with many doubts about its efficacy. When the therapist is relatively inexperienced in this treatment format and also enters into the contract with doubt about its efficacy, the stage is set for minimal outcomes. While such outcomes may manifest themselves in a variety of ways when clients and therapists evaluate the treatment, they may emerge most saliently in terms of clients' reactions to their therapists. That is, the clients tend to feel the therapist does only a fair job in helping promote self-understanding and in creating an emotionally safe atmosphere.

In contrast to the therapist who lacks confidence in the efficacy of brief and/or time-limited therapy, one might scan the clinical and theoretical work of leading authorities in the field such as Mann, Bellack, Sifneos, and Malan. If there is one distinctive element of the work of these therapists, it is the confidence they exude in the treatment they offer, even when their patients are quite chronically troubled individuals, and even when the patients doubt if they could be helped in a brief treatment format. At the same time, it would be highly inappropriate on the basis of our data to proclaim that the basic problem of TLT with the more disturbed client is the therapist's lack of confidence. That lack of confidence may indeed be detecting something accurately, that is, very brief TLT is at best difficult to carry out successfully with the more disturbed client, and with some clients it is simply not enough treatment to provide significant help.

It will be recalled that we found the usual modest relationships between duration of treatment and client and therapist judged outcome. More surprisingly, however, and germane to the present discussion, this relationship seemed strongest and clearest in the 8-session TLT group even with the obvious restriction in range. *Within* this group, duration was positively related to therapists' evaluations of client personality change ($r = .61$) and behavior change ($r = .43$) due to counseling. Additionally, 18 months after termination, duration correlated with clients' ratings of the effect of counseling on feelings (.43); their belief that counseling lasted long enough to meet their needs (.48); overall change due to counseling (.43); perceptions of therapist helpfulness in generating self-understanding (.59), in resolving problems (.43), and in creating a safe atmosphere (.65); and to clients' descriptions of the most noticeable change during counseling (.46) as well as what the counseling experience meant to them (.49). A tenable hypothesis from these findings is that clients tend to terminate brief TLT much sooner than the duration limit warrants when they and perhaps their counselors doubt if the treatment will help, for example, when the client is poorly adjusted initially. The consequence is that both participants have lowered estimates of the resulting helpfulness of the treatment. Whatever the explanation, this constellation of client expectancy, counselor expectancy, and early termination deserves serious research efforts. A useful question for researchers revolves around whether brief TLT with more disturbed clients could demonstrate greater perceived efficacy with increased therapist confidence and/or if clients were encouraged to continue in treatment to the point of the duration limit.

Some Additional Findings Worth Attention

Before concluding, we would like to examine some remaining findings that appear deserving of attention. First, an apparent paradox in the data is that clients in TLT showed no tendency at all to indicate that their treatment did not last long enough to help in the way they wanted/needed to be helped. Neither were such reactions apparent from their essay comments 18 months after termination. Thus, while TLT clients tend to evaluate their treatment less positively than TUT clients, especially 18 months after termination, such evaluations do not manifest themselves in negative feelings or doubts about the duration of treatment, *at least not more than with TUT clients.*

Regarding that contradiction, it will be recalled that most clients, especially when queried 18 months after termination, indicated that they were "not sure" if counseling lasted long enough (Item IV of CCFQ). It may be that clients gear their expectations to the treatment modality. Such a phenomenon would be consistent with what Johnson and Gelso (1980) have labeled the "shifting criterion" hypothesis, the tendency for evaluators (counselors, clients, and so forth) to employ different internal norms when evaluating TLT versus TUT. Such a hypothesis appears to account partially for what seem to be inflated evaluations of the effectiveness of TLT in some studies. Relatedly, clinical experience suggests that open-ended work often tends to sharpen clients' awareness of problems, that is, problems they may have been unaware of prior to treatment. As a consequence, clients who terminate after 20 sessions (the mean for TUT clients) will feel equally unsure that their therapy has lasted "long enough" as those whose counseling is time limited and who terminate after 6–9 sessions (the means for our TLT groups). Finally, it may be that clients in our TUT group were at times terminating in the midst of difficulties. Remember, they only had a mean of 20 sessions, and for some clients that may only be long enough to create an awareness of the problems that do exist. It is also possible that some clients' treatment was terminated artificially by, for example, graduation or the end of the academic year.

A second finding worth elaborating pertains to the nature of postcounseling help-seeking of clients in the three treatments. Although clients in the briefest treatment mode were more likely to seek additional counseling in the 18 months between termination and follow-up, some preliminary data indicate that the counseling they received was of much briefer duration than additional counseling received by clients in the TUT condition. Based on our own clinical experience as well as therapists' reports of greater activity level and structuring in TLT versus TUT, we would like to offer the hypothesis that treatments of differing predetermined durations teach clients corresponding ways of thinking about their problems and formulating solutions to them. Thus, for better or worse, very brief TLT may teach clients to conceptualize their difficulties in a more structured way and take a more problem-solving tack to solutions, as opposed to a tack involving deeper self-exploration, the resolution of unconscious conflicts, and so forth. If such a formulation is correct, it would make sense that when such clients sought further counseling it would be of a brief nature.

Finally, extrapolating from treatment durations of the three treatment groups along with the durations of the therapeutic experiences obtained by clients during the 1½ years following termination, it appears that despite the fact that clients who receive brief TLT are more likely to return for additional counseling than are those receiving TUT, the *total* number of sessions (including subsequent counseling) received by TLT clients is substantially less than received by clients in open-ended work. Such extrapolations reveal the following total treatment means for clients in 8-session TLT, 16-session TLT, and TUT, respectively: 8.22, 13.00, 25.32. *Thus, while setting a duration limit that is markedly lower than the typical duration at a given agency will probably result in increased return for more counseling, time-limited procedures will still save considerable agency time, even if the returners all were to seek their additional help at the original treatment agency.*

Some Implications and Conclusions

How might the present findings be integrated with existing research on TLT, other than the research employing self-report? Of the five comparative studies using criterion sources beyond self-report (outside observers or psychological tests), four found no differences between TLT and TUT at follow-up points ranging from 6 months to 2½ years (Keilson et al., Chapter 1; Phillips & Johnston, 1954; Reid & Shyne, 1969; Shlien, Mosak & Dreikurs, 1962). One study (Henry & Shlien, 1958) found no differences at termination, but a decrement in TLT clients 6 to 12 months later.

Scrutiny of those studies indicates that comparison is difficult at best. For example, as indicated, Keilson et al. excluded clients who were in the lower quarter on initial adjustment; Reid and Shyne studied community families; Phillips and Johnston studied a special form of behavioral treatment and did not report mean number of sessions for TLT and TUT clients; Henry and Shlien apparently reported on the same group of clients as Shlien, Mosak, and Dreikurs, and found no differences on one measure but differences favoring TUT on another.

Given the primitive state of this research domain, probably the most tenable conclusion is that upon follow-up assessment there are no clear differences between TLT and TUT from the vantage points of observers or from psychological tests. Both seem to have salutary effects. In the eyes of clients, and possibly therapists (see Johnson & Gelso, 1980, for further elaboration), there is a tendency to perceive TLT as being less desirable and helpful than TUT, although still helpful. These perceptions on the part of the counseling participants may occur especially when the client is more disturbed initially, when the therapist is less experienced and confident in TLT, or when the treatment terminates much sooner than the duration limit warrants.

It should be noted that we have been discussing TLT as if it were a unitary treatment while in fact approaches vary widely (Patterson & O'Sullivan, 1974). Among existing research studies, the time limit alone has varied from 4 to 30 or so sessions! Again, we make a plea for caution in generalizing about the value of TLT, in itself or relative to TUT.

When current findings are integrated with existing research, can implications be drawn for agency practice? Tentatively, we suggest that at least with the better adjusted clients, an agency can save considerable time, and thus tackle vexing waiting list problems, by conducting TLT—and at the same time provide a service that these clients and their therapists perceive as helpful. This is so despite the probability that the service will not be seen as equally helpful in comparison to the longer TUT. (Note that not all our main effects favoring TUT could be explained by the initial adjustment by treatment group interaction pattern.) It should be noted that this picture might change importantly if therapists were employed who were experienced and confident in the use of TLT.

For the more disturbed client, we cannot currently recommend TLT, at least for efficacy reasons alone, and when client reactions are the central criterion. If an agency deems it important to abbreviate treatment duration because clients must wait too long for treatment when it is open ended, then TLT with the more disturbed client might best be viewed as either crisis oriented or preparatory to referral and long-term treatment. Are there therapist techniques or attitudes that might make for more effective help in the eyes of the more disturbed clients receiving TLT? Again, further treatment experimentation and empirical study with this population are warranted.

Addendum: Toward an Agency Reorientation Partially Based on Research Findings

It will be recalled from the Introduction to this book that a primary reason for doing the study reported in this chapter was an agency issue. That is, the Center had a severe waiting list problem. The study reported in Chapter 1 provided a hopeful beginning, but we felt additional data were required, particularly data from the vantage points of clients and therapists, before a major change in treatment policy could be undertaken.

The way in which agency policy was changed may be a good lesson in how scientific findings become melded with clinical observation and practical concerns. It is probably true that, given the findings reported in chapter 1 and the pressing waiting list problems of our agency, the client and therapist reports presented in this chapter would have to markedly *disfavor* TLT for at least some agency change *not* to have occurred. Yet we feel that the research findings did influence agency change in a salubrious manner. Since all of us have so often heard how scientific findings fail to alter practice, we would like to present here what we think is an accurate view of how the findings reported in this chapter, when combined with those in Chapter 1 as well as existing literature, did alter agency procedure.

The therapists in the studies reported in chapters 1 and 2 were agency practitioners and interns. Through participation in the researches, they were accumulating clinical experience in and observations about TLT. When those experiences and observations were added to the data that began to emerge, for example, through preliminary reports, it appeared that very brief (for example, 8-session) TLT may have been too brief for too many clients. At the same time, theoretical material compatible with the staff's clinical orientation began to emerge (especially Mann, 1973). Mann's work entailed a time limit of 12 sessions, with a clear beginning, middle, and end phase. A staff decision was made to institute a 12-session time limit and, concomitantly, to accelerate in-service training efforts in TLT that were already in operation. Just as one example, we altered our usual case conference format such that two senior therapists each presented in weekly meetings one 12-session TLT case from beginning to termination. This change was an effort to better understand the process of TLT.

But what of the finding that the initially more disturbed client may not do as well in TLT, in his or her own eyes as well as those of the therapist? Additionally, since clients in brief TLT so often return for more treatment, how could the agency accomodate this pattern without subverting the potential effectiveness of time limits? The agency, with full staff participation, decided to respond to these questions in a variety of ways. First, it was decided that a certain proportion of therapists' caseloads would not be time limited, and the decision was left up to the therapist regarding who those clients would be. Clients were informed in written material prior to an intake interview that they would *probably* be seen for a limit of 12 sessions. They were again given this message during the intake session. But the final decision was based on the clinical judgment of the therapist to whom the client was finally assigned. The percentages of one's caseload that were not time limited varied according to the therapist's position, that is, senior staff, affiliate, intern, practicum student. Generally, however, that percentage was approximately 25.

To deal with the joint issue of clients' tendency to return for more counseling on the one hand, and the need to maximize the potency of time limits (or at least not subvert it) on the other, we developed a policy that (a) permitted students a maximum of 12 sessions in a calendar year, and (b) required at least a 4-month period between termination and further counseling. Of course, such policies were to be modified to accomodate clinical exigencies, for example, clients in crises were always eligible for treatment, and such crises work was often accompanied by outside referrals after the emotional turmoil subsided.

Additional modifications of the basic 12-session policy were created in an effort to produce maximal flexibility while, at the same time, continuing to keep the waiting list as small as possible. The details of the modifications do not belong in this chapter. Again, what we wish to clarify here is how agency practice was shaped by research findings, and how practical agency needs, clinical observation and judgment, and research can be, and in this case were, integrated in shaping treatment procedures.

Finally, we would like to underscore that it takes patience to wait for data before instituting change. In the current case, at least 2 years passed before preliminary data could be fed into our system. Yet we think that the patience is well worth it. The major changes in agency practice that we have been writing about have been in practice for over 6 years. While of course such procedures will and should continue to change with additional experience and research, we suggest that in the current case the research helped create a solid basis for change; we have managed to avoid the rather capricious-like change that agencies sometimes manifest when procedures are a result only of clinical impression. In addition, a waiting list (that earlier hovered around the 200 mark) now is considered dangerously high when it approaches 25, while we have actually increased slightly the number of clients seen at the agency. Most importantly, follow-up data, some of which are presented in the next chapter, indicate that clients perceive our services positively, as positively as when treatment was exclusively open ended and when clients often had to wait several weeks before they could be seen.

Notes

[1]Of course, we could have continued assigning clients until our desired sample size of 90 was attained, and until each therapist did see two clients under each condition. As it was, however, our efforts to provide some balance, along with the decision to use interns over 2 academic years, resulted in the assignment phase of the study persisting over a 28-month period. Given the desirability of a long-term follow-up, and the fact that some clients in the TUT condition were seen for more than 2 years, continuing the assignment phase for an even longer duration (thus increasing even more the time between the beginning of the study and the 18-month follow-up) was more than the researchers felt either willing or able to bear. This is yet another example of how human factors may enter into the presumably objective design of experiments.

[2]Because of the possibilities of Type I statistical errors (concluding that statistically significant differences occur when they do not) resulting from the use of numerous analyses of variance (ANOVA's) on the same data, we also analyzed data for the 1-month and 18-month follow-ups through the use of multivariate analysis of variance (MANOVA). MANOVA tends to be a more conservative test of significance; it allows for examination of the effect of one or more variables on a *combination* of dependent or outcome variables. In deciding on which combinations of outcome measures to use in the MANOVA's we followed Biskin's (1980) reasoning. That is, we used combinations from the CCFQ for which it made

conceptual sense to combine, as follows: Ia, b, c, d, and e; IIa, b, c, d, and e; III and V; VIa, b, and c.

The results for the main effects of treatment and the initial adjustment ✕ treatment interactions were similar to those obtained through the ANOVA's presented in the text. The multivariate F tests (Wilk's lambda criterion using Rao's approximate F test) for each combination and the probability levels were: For the *1-month follow-up*—Items Ia, b, c, d, and e (F for treatment main effect = 2.58, p = .007; for the interaction = .97, p = .47); Items IIa, b, c, d, and e (F main effect = 1.12, p = .35; for interaction = .66, p = .76); Items III and V (F main effect = 1.71, p = .15; for interaction = 1.39, p = .24); Items VIa, b, and c (F main effect = .89, p = .51; for interaction = 1.86, p = .09).

These same analyses for the *18-month follow-up* were: Items Ia, b, c, d, and e (F main effect = .33, p = .97; for interaction = 1.27, p = .25); Items IIa, b, c, d, and e (F main effect = 1.74, p = .08; for interaction = .77, p = .66); Items III and V (F main effect = .79, p = .53; for interaction = 2.02, p = .09); Items VIa, b, and c (F main effect = .31, p = .93; for interaction = 1.73, p = .10).

Note that MANOVA's were not done on Items VII a through q, because each item was answered by different subjects.

REFERENCES

BERGIN, A. E., & LAMBERT, M. J. The evaluation of therapeutic outcomes. In S. L. Garfield and A. E. Bergin (Eds.), *Handbook of psychotherapy and behavior change* (2nd ed.). New York: Wiley, 1978.

BISKIN, B. H. Multivariate analysis in experimental counseling research. *The Counseling Psychologist*, 1980, *8*, 69–73.

GARFIELD, S. L. Research on client variables in psychotherapy. In A. E. Bergin and S. L. Garfield (Eds.), *Handbook of psychotherapy and behavior change*. New York: Wiley, 1971.

GARFIELD, S. L. Research of client variables in psychotherapy. In S. L. Garfield and A. E. Bergin (Eds.), *Handbook of psychotherapy and behavior change* (2nd ed.). New York: Wiley, 1978.

HENRY, W. E., & SHLIEN, J. M. Affective complexity and psychotherapy: Some comparisons of time-limited and unlimited treatment. *Journal of Projective Techniques*, 1958, *22*, 153–162.

HOWARD, K. K., ORLINSKY, D. E., & TRATTNER, J. H. Therapist orientation and patient experience in psychotherapy. *Journal of Counseling Psychology*, 1970, *17*, 263–270.

JOHNSON, D. H., & GELSO, C. J. The effectiveness of time limits in counseling and psychotherapy: A critical review. *The Counseling Psychologist*, 1980, *9*, 70–83.

LAMBERT, M. J. Characteristics of patients and their relationship to outcome in brief psychotherapy. *Psychiatric Clinics of North America*, 1979, *2*, 111–123.

LORR, M. A. *Comparison of time-limited and time-unlimited psychotherapy.* Paper presented at the Annual VA Conference on Cooperative Studies in Psychiatry, Denver, 1967.

MANN, J. *Time-limited psychotherapy.* Cambridge, Mass.: Harvard University Press, 1973.

MUNRO, J. N., & BACH, T. R. The effect of time-limited counseling on client change. *Journal of Counseling Psychology,* 1975, *22,* 395–398.

PATTERSON, V., & O'SULLIVAN, M. Three prespectives on brief psychotherapy. *American Journal of Psychotherapy,* April 1974, 265–277.

PHILLIPS, E. L., & JOHNSTON, M. H. S. Theoretical and clinical aspects of short-term, parent-child psychotherapy. *Psychiatry,* 1954, *17,* 267–275.

REID, W. J., & SHYNE, A. W. *Brief and extended casework.* New York: Columbia University Press, 1969.

SHLIEN, J. M., MOSAK, H. H., & DREIKURS, R. Effects of time limits: A comparison of two psychotherapies. *Journal of Counseling Psychology,* 1962, *9,* 31–34.

SIEGEL, S. *Nonparametric statistics for the behavioral sciences.* New York: McGraw-Hill, 1956.

STRUPP, H. H., & HADLEY, S. W. A tripartite model of mental health and therapeutic outcomes. *American Psychologist,* 1977, *32,* 187–196.

SUNDLAND, D. M. *Therapist Orientation Questionnaire, Up-to-date.* Paper presented at the Third Annual Meeting of the Society for Psychotherapy Research, Nashville, June 1972.

SUNDLAND, D. M., & BARKER, E. N, The orientations of psychotherapists. *Journal of Consulting Psychology,* 1962, *26,* 201–212.

WOOD, B. L. *The relationship of selected counselor, client, and treatment factors to clients' post-counseling satisfaction.* Unpublished doctoral dissertation, University of Maryland, College Park, 1979.

3

The Change Process Following Time-Limited Therapy

Diane M. Adelstein, Charles J. Gelso, James R. Haws,
Kathryn G. Reed, and Sharon Baron Spiegel

The large-scale field experiment reported in Chapter 2 suggested that, well after counseling termination, clients who received TLT (a) tended to feel positively about the experience, although (b) they did not feel as positively as did clients receiving TUT. That experiment, however, was viewed as a conservative test of the comparative effectiveness of TLT, since the therapists were obviously and notably less experienced in the practice of TLT than of TUT. The present study was the first agency field investigation focusing on outcomes after the implementation of the TLT program had been in operation for over 3 years. Thus, agency practitioners were quite experienced in this treatment modality, although it is probably safe to say that their clinical preferences were still for moderately long-term, open-ended work. Thus, the present investigation examines clients' and therapists' reports of the efficacy of TLT in an agency in which that mode has been the predominant treatment.

Through a careful examination of existing theoretical and empirical literature, we became impressed with the possibility that the most beneficial effects of TLT

The order of authorship is alphabetical and does not reflect our relative contributions to the project, which we feel were approximately equal.

become evident *after* termination. Thus, TLT was conceptualized as setting in motion a change process—a process whose effects gradually accumulate after the end of treatment. The possibility that the bulk of positive change might occur following termination of TLT may partially account for the fact that therapists often eschew this treatment format, more so than is appropriate on the basis of client reports, observer ratings, and test data (see Johnson & Gelso's [1980] review).[1] This phenomenon was in contrast to that conceptualized for TUT, where the extended time in treatment allows the therapist to witness directly more of the client's growth.

With the above considerations in mind, the present study generally aimed at assessing clients' retrospective perceptions of (a) their growth that occurred over an approximately 1-year period between TLT termination and follow-up, and (b) the extent to which that growth was attributed to counseling. Secondarily, the investigation sought to assess clients' and therapists' views of client change *during* counseling, the relationship between the perceptions of these two groups, and the relationship between each group's perceptions of change during counseling and of change between termination and the 1-year follow-up.

Along a somewhat different vein, some of the findings in Chapter 2 as well as earlier literature discussed by Johnson and Gelso (1980) suggest that if TLT is to have a durable impact the client must participate in it beyond the initial few sessions. That is, some undesignated amount of time in treatment is necessary if the aforementioned change process is to become initiated. Relatedly, one may raise the question of whether clients who only have a few sessions (i.e., much fewer than the duration limit permits) are psychologically involved in TLT. For that group, the duration limits may be practically and psychologically inconsequential, for such clients may only be wanting a few counseling sessions to begin with. Thus the study employed only former clients who had received a minimum of 8 sessions of TLT (where the actual duration limit was between 12 and 16 sessions).

While much of our research program at Maryland has tended to focus on clients' perceptions, none of the research heretofore examined such perceptions in an in-depth way. Thus, we had relied almost exclusively on readily quantifiable questionnaire responses. Along with such responses, the present study entailed semistructured interviews with a small number of former clients. Our hope was to generate hypotheses that would help us understand the nature of the change processes that are mobilized in TLT. Thus, we selected only clients whose earlier questionnaire responses reflected their sense that such a process was indeed set in motion; our questions were designed to illuminate the nature of this phenomenon.

As was the case in Chapter 2, part of the present data gathering was aimed at uncovering client factors related to perceived outcome. Thus, therapists completed a 30-item questionnaire assessing various aspects of client change. The findings from that phase of the study are reported in Chapter 5.

Method

The Clients

Subjects for the study were 38 students who had completed TLT on an average of 12 months (range of 8–14 months) prior to the follow-up. To be selected for the study, clients had to meet the following additional criteria: (a) be judged by the intake therapist and the therapist to have a personal problem (i.e., versus a problem in educational or vocational choice); (b) have received between 8 and 16 sessions of TLT at the Center (as indicated by the therapist's report), (c) be either freshmen, sophomores, juniors, or graduate students when counseling occurred (seniors being eliminated because of anticipated follow-up difficulties after their graduation 1 year later); and (d) have been seen by therapists who were senior staff, interns, or advanced graduate students at the Center.

Forty former clients met the criteria, and we were able to locate 38 of them. The modal client was a sophomore or junior (61%) female (71%) who had not received previous counseling (82%). The mean number of sessions the clients received was 11 (range of 8–15).

The Therapists

The therapists were nine senior staff members, six interns, and six advanced practicum students who had received at least 1 year of practicum supervision in TLT prior to the counseling done in the study. The senior therapists were PhD's in clinical or counseling psychology with an average of 11 years of postdoctoral experience (ranging from 4 to 20). The description of theoretical orientations reported in chapter 2 is quite fitting for this group. By the time of the counseling done in the present study, however, these practitioners had all had at least three consecutive years of intensive experience in TLT, mostly with a 12-session limit. Although data were not gathered on staff's attitudes toward TLT, it was our impression that the staff still had a preference for longer-term TUT. At the same time, a clear impression was that the staff possessed a positive view of the efficacy of TLT.

The interns were in the final (4th or 5th) year of their doctoral training in counseling psychology, and the practicum students had a minimum of 1 year of practicum prior to the counseling. During that year, and during the counseling, these students received careful supervision in TLT from senior staff.

Instrumentation

The study entailed the use of two therapist-completed questionnaires, one client-completed questionnaire, and a questionnaire used for the semistructured interviews.

CLIENT-COMPLETED QUESTIONNAIRE.   Former clients responded to the *Client-Rated Counseling Outcome Questionnaire* (Appendix H). This form required subjects to rate on 7-point Likert scales (a) *change during counseling* in terms of feelings, behavior, self-understanding, overall change; and (b) *change between the end of counseling and now* in terms of feelings, behavior, and self-understanding. Following these estimates, subjects made estimations of the extent to which "change between the end of counseling and now" was attributable to the following nine factors: passage of time, changes in life circumstances, the counseling received at the Center, further counseling or therapy, self-awareness, family, friends, religion, other. Subjects rated the effect of each factor on a 4-point scale (none, low, medium, high).

Reliability data were not gathered on client-completed questionnaires in the present study. Data presented in chapter 2 on very similar items, however, strongly supported the reliability of such items.

THERAPIST-COMPLETED FORMS.   Therapists responded to two questionnaires at the time their former clients were contacted for follow-up (Appendixes I & J). The *Counseling Outcome Measure* asked therapists to rate, on 7-point Likert scales, the degree of improvement during counseling in clients' feelings, behavior, self-understanding, and overall change. The second instrument, entitled *The Client Change Inventory* is discussed in detail in chapter 5, where we examine the aspect of the study pertaining to client factors influencing change.

To determine the retest reliability of the two therapist-completed questionnaires, these forms were administered to a separate group of 24 therapists 2–3 weeks apart. This group contained 15 males and 9 females, 6 senior staff and intern therapists, and 18 graduate students who had enrolled in beginning or advanced practica during the prior semester. During the first administration, therapists were asked to complete the measure with regard to one of their clients who had recently completed counseling. Then, 2–3 weeks later these therapists were asked to again complete the questionnaires with reference to this same client.

The retest reliabilities (Pearson r's) for the four items of the *Counseling Outcome Measure* were, respectively, .81, .74, .63, and .73 (all p's $< .001$). Reliability data on the second instrument is presented in Chapter 5.

THE SEMISTRUCTURED INTERVIEW QUESTIONNAIRE.   This questionnaire, which was employed during interviews, consisted of 15 questions aimed at gathering former clients' perceptions of how they changed during and after counseling and, most centrally, what might have operated during counseling to initiate the change process about which we were concerned. The questions were devised by the research team, four of whom had considerable experience in TLT. As can be seen in Appendix K, the questions require rather brief answers for the most part, although all of them require a good bit of client reflection on his or her development during and after counseling.

Procedure

All 38 locatable clients were telephoned by a member of the research team. The phone call attempted to solicit client cooperation in completing the *Client-Rated Counseling Outcome Questionnaire*, and callers generally followed a prearranged script in making their request. All clients agreed to complete the questionnaire, which was then mailed to them immediately. Seventy-five percent of the subjects returned their completed questionnaires within 2 weeks. The remaining subjects were again called as a reminder, and these subjects returned the completed forms. Thus, the return rate was 95% of the potential subjects and 100% of those we could locate.

It should be noted here that when rating the effect of their counseling, clients were explicitly asked to evaluate the counseling experience under investigation, and not prior or subsequent experiences. This distinction is important because, as is discussed later, a sizable percentage of clients did receive later counseling.

The 21 therapists who treated these clients were asked to complete the two therapist questionnaires. Therapists were given their clients' folders so that the work could be reviewed. (Remember, the client had been seen approximately a year earlier.) Therapist-rated forms were completed for all 38 former clients.

Of the clients who exhibited a clear change process following termination, and who attributed that change to the counseling they received, six were randomly selected for the semistructured interviews. These six were contacted by telephone and asked to participate in a 60-minute interview with one of the researchers (either senior staff or interns at the Center). Clients were informed that the purpose of the interviews was to assess how change had occurred in former clients who, according to earlier questionnaire reults, indicated that they had grown considerably since counseling. All six clients agreed to the interviews, although only four actually attended.

The specific selection criteria for these clients were (a) self-ratings indicating either no change or positive change from the beginning to end of counseling on the four Likert scales assessing such change in the Client-Rated Counseling Outcome Questionnaire; (b) at least moderate change between termination and follow-up on two of the three items assessing postcounseling change (moderate change required responses of 6 on the 7-point scales) and no evidence of deterioration on the third item; and (c) at least a "medium" attribution of postcounseling change to the counseling received at the Center (medium equaled 3 on a 4-point scale, where 1 = no attribution to counseling, 2 = a low attribution, and 4 = a high attribution).

The four former clients were interviewed by one of the members of the research team along with a graduate student in counseling psychology. The use of co-interviewers was felt to be important to assure that clients responses were clear (i.e., to an observer as well as the interviewer) and to facilitate recording. The co-interviewer wrote the client's responses verbatim and, following the interview, checked his or her responses with the interviewer to make sure they both heard the same responses. Interviews lasted between 45 minutes and an hour and a half.

Results

For the sake of clarity, the results are presented according to the primary and secondary questions the study addressed. Impressions from the semistructured interviews are noted at the end of the Results section.

1. *Do clients improve during TLT in terms of feelings, behavior, self-understanding, and overall change as perceived by themselves and their therapists?*

Although the primary data of interest pertain to client change *following* counseling, we first report ratings of change during treatment (beginning to end), again for the sake of clarity. Such data provide a frame of reference against which subsequent change or lack of it can be evaluated.

Table 3–1 presents means and standard deviation of clients' and therapists' ratings of client change during counseling. Regarding client-rated change, Table 3-1 indicates that clients approximately one year after counseling, saw themselves as having improved slightly to moderately (during the time of counseling) on feelings, behavior, self-understanding, and overall change. Correlational analysis (Pearson r's) reveals a strong relationship among clients' assessments on these four measures, as the coefficients ranged from .61 to .82. Further, t tests of the difference between correlated means indicated that clients' ratings of themselves on the four dimensions do not differ from one another. Thus, clients saw themselves improving during counseling about equally in their feelings, behavior, self-understanding, and overall.

Therapists' ratings exhibited a somewhat different pattern. Like the clients, therapists tended to rate client change as slight to moderate. On the other hand, the therapists were not quite as optimistic; as the table shows, therapists reported less improvement (than clients) in client self-understanding ($p < .02$), and perceived less overall change ($p < .05$). Therapist and client ratings do not differ on behavior change and feeling improvement.

Like the clients, therapists' ratings of behavior change, self-understanding improvement, and overall change were highly interrelated (r's from .70 to .79). The relationship of feeling improvement with these three other variables, however, was not as strong, although still well beyond chance. Thus, the correlations of feeling improvement with the other three variables were: behavior change = .52, self-understanding = .36, and overall change = .54. Finally, therapists viewed their clients as exhibiting greater feeling improvement than behavior change ($t = 3.03, p < .01$), self-understanding improvement ($t = 2.74, p < .01$), or overall change ($t = 3.03, p < .01$).

In sum, while therapists and clients exhibited somewhat different patterns of ratings, both groups viewed clients as having changed slightly to moderately on four change dimensions. Further documentation comes from the small number of former clients who were rated by themselves or their therapists as not improved or deteriorated on the four dimensions. Thus, of the 38 clients, only 4 (11%) were in

Table 3–1. Clients' and Therapists' Ratings of Client Change
During Counseling in Terms of Feelings, Behavior,
Self-Understanding, and Overall Change

| Item | | Rating source | | t | p |
		Client rating	Therapist rating		
Feeling improvement	X̄	5.68	5.58	.46	.65
	SD	1.19	.76		
Behavior change	X̄	5.58	5.21	1.85	.07
	SD	.95	.78		
Self-understanding	X̄	5.71	5.13	2.49	.02
improvement	SD	1.04	.99		
Overall change	X̄	5.66	5.21	2.02	.05
	SD	1.04	.81		

Note. In both client and therapist rating scales, 4 = no change, 5 = slight improvement, 6 = moderate improvement, and 7 = much improvement.

this negative category on feeling improvement, 4 (11%) on behavior change, 5 (13%) on self-understanding improvement, and 4 (11%) on overall change according to the clients' own ratings. The corresponding frequencies and percents of therapist-rated changes were: 2 (5%), 6 (16%), 10 (26%), and 6 (16%). It can be seen from these figures, as well as those presented previously, that therapists were less positive than were clients in their judgments of self-understanding improvement (and than themselves on the other dimensions). Thus, over one-quarter of the clients were seen by their therapists as not improving in self-understanding during TLT.

2. *What are the interrelationships of therapist and client ratings of feeling improvement, behavior change, self-understanding improvement, and overall change during counseling?*

Table 3–2 presents data on the intercorrelations among the ratings made by therapists and clients. The coefficients in Table 3–2 indicate at least modest agreement between client and therapist ratings of change. The coefficients in the diagonal (underlined) are for therapist and client ratings of the same dimension. It can be seen that the correlations for behavior change and overall change are beyond chance. Apparently, therapists and clients rely on different data or employ different criteria when rating client self-understanding improvement and feeling improvement, at least in relatively brief TLT. Finally, Table 3–2 reveals that when rated by one member of the therapy pair (e.g., the therapist) most of the three change dimensions are significantly related to the overall change dimension as seen by the other member of the pair (e.g., the client).

3. *Do former clients, according to their own reports, continue to manifest feeling improvement, behavior change, and self-understanding improvement during the year following termination of TLT?*

This question and the next one, pertinent to change attribution, are central to our interest in finding out if TLT is effective in setting in motion a change process that continues well after termination. We answer the questions in a variety of ways.

The simplest method of answering Question 3 is to inspect clients' responses to the first two parts of the *Client-Rated Counseling Outcome Questionnaire* (Appendix H). The first part asks former clients to rate themselves from the beginning to the end of counseling on the three dimensions of change, while the second part asks for the same items to be rated for the period from termination to now (the time follow-up). Inspection of the means of the first two columns of Table 3–3 (Change During Counseling and Change After Counseling) reveals that changes during counseling were matched in magnitude by those between termination and follow-up. Thus, on our three change dimensions these former clients saw themselves, on the average, changing between a slight and moderate amount (5 = slight, 6 = moderate), and essentially they perceived themselves changing the same amount between termination and follow-up one year later.

Table 3–2. Correlations of Client- and Therapist-Rated Change on Four Change Dimensions

	Therapist ratings			
Client ratings	Feeling improvement	Behavior change	Self-understanding improvement	Overall change
Feeling improvement	.30	.25	.24	.30
Behavior change	.46**	.34*	.23	.40*
Self-understanding improvement	.22	.28	.14	.27
Overall change	.50**	.50**	.37*	.48**

* = $p < .05$
** = $p < .01$

Table 3–3. Clients' Ratings of Change During Counseling, Between the End of Counseling and the One-Year Follow-Up, and a Measure of Cumulative Change

| | Change period | | | | | |
| | Changes during counseling | | Changes after counseling | | Cumulative change | |
Item	$\bar{X}$	SD	$\bar{X}$	SD	$\bar{X}$	SD
Feeling improvement	5.68	1.19	5.55	1.52	7.24	1.78
Behavior Change	5.58	.95	5.61	1.15	7.18	1.70
Self-understanding improvement	5.71	1.04	5.82	1.06	7.53	1.64

A second method of answering Question 3 is to determine if the change following counseling significantly adds to that occurring during counseling. Here we formulated an index of cumulative change by additively combining each client's responses to Items 1, 2, and 3 (change during counseling on the three dimensions) with those to 5, 6, and 7 (change after counseling on the same dimensions). On these latter items a response of 4 (no change) was recoded as 0, 5 (slight improvement) as 1, 6 (moderate improvement) as 2, 7 (much improvement) as 3. For example, if a client circled 5 for feeling improvement during counseling and 6 (recoded as 2) for feeling improvement after counseling, his or her cumulative change score would be 7. The right-hand column of Table 3 presents these cumulative change scores. Correlated t tests were computed to assess the significance of the differences between the means for change during counseling and cumulative change. Highly significant differences emerged for the three items as follow: Feeling improvement ($\bar{X}$'s = 5.68 vs. 7.24, t = 8.84, p <.001), behavior change ($\bar{X}$'s = 5.58 vs. 7.18, t = 10.27, p <.001), and self-understanding improvement ($\bar{X}$'s = 5.71 vs. 7.53, t = 10.16, p <.001). Thus, on all three change measures, the change occurring between termination and follow-up was a statistically significant increment to that emerging during counseling.

A final way of answering Question 3 involves an inspection of the patterns of change during counseling and after counseling, and permits a more direct test of the "change in motion" hypothesis than do the other methods. Here we roughly categorized clients as those who got better, stayed the same, or got worse during counseling and after counseling on each item. Responses below 4 on our scales placed subjects into the "worse" category, responses of 4 placed them into the "same" category, and those above 4 into the "better" category. This method produces a 3 × 3 matrix where clients are categorized as better, the same, or worse during and after counseling.

Table 3–4 presents these 3×3 matrices for each of the three items. Examination of the table reveals that the large majority of former clients changed for the better both during and after counseling (see the lower right-hand cell of each matrix). Now, the "change in motion" hypothesis would appear to fit clients in two categories in Table 3-4, those who changed for the better both during and after counseling (bottom right-hand cell of each matrix), and those who were the same during counseling but changed for the better after counseling (bottom center cells of the matrices). It can be seen that the number and percentages of these clients for each item are: Feeling improvement, 27 (71%); behavior change, 30 (79%); and self-understanding improvement, 32 (84%). Chi square tests (with Yates correction) comparing these frequencies of clients exhibiting the "change in motion" pattern with those who did not (frequencies of all other cells) revealed statistical significance for each item (feeling improvement, $\chi^2 = 6.74$, $p < .01$; behavior change, $\chi^2 = 12.74$, $p < .001$; self-understanding improvement, $\chi^2 = 17.99$, $p < .001$). Thus, this third method of analysis strongly supports the "change in motion" hypothesis, and further elucidates the manner in which it is manifested.

In sum, our three methods of examining the data all strongly support a positive response to Question 3, and in the process lend support to the "change in motion" hypothesis. When queried approximately a year after ending counseling, the large majority of clients feel they have changed for the better on relevant change dimensions both during and after counseling. On the whole, the change does not appear to be dramatic during counseling, but it does occur and is continued to about an equal extent after termination. This continuation of change is manifested by a very large percentage of clients, well beyond what would be expected by chance.

4. *To what extent are changes during the year following counseling attributed to that counseling as opposed to other processes and events?*

We attempted to answer this question in two ways. Item 8 of the *Client-Rated Counseling Outcome Questionnaire* asked clients to rate the extent to which they attributed "changes between the end of counseling and now" to eight different factors (see Table 3–5), and our analysis will focus on clients' responses to those eight factors.

Our first step entailed determining the number and percent of clients who fit into the "change in motion" category as discussed under Question 3 and who indicated that the change they experienced between termination and follow-up was attributable, to a "medium" or "high" extent, to counseling at the Center. This determination was made for each of the three change items—feeling improvement, behavior change, self-understanding improvement. For "feeling improvement," 19 of the 27 (70%) clients who fit into the "change in motion" category attributed their postcounseling change, to a medium or high degree, to the counseling. The corresponding frequencies and percentages for "behavior change" and "self-understanding improvement" were, respectively, 23 of 30 (77%) and 24 of 32 (75%). Thus, although the exact figures depend on the

Table 3–4. Patterns of Change During and After Counseling on Three Dimensions of Change

Item	Time		During counseling		
			Worse	Same	Better
Feeling improvement	After counseling	Worse	0	0	5 (13)
		Same	0	0	4 (11)
		Better	2 (5)	2 (5)	25 (66)

Item	Time		During counseling		
			Worse	Same	Better
Behavior change	After counseling	Worse	0	0	1 (3)
		Same	0	3 (8)	4 (11)
		Better	0	1 (3)	29 (76)

Item	Time		During counseling		
			Worse	Same	Better
Self-understanding improvement	After counseling	Worse	0	0	1 (3)
		Same	0	0	4 (11)
		Better	1 (3)	4 (11)	28 (74)

Note. Percentages are in parentheses adjacent to frequencies.

particular change item being evaluated, approximately three-fourths of the clients in the "change-in-motion" category attributed at least an important amount of that postcounseling change to the TLT they received.

The second step in answering Question 4 was to determine the frequencies and percentage of clients who attributed various amounts of postcounseling change (on a scale labeled "none," "low," "medium," and "high") to the eight factors. Table 3–5 presents the results of this analysis. The column on the right-hand side of the table presents the percentages of clients who rated the effect of each factor as either "medium" or "high."

The data in Table 3–5 reveal a clustering of effects. That is, factors such as the passage of time, changes in life circumstances, counseling at the Center, and self-awareness each received a similarly high attribution percentage. The remain-

Table 3–5.   Frequencies (and Percentages) of Former Clients'
Attributions of Change to Eight Change Factors
and Percent Making Medium or High
Attributions to Each Factor

Factor	Effect of each factor				Percentages indicating a medium or high effect
	None	Low	Medium	High	
1. Passage of time	4 (10.5)	8 (21.1)	20 (52.6)	6 (15.8)	68.4
2. Changes in life circumstances	3 (7.9)	4 (10.5)	16 (42.1)	15 (39.5)	81.6
3. Counseling received at the Counseling Center	3 (7.9)	7 (18.4)	22 (57.9)	6 (15.8)	73.7
4. Further counseling or therapy	24 (63.2)	1 (2.6)	5 (13.2)	8 (21.1)	34.3
5. Self-awareness	0 (0)	10 (26.3)	20 (52.6)	8 (21.1)	73.7
6. Family	13 (34.2)	8 (21.1)	10 (26.3)	7 (18.4)	44.7
7. Friends	8 (21.1)	9 (23.7)	14 (36.8)	7 (18.4)	55.2
8. Religion	30 (78.9)	4 (10.5)	2 (5.3)	2 (5.3)	10.6

ing factors, further counseling, family, friends, and religion, receive lower ratings.

Chi-square analyses were performed by comparing the frequency of subjects making medium and high attributions with those responding in the "low" and "none" categories. Of central interest was that none of the factors received significantly higher attributions than did counseling when the data were analyzed in this way. Counseling, on the other hand, was more often viewed as affecting postcounseling change than were family, further counseling, and religion.

It should also be noted that while the factor "further counseling or therapy" did not receive a high attribution percentage, 14 (37%) rated the effect as greater than "none." This may indicate that at least 14 of the clients in fact sought further counseling or therapy. A plausible inference from these data is that when further counseling is sought, it tends to be evaluated positively in terms of its effects. (Note that 8 of the 14, or 58%, rated the effect as "high.")

In summary, the data in this section indicate that at least an important amount of change after TLT is attributed to the TLT experience. This postcounseling change, in the eyes of clients, is influenced by a group of related factors of which the counseling is one. Such factors as the passage of time, changes in life circumstances, self-awareness, and further counseling (when it is sought) all seem to contribute to the change that begins during counseling.

5. *Is the change that occurs after counseling predictable from clients' and therapists' evaluations of change that emerges during counseling?*

In response to this question, it appears that clients' and therapists' evaluations of change during counseling are not predictive or minimally predictive of the amount of client-rated change between counseling termination and follow-up approximately one year later. Thus, the correlations between the during- and after-counseling ratings are negligible and statistically nonsignificant, as Table 3–6 indicates. The generally weak relationships (regardless of statistical significance) noted in the above analysis lead to the important question of just what factors, if any, do predict postcounseling change. That is the subject of our analyses of the data in this study reported in Chapter 5.

6. *Do the semistructured interviews suggest client, therapist, or treatment factors that might be part of or underlie the extent to which TLT is effective in setting in motion a change process that continues or accelerates following termination?*

Table 3–6. Correlations of Client and Therapist Ratings of Change During Counseling with Clients' Ratings of Change Between Termination and Follow-Up

		Client rated change between termination and follow-up		
Change during counseling	Rating Source	Feeling improvement	Behavior change	Self-understanding improvement
Feeling improvement	Therapist	*– .31	– .04	– .27
Behavior change	Therapist	.04	.22	.11
Self-understanding	Therapist	.06	.14	.20
Overall change	Therapist	.00	.15	.11
Feeling improvement	Client	– .15	– .12	– .03
Behavior change	Client	.18	.29	.20
Self-understanding	Client	.06	.11	.22
Overall change	Client	– .17	.17	.04

$* = p < .05$

Three members of the research team studied the typed transcripts from the interviews that were held with the four former clients. (See Appendix K for the interview questions.) These three researchers, all experienced in the conduct of TLT as well as open-ended counseling (3–16 years of clinical experience), reviewed the client protocols both individually and then collaboratively in order to share observations and derive hypotheses from them. What follow are the shared observations of the three members.

First and perhaps foremost, it is clear that *the four clients were constantly, actively, and intensely involved in their therapy during the time of treatment*. They thought about the work actively between sessions, mentally prepared for sessions, and often took notes based on the sessions. In a word, these seemed to be highly motivated clients who worked hard at learning about themselves and applying what they learned.

After termination, these individuals thought about what happened in the therapy much less than they did during the work, as might be expected. At the same time, it was evident that the therapy/therapist was internalized by the clients. Clients noted that conscious thoughts of the therapy/therapist emerged especially when they encountered troubles that had been previously explored during treatment. (Three of the four quantified their answer to this question, Item 1, saying that they thought or talked about what happened in counseling about once a month.)

The themes in all protocols suggested that, in the clients' eyes, this intense involvement was occurring with a person, the therapist, who was supportive, willing to reinforce the clients' progress and accomplishments, and able to provide a structure within which clients could both understand and begin to tackle their problems. Techniques that were structure-providing varied, according to the clients, but most often mentioned were structuring interpretations, questions that challenged unhelpful and unexamined assumptions, and at times active suggestions.

Along with the above data on clients' impressions of their therapists, it was abundantly clear that these individuals valued their therapists. There was no evidence at all of the kinds of power struggles that may emerge and get helpfully worked through in long-term therapy. Rather, the clients' comments suggested a quick development of a working alliance with a real person. This was so despite the fact that there was also sound evidence for the manifestation of transference reactions in three of the cases, that is, in their comments about their therapists. The transferences, however, seemed consistently positive and probably fed and were fed by a sound working alliance. (See Greenson's [1978] explorations of the interplay of the working alliance, the real relationship, and the transference relationship in psychoanalytic therapy.)

It was evident in three of the cases that the therapy and therapist were missed after the experience ended. The practice and preparation that occurred during treatment seemed to continue, and the clients took pride that the changes occurring in the therapy were internalized and continued. At the same time, this pride was mixed with a sense of loss. The relationship was special to these people, and three of them left it with some sense of anxiety and pressure, as well as loss. Confidence following termination, however, was actually enhanced by the successes these clients experienced on their own.

What kinds of changes occurred in these individuals during and after treatment? Probably the most notable and clearest pattern was that the changes were global rather than circumscribed. We were unable to detect any consistent differences in the kinds of change emerging during as against after therapy, as the posttherapy experience seemed to serve to deepen, extend, or fortify those changes that emerged during treatment. All clients felt they understood themselves better as a result of treatment, although the researchers felt the insights commented on by these individuals had a more "brittle" or "precarious" quality than those the researchers felt occurred in the long-therapy they conducted.

In addition to insight, changes commented on by at least three of the clients included a reduction in guilt, more appropriate assertiveness and expressiveness (less in one case), and enhanced self-concept, for example, greater confidence in self, enhanced self-esteem. Idiosyncratic changes ranged from improved work effectiveness, and appropriately increased separation from parents on the one hand to an improved sense of humor and a difference in the content of fantasies on the other. Finally, it was clear that all clients ran into problems during the year after termination, and sometimes these problems attained crisis proportions. The clients seemed, however, (and they commented on this) better able to cope with their problems without letting the problems erode their self-esteem.

In summary, some clear impressions emerged from our analysis of the four interview protocols. The following observations may serve as hypotheses about what happens in TLT (at least) that underlies or is part of its effectiveness in setting in motion a change process that continues after termination: (a) The clients were highly motivated, and during treatment were constantly, actively, and intensely involved in the work; (b) they quickly became involved in a positive and meaningful relationship with a therapist who was seen as supportive, reinforcing, and helpfully structuring; (c) the changes that occurred during treatment were global rather than circumscribed—generally including self-understanding, self-esteem, guilt reduction, and expressiveness/assertiveness; (d) many indosyncratic changes were noted, for example, sense of humor, content of fantasies; (e) the changes following treatment seemed to be an extension or continuation of those emerging during counseling; (f) while the termination was not traumatic, it was experienced as a loss and often as anxiety provoking; and (g) at the same time, clients felt they gained, for example, confidence, from the successes they experienced on their own after treatment.

Discussion and Some Conclusions

The basis for the present study was the hypothesis that TLT is effective in beginning or setting in motion a change process whose effects gradually accumulate after treatment termination. In presenting this hypothesis in the introductory section of this chapter we proposed that the bulk of positive change or the most beneficial effects of TLT might occur *following* termination. We felt that TLT might begin or set in motion a change process, but that most of the change would occur after treatment. Such a phenomenon might help explain why therapists are so often more negative about TLT than are their clients (Johnson and Gelso's [1980] finding). That is, since TLT only begins a change process, therapists do not have the opportunity to witness directly the major changes resulting from this treatment—in contrast to open-ended or longer-term counseling where therapists do get a first-hand view of at least more of their clients' changes.

Is the "change in motion" hypothesis supported by our data? It seems clear from the data that the portion of the hypothesis stating, in effect, that greater changes emerge after than during treatment *was not supported*. Rather, clients who become involved enough in TLT to participate in a number of sessions approaching the duration limit exhibit between a "slight" and "moderate" amount of change on several relevant dimensions during counseling, and they manifest, according to their own reports, about an equal amount of change between termination and a follow-up one year later. Thus, our "change in motion" hypothesis requires some revision, and may be stated as follows: *Time-limited counseling is effective in beginning or setting in motion a change process that continues at an approximately equal rate following termination, to a point at least one year following that termination.* It is important to add that this is an "on-the-whole" statement, and that much individual variability exists in posttherapy change. Also, it must be kept in mind that our client-selection procedures make the hypothesis clearly fitting only for the subgroup of clients who continue in TLT beyond the initial stage. For clients in general, the "equal rate" hypothesis may represent the upper limit of posttherapy change. Clearly this is a question deserving of additional research attention.

It might be worth underscoring that the amount of overall change as well as the amount of change on dimensions such as feeling improvement, behavior change, and self-understanding improvement is indeed not dramatic, either during or after counseling. Yet, according to clients and their therapists, change does occur during treatment, and the clients feel it does continue. Our interview data suggest that the "during" and "after" treatment changes are not qualitatively different from one another. Instead, the posttreatment period serves to help clients fortify, extend, or perhaps deepen the growth that emerges during counseling. While some clients report improvement in their *feelings* during counseling followed by a worsened state afterwards (13%; see Table 3–4), this improvement-deterioration cycle rarely occurs on dimensions such as "behavior change" and "self-understanding." On these latter dimensions, approximately 80%–85% of the clients report improvement between termination and follow-up, and about 10% more report improvement during counseling followed by no change (stabilization?) afterwards.

The data in this chapter are a far cry from the fears often expressed by therapists that brief TLT only serves as a temporary solution to clients' problems. While we have had to revise our "change in motion" hypothesis as a result of the data, it may still be true that therapists' concerns about brief TLT are tied to the likelihood that in such work the therapist witnesses less client growth directly than in longer-term treatment. One practical and partial solution to this problem is a procedure that some of us have found useful clinically in understanding the effects of TLT. This procedure is a periodic (for example, 3- to 6-month) follow-up of clients we have treated. More often than not we have been surprised at the extent to which former clients continue to grow on their own after counseling.

We have been discussing continued growth after counseling as if it is a sole result of that counseling. The data do suggest that the large majority of former clients do attribute at least an important part of posttherapy growth to the therapy experience (although a small proportion, 8%, did report that *none* of the change they experienced following therapy was attributable to the treatment). For the most part, however, the therapy experience becomes melded with several psychological and situational factors in accounting for posttherapy growth. Thus, the therapy experience, the passage of time, changes in life circumstances, and the former clients' own self-awareness all seem to play an important role, in clients' eyes, in continued growth after treatment. Furthermore, family and friends seem to play an important role for about half the clients. We suspect that it would be exceedingly difficult to unravel the complex causal network in which these variables are probably imbedded. For now it must suffice to say that counseling does appear to have an effect on postcounseling growth in clients' eyes, and that it is part of a host of factors that influence such growth and also in some cases produce the deterioration that has been the subject of recent research (Bergin & Lambert, 1978) and debate (Bergin, 1980; Mays & Franks, 1980).

For a sizable minority of clients, perhaps up to a third, some amount of additional counseling following TLT termination may be an important part of continued growth. One might wonder here if TLT is any different from open-ended counseling, since clients who have received TLT simply seek more counseling when they want it, and at a rather high rate.

In formulating an answer to that question, two pieces of data seem particularly relevant. First, the rates with which students return for more counseling as reported in Chapter 2 for 8-16-session TLT were approximately 50% and 25%, respectively. The fact that the return rate found in the present study (where a 12-session limit was largely used) was about midway between these two rates lends itself to the following hypothesis: *the return rate is inversely proportional to the duration limit in TLT*. Now, this hypothesis results from our combining disparate time periods between termination and follow-up, so what we have here is an interesting and researchable hypothesis, and nothing more. Also, about a quarter of the TUT clients in Chapter 2 sought additional counseling. At some point, probably a point at which the session limit exceeds the mean number of sessions at a given agency, we would thus expect the inverse relationship pointed to by the hypothesis to fade or disappear.

The inverse relationship between duration limit and return rate in TLT seems to suggest TLT and TUT are essentially the same process—and take the same amount of total counseling time. A second piece of data, however, negates such a conclusion. Data in Chapter 2 suggest that although clients receiving brief TLT return for counseling at a greater rate than clients in TUT, the subsequent counseling they receive is of much briefer duration than that of the TUT returners. The net result is that the total amount of counseling received by TLT clients is appreciably less than that received by TUT clients. Thus, our tentative answer to whether TLT and TUT are essentially the same is negative. Even given the higher "recidivism" or return rate, TLT consumes appreciably less counselor time.

Based on the research team's analysis of interview protocols, we suggested that the insights developed by TLT clients seemed more "brittle" or "precarious" than those of TUT clients. While the meaning of this impression is difficult to put into words without going into detailed case material, two findings of the present data analysis seem to fit the impression. First, clients saw themselves improving in self-understanding during counseling significantly more than their therapists saw them improving (see Table 3-1). Second, of all the interrelationships among therapist and client ratings of change during treatment, the correlation between these therapy participants' ratings of self-understanding improvement was lowest ($r = .14$, see Table 3-2). Thus, at least in TLT, therapists do not see their clients gaining as many insights as do the clients, and indeed clients and therapists do not appear to be responding to the same stimuli when making judgments about insight development. At the same time, it is important to note that the therapists *did* perceive their clients as improving in self-understanding (as did the research team who interviewed the four clients). One might speculate that these clients gained at least enough insight to allow for continued posttherapy growth. Relatedly, even within the realm of psychoanalytic theory of treatment, current researches (e.g., Horwitz, 1974; Strupp, Fox, & Lessler, 1969) suggest that depth insight is not a requisite for lasting personality and behavior change.

We conclude this discussion by noting that the present study was naturalistic in that no independent variables were manipulated, and comparisons were not made with the reports of former clients either randomly or nonrandomly assigned to open-ended counseling. It follows that we cannot make conclusions about the relative effects of TLT and TUT. Furthermore, as the Addendum to chapter 2 indicates, a 12-session duration limit was employed at the Center for the large majority of clients. Clients seen in open-ended work were usually either the most disturbed individuals and/or those most suitable for training purposes.

We could not draw conclusions about clients in general based on the above data. Rather, the most tenable conclusions from the present data are that TLT tends to be effective, in clients' and experienced therapists' eyes, in an agency situation in which most but not all clients are assigned to that mode and for clients who continue in the treatment beyond the initial, preliminary stage. (As has been pointed out in Johnson and Gelso's [1980] review, clients in TLT tend to complete treatment or go beyond the preliminary stage more than those in TUT.) From the clients' viewpoints, those changes occurring during treatment do continue afterwards, and the continued growth after treatment, at least to an important extent, is indeed attributable to the counseling experience. Through semistructured interview data with a small number of clients we have developed hypotheses about what factors underlie or are part of the capability of brief TLT to induce the kinds of change that continue well after termination (see Question 6 in this chapter). Hypotheses about client, therapist, and treatment-situation variables were offered. The next two chapters provide further exploration of factors that influence the outcomes of TLT.

Note

[1]We would like to acknowledge the inconsistency of some of these observations with some of the results reported in Chapter 2. In this respect, it should be noted that the present study was organized prior to the final analysis of the results in Chapter 2.

REFERENCES

BERGIN, A. Negative effects revisited. *Professional Psychology,* 1980, *11,* 93–100.

BERGIN, A., & LAMBERT, M. The evaluation of therapeutic outcomes. In S. Garfield and A. Bergin (Eds.), *Handbook of psychotherapy and behavior change* (2nd ed.). New York: Wiley, 1978.

GREENSON, R. R. *Explorations in psychoanalysis.* New York: International Universities Press, 1978.

HORWITZ, L. *Clinical prediction in psychotherapy.* New York: Jason Aronson, 1974.

JOHNSON, D. H., & GELSO, C. J. The use of time limits in counseling and psychotherapy: A critical review. *The Counseling Psychologist,* 1980, *9,* 70–83.

MAYS, D., & FRANKS, C. Getting worse: Psychotherapy or not treatment. The jury should still be out. *Professional Psychology,* 1980, *11,* 78–92.

STRUPP, J., FOX, R., & LESSLER, K. *Patients view their psychotherapy.* Baltimore: Johns Hopkins University Press, 1969.

Client and Therapist Factors Influencing the Outcomes of Time-Limited Therapy

Introduction to Part Two

Part One of the book presented three studies focusing primarily on the outcomes of TLT. Part Two consists of two chapters that analyze the relationships between characteristics of the client and therapist on the one hand and treatment outcomes on the other.

Although there exist few clear and consistent research findings in the general counseling and therapy literature on the client and therapist factors that seem to influence the treatment process and its outcomes, studies on these factors *have* been done and have accumulated over the years. Thus, factors such as the client's motivation to change, likeability, degree of disturbance, and the therapist's level of experience and theoretical orientation have at least been studied to the point that reviewers of the research scene have been able to make summary statements of their role in therapy process and outcome (e.g., Auerbach & Johnson, 1977; Garfield, 1978; Luborsky et al., 1971; Meltzoff & Kornreich, 1970; Parloff, Waskow, & Wolfe, 1978). The scene is not nearly so favorable in the domain of TLT. Lambert (1979) calls the state of this research area primitive. Although much clinical speculation has occurred over the years on client and therapist factors influencing TLT, we have next to no research on this matter, to say nothing of whether such client and therapist variables operate differently in TLT as opposed to open-ended therapy.

Chapters 4 and 5 provide a preliminary look at characteristics in the client and counselor that appear to affect TLT outcome. Chapter 4, written by Charles J.

Gelso, David H. Mills, and Sharon Baron Spiegel and presenting data gathered in the investigation reported in detail in Chapter 2, examines the relationship between a host of client and therapist factors on the one hand and outcome on the other (1 month and 18 months after treatment termination). The client and therapist factors generally reflect therapists' theoretical orientation to counseling, therapists' experience in and attitudes toward TLT, and therapists' initial impressions of such client characteristics as severity of disturbance, willingness to change, and motivation for counseling.

Chapter 5, written by Diane M. Adelstein, Charles J. Gelso, James R. Haws, Kathryn G. Reed, and Sharon Baron Spiegel, examines whether certain client factors that emerge in TLT are predictive of continued growth a year after treatment termination. The data presented in that chapter are based on the study reported in detail in Chapter 3. Unlike existing research, that study employs multivariate as well as univariate correlational procedures in seeking to uncover the relationship among client characteristics emerging during treatment and continued post-therapy growth.

REFERENCES

AUERBACH, A. H., & JOHNSON, M. Research on the therapist's level of experience. In A. S. Gurman and A. M. Razin (Eds.), *Effective psychotherapy: A handbook of research,* New York: Pergamon, 1977.

GARFIELD, S. L. Research on client variables in psychotherapy. In S. L. Garfield and A. E. Bergin (Eds.), *Handbook of psychotherapy and behavior change* (2nd ed.). New York: Wiley, 1978.

LAMBERT, M. J. Characteristics of patients and their relationship to outcome in brief psychotherapy. *Psychiatric Clinics of North America,* 1979, *2,* 111–123.

LUBORSKY, L., CHANDLER, M., AUERBACH, A. H., COHEN, J., & BACHRACH, H. Factors influencing the outcome of psychotherapy: A quantitative review. *Psychological Bulletin,* 1971, *75,* 145–185.

MELTZOFF, J., & KORNREICH, M. *Research in psychotherapy.* Chicago: Aldine, 1970.

PARLOFF, M. B., WASKOW, I. E., & WOLFE, B. E. Research on therapist variables in relation to process and outcome. In S. L. Garfield and A. E. Bergin (Eds.), *Handbook of psychotherapy and behavior change* (2nd ed.). New York: Wiley, 1978.

4

Client and Therapist Factors Influencing the Outcomes of Time-Limited Counseling One Month and Eighteen Months After Treatment

Charles J. Gelso, David H. Mills, and Sharon Baron Spiegel

Counseling and psychotherapy research finally appear to have gotten satisfactory answers to the highly global question of "does counseling/psychotherapy work" (see Bergin & Lambert, 1978; Gelso, 1979a, 1979b). As that occurred, we began to study wholeheartedly the questions of the type posed a number of years ago by Krumboltz (1966) and which Gelso (1979a) has referred to as "who, what, when, and where?" questions. These studies address the issue of what kinds of treatments offered by which therapists to which clients are most beneficial in terms of a particular criterion. As presented in Chapters 1 and 2, the comparison of TLT of different durations with TUT and with a no-treatment control for initially better and more poorly adjusted clients is in keeping with these "who, what, when, and where?" questions. The data presented in this chapter are intended to take us one step further along that road.

As noted in the introduction to Part Two, almost no empirical research has been done on factors associated with the outcomes of time-limited treatment. We were not able to locate a single study assessing the *differential* impact of such factors on TLT compared to TUT. Thus, the present investigation serves as an early, even beginning, effort along these lines.

What factors might predict outcome in TLT? What factors might differentially predict outcome in TLT and in TUT? These are the central questions we address in this chapter. In conceptualizing these questions, we sought to study variables that both (a) would be of interest in furthering our general understanding of factors influencing the outcomes of TLT, and (b) would be practically meaningful. Regarding the latter, we selected predictor variables that might be useful to the Center in terms of facilitating improvement in agency practice. Thus, if we found, for example, that therapist directiveness was closely and positively associated with outcome, the agency could begin to examine the parameters of directiveness, and conduct in-service training procedures aimed at helping therapists learn to be appropriately directive in TLT, within the confines of their theoretical beliefs and personality styles.

Generally, several domains were selected for study, each with an array of associated variables. The first might be called the *individual therapist*. We attempted to determine if there existed an interaction between an individual therapist factor and a treatment mode (8-session TLT, 16-session TLT, TUT). Thus if we found that therapists differed among themselves on relative effectiveness in the three treatment modes, we could then study those who seemed especially competent in TLT, and attempt to train other therapists in ways consonant with the clinical style of the TLT-competent therapists.

A second class of potential "influences" that was studied centered on therapists' *theoretical orientation* to counseling/therapy. While available outcome evidence does not generally favor one theoretical orientation (Gelso, 1979a, 1979b; Smith & Glass, 1977), we expected that selected aspects of a therapist's orientation, for example, a tendency to be active and directive, might be associated with outcome in brief TLT.

Another class of influencers that might be both theoretically and practically useful is the *therapist's experience in and attitudes toward TLT*. Although the relationship of experience to outcome in therapy/counseling in general is a highly complex one, overall it does appear that experience is demonstrably related to a host of process as well as outcome factors (Auerbach & Johnson, 1977; Luborsky, Chandler, Auerbach, Cohen, & Bachrach, 1971).

Additionally, it makes at least clinical and intuitive sense that a therapist's attitude toward the treatment she or he offers will influence that therapist's behavior and the product of that therapy. Thus, since therapists' experience and attitudes appeared to be relevant to outcome generally, it seemed important to assess their relationship to TLT outcome in the present study.

A final class of variables we studied was reflected in the *therapists' evaluation after an initial meeting* with the client. Degree of client disturbance, client motivation for counseling and willingness to change, the therapist's confidence in the treatment to be offered, and therapists' expected enjoyment in working with the client were all rated by therapists after the first counseling meeting. Each of these factors has been studied in relation to outcome of open-ended counseling (Garfield, 1978; Lambert, 1979; Parloff, Waskow, & Wolfe, 1978), and, again, we hoped to get a preliminary picture of their role in TLT, in itself, and in comparison to TUT.

Before presenting the data, let us note that we have been using the term *outcome* as if it were a unitary and absolute entity. As discussed in Chapter 2, this is actually far from the truth. As we present and discuss our findings, it is important to keep in mind that by outcomes we mean client and counselor ratings of the results of treatment. Generalizations to other criterion sources should be made with caution, and always in relation to the existing research literature.

Method

Details of the methodology have been presented in Chapter 2, and here we shall only summarize the primary features. Following random assignment to one of three treatment modes (8- and 16-session TLT, TUT), clients received those treatments, and were then followed up approximately 1 month and 18 months after termination of counseling. The follow-ups solicited client reactions to the counseling they received, their judgments of the effect of that counseling, and their views of their own development following counseling. Seventy-eight clients completed the 1-month follow-up and 67 responded in the 18-month effort.

Fifteen therapists participated in the study, and counseled nearly an equal number of clients under each treatment condition. Six of the therapists actually did counsel an equal number of clients under the three conditions; those six serve as the subjects in the analysis of individual counselor effects presented below.

Procedure and Instrumentation

Following a summary of each of the therapist and client-completed instruments, we will present a more detailed look at those instruments pertinent to this phase of the study. The instruments in the following summary are of two types—three predictors (the *Pre-Counseling Assessment Blank,* the *Therapist Orientation Questionnaire,* and the *Time-Limited Therapy Questionnaire)* and three outcome measures, one from therapist ratings and two from clients (one a month after termination and the other 18 months after termination).

THE PREDICTORS. After the first interview with each client, the therapist completed the *Pre-Counseling Assessment Blank* (Appendix C), which assesses initial client status and therapist expectations about the treatment. During the first year of their participation in the project, all therapists completed the *Therapist Orientation Questionnaire* (Appendix E), which measures theoretical orientation along several empirically derived dimensions (Sundland & Barker, 1962; Sundland, 1972). All full-time and part-time senior staff and interns in the Center's Counseling Division ($n = 28$) over a two year period took the instrument, including thirteen who were not part of the study (Peabody & Gelso, 1977).

Within a month after each therapist terminated with his/her last client in the study, the therapist responded to the *Time-Limited Therapy Questionnaire*

(Appendix A). This instrument provided information on therapists' expressed theoretical orientation, years of experience, experience in time-limited and short-term therapy, and attitude toward such treatment both before and after participation in the project.

In summary, the 15 therapists completed three instruments that are employed as outcome predictors. These instruments generally sought to assess relevant client qualities, therapists' expectations for the treatment, therapists' theoretical orientation, and experience in and attitudes toward the treatments being offered.

THE OUTCOME CRITERIA.   Immediately following termination with each client, the therapist completed the *Post-Counseling Assessment Blank* (Appendix D), part of which measures the therapist's evaluation of clients' personality, behavior and feeling change as a consequence of treatment. The items relating to these three dimensions were used as the therapist-rated outcome measures. Client-judged outcomes were derived from the *Counseling Center Follow-Up Questionnaire* (Figure 2–1, Chapter 2), both 1 month and 18 months after termination. Three items assessing satisfaction with and change due to counseling were selected for use in this analysis.

INSTRUMENTATION DETAILS.   As indicated, items from three instruments were used as outcome predictors. The *Pre-Counseling Assessment Blank* contains the following five items that therapists rated on 7-point scales: (a) client's degree of disturbance or psychopathology (pervasiveness rather than acuteness); (b) client's motivation for counseling and (c) willingness to change; (d) therapist's degree of confidence that the client would profit from the treatment to be offered; and (e) the extent to which the therapist expected to enjoy working with each client.

Items that made clinical and conceptual sense in terms of their possible prediction of outcome and lack of redundancy were selected from the *Time Limited Therapy Questionnaire*. The seven selected items asked therapists (a) to identify the relative influence of four prominent theories on their orientation to counseling (behavioral, gestalt, phenomenological/existential/Rogerian, and psychoanalytic), and their relative influences were reflected in percentages (Item I.A in Tables 4–1, 4–2, and 4–3); (b) to rate their relative experience prior to the project in TLT and in structured, short-term therapy, (1 = much more than average experience, 5 = much less experience; Items II.2 and III.3 in the three tables); (c) to rate their attitude toward TLT, before and after participation (1 = very positive, 7 = very negative; Items II.4 and II.5 in the three tables); and (d) to rate their amount of learning about TLT since beginning in the project (1 = much learning, 4 = none; Item II.6 in Tables 4–1, 4–2, and 4–3). A final predictor was the therapists' amount of postdoctoral experience (interns considered as having zero years experience; see Item II.1 in the tables).

The *Therapist Orientation Questionnaire* contains 104 items and assesses dimensions along which therapists vary in their theoretical orientation to counseling/therapy. Subjects respond to each item (statement) on a Likert scale ranging from 1 (strongly disagree) to 5 (strongly agree) (Sundland, 1972). See Appendix E.

This 1972 form of the TOQ contains 61 items from Sundland's earlier factor analysis, which uncovered 10 factors. We scored the protocols according to these 10 factors (see Item I.C 1–10 in the table), and the factor labels are given in the three tables. The definitions of factors are given in Appendix L.

In addition to these 10 factors, the TOQ was scored on the five item clusters generated by the cluster analysis performed by Howard, Orlinsky, and Trattner (1970). This second analysis was performed because we suspected that at least two of the clusters, Therapist Directiveness and Inner Experience, might relate to TLT outcomes and might add additional information. Again, the cluster labels are presented in the three tables (Items B. 1–5 in the tables) and their definitions are given in Appendix L.

Items from two additional instruments were used as outcome measures. Three items from the *Post-Counseling Assessment Blank* completed by therapists after each final counseling session were used as the therapist-judged outcome measures. Therapists rated their clients on (a) the degree of *overall personality change* as a consequence of treatment (1 = no change, to 7 = much change); (b) the degree to which client is *behaving more effectively* due to counseling (1 = no more effectively, 7 = much more effectively; and (c) the degree to which client is *feeling better* (e.g., self-regard, optimism) as a consequence of treatment (1 = no better, 7 = much better).

Three items from the *Counseling Center Follow-Up Questionnaire* were used to assess client-judged outcome. The first item asks clients to rate their satisfaction with the results of counseling (1 = very satisfied, 5 = very dissatisfied; see Item III of Figure 2–1 in Chapter 2; the second item elicits a rating of the extent to which the client sees his or her life having been changed as a result of counseling (1 = no change for the better, 5 = much change for the better; see Item V, Figure 1–1, Chapter 2). The third item was the sum of five items on the CCFQ that ask clients to evaluate the change due to counseling in five separate domains—feelings, relating, accomplishing, thinking, and perception of whether others acted as though they had changed (see Item II.a through II.e, Figure 2–1, Chapter 2).

Summary of Procedure and Analysis

From those three instruments as predictors, a total of 30 items representing therapists' orientation (19 items), experience and attitudes (6 items), and expectations and judgments after the first counseling session (5 items) were drawn and then correlated (using Pearson coefficients) with (a) therapists' evaluations of clients' personality, behavior, and feeling change due to counseling, and with (b) clients' ratings of satisfaction with and changes due to counseling, the latter assessed in two ways. Therapist outcome evaluations were made shortly after termination, while clients' outcome ratings were made 1 month and 18 months after ending counseling. All correlations between predictor and outcome criteria were computed separately for clients in 8-session TLT, 16-session TLT, and TUT.

The Findings

Below we shall present, first, our findings concerning the role of the individual therapist in affecting TLT versus TUT outcomes. Then we shall present data on the relationship of the 30 predictor variables to therapists' ratings of personality, behavior, and feeling change in their clients as a consequence of counseling. The results section will be concluded by an analysis of the correlation of these same 30 predictors with client-rated outcomes 1 month and 18 months after termination.

The Individual Therapist

The six therapists studied in this phase of the analysis were all senior staff counselors, with from 2 to 16 years of postdoctoral experience ($\bar{X} = 5.7$ years). These therapists (2 males, 4 females) varied widely in their reported theoretical orientation, although none was very strongly wedded to one persuasion. When asked to express various theoretical influences on their counseling in terms of percentages, the primary influences fortuitously distributed themselves across the six therapists. Thus, one therapist each expressed the primary influence as psychoanalytic, behavioral, rational-emotive, gestalt, and phenomenological/ existential/Rogerian. A sixth therapist felt an equal influence of three different orientations.

Are there differences among individual therapists in their effectiveness in doing different kinds of therapy, specifically the three treatment-duration types in this study? To answer this question we performed 3 × 6 (treatment mode by individual therapist) analyses of variance for each of the three therapist-rated and three client-rated outcome criteria. The F ratio of interest from these analyses, the treatment mode by individual therapist interaction effect, provides a direct statistical answer to the question we have posed.

The analyses were entirely consistent in the almost complete absence of statistically significant individual therapist by treatment mode interactions. Thus, no evidence whatever emerged to suggest that therapists differ from one another in their *comparative* ability to perform time-limited versus unlimited counseling.

The only statistically significant effects coming from the above analyses indicate that therapists do in fact differ from one another in their ratings of client change in personality, behavior, and feeling due to counseling regardless of the treatment. Thus, the main effect for the individual therapist factor was highly significant ($p < .01$) for each of these items. At the same time, these same therapists did not differ in terms of *their clients' ratings* of change due to counseling and satisfaction with the experience. The implications of these findings are explored in our discussion section.

Factors Associated with Therapist-rated Outcome

The relationship of the 30 predictor items to the ratings (by all 16 therapists) of clients' personality, behavior, and feeling change due to counseling are presented in Table 4–1. We summarize here only these correlational patterns that seem most salient and conceptually intelligible. The reader is invited to study the table (as well as Tables 4–2 and 4–3) for himself or herself for whatever additional hypotheses might be derived from the remaining correlations.

THEORETICAL ORIENTATION.   Few of the correlations between theoretical orientation items (I.A, B, and C in Table 4–1) and therapist-rated outcome attain significance. Two patterns, however, seem noteworthy. The more a therapist was oriented toward gestalt therapy, the less she or he felt the client changed constructively in the briefest TLT, but the more she or he felt clients changed in TUT.

The second notable pattern was for *therapist directiveness* to be related to client change in the 8-session TLT, but not in the 16-session TLT or in the TUT (see B.5 under Theoretical Orientation). Using the definition of directiveness in Appendix L, we see that therapist-rated change in brief TLT is greatest for therapists who tend to "prescribe an actively guiding, instructing, confronting therapeutic approach to improve the patient's social adjustment"; this relationship, however, does not hold up as the length of treatment increases.

THERAPIST EXPERIENCE AND ATTITUDES.   Inspection of the data in Section II of Table 1 indicates, perhaps most notably, that therapists' attitudes toward TLT before and after participation in the project tend to be associated (significantly or nearly so) with their posttreatment judgments of clients' change in TLT, but not in TUT. Relatedy, the reported amount of learning about TLT during the project showed the same correlational pattern. At the same time, prior experience in either TLT or in structured, short-term treatment was not associated with outcome ratings of TLT, or, unsurprisingly, of ratings of TUT. Finally, experience in general (Item II.1) was related to ratings of clients' behavior change only in TUT. Apparently, the more experienced therapists were more likely to feel their clients changed their behaviors appropriately as a result of therapy only when the therapy was open ended.

RATINGS AFTER THE INITIAL SESSION.   While the relationships between therapists' theoretical orientation, experience, and attitudes on the one hand and outcome on the other tend to be either nonsignificant or, when significant, of

(continued on p. 97)

Table 4–1. Correlation of Predictors with Therapist-Judged Client Change Rated at Termination

	Therapist-judged outcome								
	Overall personality change			Behavior change			Feeling change		
Predictors	8 (n = 27)	16 (n = 28)	UL (n = 23)	8 (n = 27)	16 (n = 28)	UL (n = 23)	8 (n = 27)	16 (n = 28)	UL (n = 23)
I. *Theoretical orientation*									
A. *Stated* (in percents)									
1. Behavioral	.30	.12	.18	.20	.12	.25	.27	.06	.25
2. Gestalt	−.20	−.13	−.07	−.44*	−.12	.38	−.52**	−.07	.44*
3. Phenomenological/existential/Rogerian	−.07	−.03	.05	−.13	−.24	.01	−.04	−.18	.00
4. Psychoanalytic	−.03	−.17	−.22	.30	.03	.01	.18	−.03	.04
B. *Inventoried* (Howard, Orlinsky, & Trattner clusters for the *Therapist Orientation Questionnaire*)									
1. Psychoanalytic orientation	−.11	−.15	.12	−.19	.00	.07	−.02	.04	.24
2. Impersonal learning	−.11	−.20	−.04	−.15	.04	−.06	.11	.12	.19
3. Therapist role	−.31	−.54**	−.10	−.20	−.32	.10	.00	−.24	−.15
4. Inner experience	−.14	−.01	.02	−.02	−.03	.02	.04	.12	.08
5. Therapist directiveness	.27	.04	−.14	.57**	.07	.14	.54**	.15	.37

Table 4–1. (Continued)

C. *Inventoried (Sundland factors for the Therapist Orientation Questionnaire)*

1. Social goals & directiveness	.14	.11	– .32	.35	.25	.07	.27	.31	.04
2. Affective gains	– .13	– .36	– .13	.15	– .26	.09	.11	– .26	.18
3. Training, planning & conceptualization	.10	– .17	– .23	.16	– .06	– .13	.22	.11	– .04
4. Verbal learning & cognitive gains	– .01	– .20	– .15	.31	– .08	.09	.49**	.07	.25
5. Psychoanalytic techniques	– .16	– .12	.20	– .15	– .12	.05	– .05	– .03	– .01
6. Active, involved therapist	.22	.21	.35	.11	.08	.21	.05	.11	.30
7. Therapist security	.10	.19	– .03	– .02	.27	– .14	.03	.43*	– .10
8. Informal behavior	.05	.07	– .10	.05	– .12	– .25	– .12	– .01	– .02
9. Inherent growth	.22	.17	– .06	.23	– .07	– .02	.20	.07	.16
10. Interruptive activity	.07	– .11	– .29	.12	– .14	– .22	.11	– .22	.00

II. *Items from the TLT Questionnaire*

1. Years postdoctoral experience (interns = 0)	– .22	.00	.21	– .02	.14	.43*	.03	.08	.32
2. Amount of experience in TLT before project	– .11	.01	.23	– .04	– .15	.16	– .07	.05	.17

(continued)

Table 4–1. (Continued)

| | Therapist-judged outcome | | | | | | | | |
| | Overall personality change | | | Behavior change | | | Feeling change | | |
Predictors	8 (n = 27)	16 (n = 28)	UL (n = 23)	8 (n = 27)	16 (n = 28)	UL (n = 23)	8 (n = 27)	16 (n = 28)	UL (n = 23)
3. Amount of experience in structured, short-term therapy before project	-.05	-.19	.13	.04	.11	.08	.09	-.06	.03
4. Attitude toward TLT before project	.43*	.42*	.24	.33	.29	.08	.29	.13	.15
5. Attitude toward TLT after project	.24	.36	-.01	.32	.34	.08	.38*	.34	.13
6. Amount of learning about TLT since beginning of project	.23	.19	.19	.29	.41*	.21	.40*	.25	.05
III. Therapist-rated client characteristics (after first session)									
1. Degree of disturbance	-.15	.20	.44*	-.24	-.08	.15	-.17	.20	.14
2. Motivation for counseling	.34	.66*	.48*	.39*	.73**	.39	.41*	.68**	.60**
3. Willingness to change	.34	.44*	.18	.50**	.47*	.14	.43*	.56**	.37
4. Therapist confidence that client will profit from the treatment	.56**	.18	.57**	.65**	.36	.53**	.59**	.39*	.65**
5. Predicted therapist enjoyment in working with client	.45*	.06	.37	.59**	.28	.35	.67**	.29	.33

Note. All scales arranged for these analyses so that higher scores = greater degree of the rated quality.
[a]8 = 8-session TLT, 16 = 16-session TLT, UL = Time-unlimited Therapy
$* = p_i < .05; ** = p < .01$

modest magnitude, those between therapists' post-initial interview ratings and outcome are much more often significant and sometimes very substantial. Thus, therapists' ratings of clients' motivation for counseling, as well as their confidence that clients will profit from the offered treatment, were consistently and sometimes strongly related to outcome ratings regardless of the treatment mode. On the other hand, therapists' judgments of clients' willingness to change, as well as therapists' prediction of how much they would enjoy working with the client, were significantly related to change ratings in TLT, but not so related in TUT.

Finally, therapists' initial judgments of degree of client disturbance were positively related to ratings of overall personality change in TUT, but unrelated to such ratings in TLT.

Factors Predicting Client-rated Outcome One and Eighteen Months After Termination

Table 4–2 and 4–3 present the correlations of the same 30 predictors with three client-rated criteria—overall change due to counseling, satisfaction with the results of counseling, and a cumulative index of change due to counseling (consisting of five items, as discussed earlier). Table 4–2 presents these data for the 1-month follow-up, while Table 4–3 does so for the 18-month follow-up.

As was the case with the data on therapist-rated change, we note here only those correlational patterns that seem most conceptually meaningful and intelligible. This is done with a special eye toward the juxtaposition of the findings in this section with those just presented on the correlates of therapist-rated change.

THEORETICAL ORIENTATION. It will be recalled that the extent to which therapists felt their orientation was influenced by gestalt therapy was positively related to their ratings of client change in TUT, but negatively related in TLT. When clients' ratings 1 month and 18 months after termination are examined, a contradictory picture emerges. Thus, the therapists' espousal of a gestalt orientation was negatively related to the cumulative index of client-reported change due to counseling when the counseling was time unlimited, and unrelated to any of the outcome measures for TLT. A second contradiction pertains to the role of therapist directiveness. While directiveness was positively related to therapist ratings of client change in TLT, it is clearly unrelated to clients' perceptions of outcome.

A few additional patterns regarding the role of theoretical orientation appear noteworthy. First, the extent to which therapists viewed the therapeutic process as involving impersonal learning (emphasizing a controlled, nonevaluative, impersonal manner) was negatively related to clients' ratings of overall change due to counseling (and approaching significance on the other two outcome indices) for TUT. For TLT, however, whether the therapist subscribed to an impersonal learning approach or its opposite, a close personal relationship, was inconsequential to client-judged outcome. Second, the extent to which therapists did not admit

(continued on page 104)

Table 4–2. Correlation of Predictors with Client Ratings 1 Month After Termination

	Client-judged outcome								
	Overall change due to counseling			Satisfaction with results of counseling			Cumulative index of change due to counseling		
Predictors	8[a] (n = 27)	16[a] (n = 28)	UL[a] (n = 23)	8[a] (n = 27)	16[a] (n = 28)	UL[a] (n = 23)	8[a] (n = 26)	16[a] (n = 28)	UL[a] (n = 22)
I. Theoretical orientation									
A. Stated (in percentages)									
1. Behavioral	.00	− .07	.00	− .05	.04	.07	− .06	.09	− .04
2. Gestalt	.07	− .07	− .29	.00	.07	− .38	− .08	− .20	− .47*
3. Phenomenological/existential/Rogerian	− .14	− .21	.01	− .10	− .41*	.06	.23	− .05	.24
4. Psychoanalytic	.10	.25	.33	.19	.49**	.23	− .07	− .01	.26
B. Inventoried (Howard, Orlinsky, & Trattner clusters for the Therapist Orientation Questionnaire)									
1. Psychoanalytic orientation	.17	− .24	.00	.22	− .31	− .21	.24	.10	.05
2. Impersonal learning	.25	− .15	− .44*	.20	− .09	− .34	.31	− .08	− .41*
3. Therapist role	− .13	− .34	.17	.03	− .22	.08	.27	− .26	.18
4. Inner experience	.02	.18	− .24	− .07	.09	− .17	.10	− .02	.03
5. Therapist directiveness	− .08	.11	.18	− .02	.18	.18	− .13	− .09	.35

Table 4–2. (Continued)

C. *Inventoried (Sundland factors for the Therapist Orientation Questionnaire)*

1. Social goals & directiveness	−.19	.08	.00	.20	.14	−.12	−.37	−.12	−.11
2. Affective gains	−.02	.02	.32	−.13	.32	.21	.14	−.30	.39
3. Training, planning & conceptualization	.00	−.30	−.17	−.03	−.25	−.23	.03	−.38	−.11
4. Verbal learning & cognitive gains	−.07	.02	.01	−.03	.02	.07	.18	−.07	.10
5. Psychoanalytic techniques	−.02	−.03	.04	.02	−.21	.10	.11	.12	−.01
6. Active, involved therapist	.02	.26	.21	.04	.01	.12	−.07	.24	.17
7. Therapist security	.05	.02	−.55**	−.09	.00	−.53**	−.18	−.06	−.54**
8. Informal behavior	−.18	.04	.07	−.18	.01	−.02	−.25	−.05	−.03
9. Inherent growth	−.32	.18	−.07	−.34	.33	.18	−.37	.16	−.01
10. Interruptive activity	.09	−.25	−.05	−.01	−.06	.07	.09	−.29	−.17

II. *Items from the TLT Questionnaire*

1. Years postdoctoral experience (interns = 0)	.14	.24	.34	.24	.09	.18	.23	.09	.42*
2. Amount of experience in TLT before project	−.22	.07	.36	−.10	−.10	.29	−.08	.04	−.02
3. Amount of experience in structured, short-term therapy before project	.09	−.10	.07	.14	−.00	−.00	.17	−.11	−.25

(continued)

Table 4–2. (Continued)

Predictors	Client-judged outcome								
	Overall change due to counseling			Satisfaction with results of counseling			Cumulative index of change due to counseling		
	8[a] (n = 27)	16[a] (n = 28)	UL[a] (n = 23)	8[a] (n = 27)	16[a] (n = 28)	UL[a] (n = 23)	8[a] (n = 26)	16[a] (n = 28)	UL[a] (n = 22)
4. Attitude toward TLT before project	.19	.10	.13	.10	.05	.12	.02	.45**	.08
5. Attitude toward TLT after project	−.14	.16	−.06	−.15	−.11	.21	−.15	.41*	−.02
6. Amount of learning about TLT since beginning of project	−.09	−.00	.08	−.05	−.15	.13	.09	.20	.03
III. *Therapist-rated client characteristics (after first session)*									
1. Degree of disturbance	−.17	−.03	−.14	−.31	−.12	−.25	−.11	.17	−.07
2. Motivation for counseling	.11	.54**	.25	.29	.28	.09	.33	.46**	.40
3. Willingness to change	.28	.45*	.18	.30	.29	−.07	.32	.17	.32
4. Therapist confidence that client will profit from the treatment	.44*	.29	.14	.59**	.00	.07	.40*	.12	.28
5. Predicted therapist enjoyment in working with client	.34	.31	.13	.46*	.27	.11	.30	.17	.15

Note. All scales arranged for these analyses so that higher scores = greater degree of the rated quality.
[a] 8 = 8-session TLT; 16 = 16-session TLT; UL = Time-unlimited Therapy   * = p < .05; ** = p < .01

Table 4–3. Correlation of Predictors with Client Ratings 18 Months After Termination

	Client-judged outcome								
	Overall change due to counseling			Satisfaction with results of counseling			Cumulative index of change due to counseling		
Predictors	8[a] (n = 21)	16[a] (n = 24)	UL[a] (n = 22)	8[a] (n = 21)	16[a] (n = 24)	UL[a] (n = 22)	8[a] (n = 21)	16[a] (n = 23)	UL[a] (n = 21)
I. *Theoretical orientation*									
A. *Stated* (in percents)									
1. Behavioral	.17	−.27	.06	−.01	−.14	.01	−.11	−.03	.28
2. Gestalt	−.28	−.14	−.36	−.02	.00	−.25	−.07	−.23	−.43*
3. Phenomenological/existential/Rogerian	−.06	.11	.04	−.13	−.17	.01	−.07	−.01	−.06
4. Psychoanalytic	.27	.27	.23	.14	.38	.20	.02	.33	.13
B. *Inventoried* (Howard, Orlinsky, & Trattner Clusters for the *Therapist Orientation Questionnaire*)									
1. Psychoanalytic orientation	.04	−.07	.21	.30	−.18	−.05	.17	−.14	.15
2. Impersonal learning	.19	−.28	−.29	.15	−.25	−.17	.11	−.21	−.20
3. Therapist role	.21	.02	.24	.27	−.09	.18	.24	−.25	.02
4. Inner experience	.10	.39	−.06	.05	.20	.08	.05	.22	−.16
5. Therapist directiveness	.25	.19	.35	.11	.20	.23	−.05	.22	.35

(continued)

Table 4–3. (Continued)

Client-judged outcome

Predictors	Overall change due to counseling			Satisfaction with results of counseling			Cumulative index of change due to counseling		
	8[a] (n = 27)	16[a] (n = 28)	UL[a] (n = 23)	8[a] (n = 27)	16[a] (n = 28)	UL[a] (n = 23)	8[a] (n = 26)	16[a] (n = 28)	UL[a] (n = 22)
C. *Inventoried* (Sundland factors for the *Therapist Orientation Questionnaire*)									
1. Social goals & directiveness	.02	−.31	−.04	−.04	−.21	−.19	−.18	−.14	−.03
2. Affective gains	.24	.44*	.28	.12	.37	.41*	.14	.22	.13
3. Training, planning & conceptualization	.40	−.13	.01	.32	−.14	−.01	.22	−.35	−.06
4. Verbal learning & cognitive gains	.34	.17	.22	.19	.09	.29	.12	.03	.14
5. Psychoanalytic techniques	−.13	.27	.21	−.05	.11	.26	−.06	.06	.04
6. Active, involved therapist	−.14	.32	.09	.00	.48*	.30	−.06	.25	.17
7. Therapist security	.07	−.40*	−.22	.02	−.24	−.30	−.20	−.25	−.11
8. Informal behavior	−.06	.30	.03	.11	.22	.12	.08	−.04	−.12
9. Inherent growth	−.23	−.05	−.08	−.11	.03	−.05	−.31	.24	−.08
10. Interruptive activity	.24	−.33	−.13	−.06	−.31	−.05	.12	−.32	−.06

II. *Items from the TLT Questionnaire*

1. Years postdoctoral experience (interns = 0)	.20	.29	.41*	– .07	.26	.34	.10	.16	.36
2. Amount of experience in TLT before project	– .10	.21	.05	– .26	– .07	.37	.05	– .04	.05
3. Amount of experience in structured, short-term therapy before project	.34	– .01	– .08	– .04	– .05	.25	.16	– .12	.03
4. Attitude toward TLT before project	.14	.06	– .00	.20	.02	– .00	.21	.25	.32
5. Attitude toward TLT after project	.02	– .08	– .16	.06	– .21	– .15	.07	.04	– .01
6. Amount of learning about TLT since beginning of project	.16	– .09	– .03	.08	– .25	– .01	.14	.11	– .10

III. *Therapist-rated client characteristics (after first session)*

1. Degree of disturbance	– .16	– .10	.04	– .14	– .21	.00	– .22	.09	.33
2. Motivation for counseling	.52*	.30	.14	.43*	.31	.43*	.32	.58**	.42
3. Willingness to change	.61**	.26	.20	.48*	.55**	.41*	.43*	.41*	.35
4. Therapist confidence that client will profit from the treatment	.69**	.02	.16	.54*	.13	.35	.51*	– .01	.31
5. Predicted therapist enjoyment in working with client	.57**	.00	.03	.43*	.24	.21	.33	.08	.00

Note. All scales arranged for these analyses so that higher scores = greater degree of the rated quality.
[a]8 = 8-session TLT, 16 = 16-session TLT, UL = Time-unlimited Therapy   * = $p < .05$; ** = $p < .01$

to feelings of insecurity, discomfort, and/or nonunderstanding in some therapeutic relationship (see C.7, Therapist Security) was negatively related to client-rated outcome on all three indices in TUT; but again, in TLT this factor was not predictive of outcome. The two correlational patterns just noted emerged at the 1-month follow-up. While trends still existed after 18 months, however, these relationships reduced to the point of statistical nonsignificance.

THERAPIST EXPERIENCE AND ATTITUDES.   While therapists' expressed attitudes toward TLT tended to predict their outcome ratings in TLT, these attitudes had no bearing on their clients' ratings of outcome, as Section II in Tables 4–2 and 4–3 indicates. Also, therapist experience in TLT and in short-term work was uncorrelated with clients' outcome ratings (as well as therapists' ratings). The one significant pattern that did occur in this section was the relationship between overall experience and outcome. Thus, as occurred for therapist-rated outcome, client-rated outcome in TUT was usually either marginally ($p < .10$) or clearly related to therapists' overall experience level, both 1 month and 18 months after termination. Outcome was not related to any experiential variable, however, when the treatment mode was TLT.

RATINGS AFTER THE INITIAL SESSION.   Therapists' ratings of degree of disturbance after the initial session did not correlate with any of the client-judged outcome items, either 1 month or 18 months after termination. The lack of statistical significance ends here, however, as the remaining four items, in varying ways and to differing degrees, do predict outcome.

As was the case for therapist-rated outcome, therapists' initial ratings of client motivation for counseling correlated significantly (or nearly) and positively with client-rated outcome indices. These relationships seemed to cut across the three outcome measures, and were maintained with equal magnitude in the 18-month follow-up.

Regarding the three remaining items, Tables 4–2 and 4–3 display what appears to be a notable pattern. That is, the correlations of client-rated change with these three predictors (willingness to change, therapist confidence that the client will profit from the treatment to be offered, and therapists' predicted enjoyment in working with the client) tended to attain or approach significance for TLT, especially the briefest TLT, but not for TUT. Thus, it appears that these items relate to a positive prognosis when using brief TLT. At least for two of these items, willingness to change and predicted therapist enjoyment, these fndings are very similar to those noted in the presentation of therapist-rated outcome.

A final pattern worth noting is the surprising finding that therapists' ratings after an initial interview seem *more* related to client outcome ratings 18 months after termination than 1 month after ending counseling. Thus, despite the somewhat reduced n's in the 18-month follow-up (and the resulting larger correlation coefficients needed for statistical significance), 15 of the correlations were significant at 18 months, whereas only 7 were so after 1 month. The magnitude of some of the correlations at 18 months (e.g., r's from .50 to .69) seems especially notable when one considers that we are relating *client* self-ratings well after termination to *therapist* ratings after an initial meeting.

Discussion

There appear to be two prominent and important patterns in our findings. The first pattern actually pertains to the lack of statistically significant findings. That is, the results consistently failed to isolate general factors or qualities within that the therapist related to either client or therapist outcome ratings in time-limited therapy. In contrast to our expectations, we did not find that some therapists are especially effective in TLT; therapists' theoretical orientations (either toward broadly defined approaches such as psychodynamic therapy, or toward more specific elements such as focusing on inner experience) evidenced no consistent relationships with client or therapist judged outcome in TLT versus TUT; and while therapists' attitudes toward TLT did relate to their outcome ratings in that treatment format, such attitudes did not relate to their clients' outcome evaluations.

In contrast to the nonsignificance noted, the second prominent pattern in the data was that therapists' ratings (after the first counseling session) of client qualities as well as their own feelings and expectations did appear to relate to TLT outcome, sometimes strongly. These ratings, if anything, seemed more predictive of client-judged outcome at the 18-month than at the 1 month follow-up, suggesting the likelihood of a "sleeper" effect, to be examined later in this discussion.

In the sections that follow we examine and offer interpretations of the results under four headings: The individual therapist, the role of the therapists' theory, therapists' experience in and attitudes toward TLT, and the utility of clinical judgments after an initial interview.

The Individual Therapist: Are Some Better than Others at Time-Limited Therapy?

Some therapists seem to think they are better than others, both in TLT and TUT. Thus, some therapists evaluate their clients as more improved than do others. These between-therapists differences, however, are not systematically supported by clients' outcome ratings. Probably more germane to the current research effort, none of the six therapists used in this analysis appeared to be particularly effective at TLT relative to TUT, or vice versa, either according to their own evaluations or those of their clients.

The fact that a group of relatively experienced therapists exhibit clear differences in their outcome ratings—differences that are not supported by their clients' ratings—suggests the existence of something like a therapist response set with respect to outcome. Some therapists may be more sanguine in their outcome assessments, while others may make "tougher" evaluations. While this phenomenon is not especially relevant to the comparative study of TLT versus TUT, it is a finding that should be taken into account more generally when therapist evaluations are used as outcome criteria.

Regarding the lack of differences among therapists in their *relative* effectiveness in TLT and TUT, it must be remembered that we are dealing with a small sample of therapists and clients in this phase of the analysis (6 therapists and 36 clients). Also this was a moderately experienced group of therapists, averaging about 6 years of postdoctoral clinical experience. Finally, since therapist participation in the study was fully voluntary, it seems likely that those who felt most uncomfortable with TLT did not participate (though, since these nonparticipants numbered only 2 of the 12 senior staff, the generalizability of the results is not greatly hampered).

All of the above caveats nonwithstanding, we suggest that the most plausible conclusion regarding an "individual therapist" factor is that within a group of relatively experienced practitioners there are at least not likely to be dramatic differences in effectiveness in TLT versus TUT. Contrary to our expectation, it does not appear true that some are especially good at TLT, while others display clearly greater effectiveness in TUT. Although some therapists, according to their own outcome evaluations, may see themselves as better than others in *both* TLT and TUT, probably in fact the large majority of experienced practitioners who are willing to do both TLT and TUT are about equally effective at both. However, the reader should remember the possible constraints of the treatments themselves, for example, TUT generally may be more effective than TLT with the most disturbed clients (see Chapter 2).

The Role of Theoretical Orientation

It may be important to note that all the measures of theoretical orientation in this study are self-report measures and, as such, may reflect *beliefs* rather than *behavior*. However, possibly the most appropriate and significant conclusion regarding the role of the therapists' reported theoretical orientation is that it appears relatively inconsequential regarding both effectiveness in doing TLT and comparative effectiveness in TLT and TUT.

At a more specific level, the researchers had expected that aspects of theoretical orientation revolving around, for example, "directiveness," would relate to TLT efficacy, that is, that the therapists who were generally more directive would be more effective in TLT than those who reported being generally less directive. This expectation was partially upheld when the therapists themselves rated outcomes. Yet the clients appeared to have felt otherwise, since the factor "therapist directiveness" was unrelated to their outcome evaluations for any of the treatment modes. Thus, the more directive therapists report that their TLT cases fare better than do the generally less directive therapists. The clients themselves, however, do not reflect such differences.

It will be recalled from Chapter 2 that therapists reported greater directiveness (activity and structuring) in TLT than TUT. This suggests that therapists do adjust to the demands of the treatment situation (consonant with Butcher and Koss's [1978] review of therapist behavior in brief therapy). Nonetheless, we cannot say, based on the data, that therapists should be more directive in TLT than in TUT in that the findings suggest that directiveness has little if any bearing on outcome.

In general, therapy research literature suggests that theoretical orientation is unrelated to treatment success (Sundland, 1977; Parloff, Waskow, & Wolfe, 1978); this conclusion was certainly substantiated in the present study. The likelihood, however, that as discussed above therapists adjust their general orientation to the demands of the treatment situation may help explain the lack of significance in the theoretical orientation data. At the same time, a few findings that deserve attention did emerge. The findings about the gestalt orientation are particularly interesting and perplexing. The more a therapist reported being influenced by gestalt therapy principles the less that therapist was likely to rate his or her brief TLT clients as exhibitng either behavior or feeling change due to counseling. This negative relationship, however, does not occur on client-rated outcome indices. What does emerge on these indices is a *inverse* relationship between the degree of gestalt orientation and cumulative change reported by the clients 1 month and 18 months after termination in *time-unlimited therapy!* To complicate the picture further, gestalt orientation was *positively* related to feeling change in TUT when the therapists were performing the ratings!

What sense, if any, can be made of the above puzzle? We have some tentative explanations. Gestalt therapy, at least as practiced in the early to mid-1970s (when these data were gathered), seems to us to have a strong "do your own thing" element in its philosophy of treatment. It may be that setting a limit to treatment, and a brief one at that, was experienced as inimical to the approach since the limit was established by someone (the researchers, random assignment) other than the therapist. Perhaps this loss of therapist freedom or autonomy accounts for the negative association between therapists' degree of gestalt orientation and their judged outcomes in brief TLT. Since their clients did not share this ideology, it follows that they would not necessarily exhibit lower ratings of brief TLT—thus the lack of significant relationship between client-rated outcome in brief TLT and the gestalt orientation, just as with other orientations.

The positive association of the gestalt orientation with therapist-rated feeling change in TUT may be viewed as a kind of "overconfidence' among the more gestalt-oriented practitioners, particularly since their clients' ratings were in the opposite direction, that is, the more gestalt-oriented the therapist, the less change reported by the client in TUT. Again we invoke a temporally bound explanation of this phenomenon. At least in the early and mid-1970s much of gestalt therapy, particularly the Perls variety, indeed seemed to exude a kind of overconfidence well illustrated in recent analyses of Perls's approach to therapy and other aspects of his life (Dolliver, 1981; Dolliver, Williams, & Gold, 1980). At the same time, this highly aggressive and confrontive approach may not have been well suited to the Counseling Center clients since they were assigned randomly to their therapists with no mutual selection process as often occurs in other agencies and in private practice. The aggressiveness and confrontiveness of Perls's gestalt therapy (Dolliver, Williams, & Gold, 1980), in conjunction with the negative relationship of gestalt orientation to client-judged outcome in the current study, harkens back to Lieberman, Yalom, & Miles' (1973) findings about the kinds of encounter group leaders whose groups had high rates of psychological casualties. The most damaging leader style, the "aggressive stimulator," manifested an aggressive, intrusive approach involving considerable challenging and confronting. Such leaders were impatient and pushed for early disclosure and emotional expression from the group members.

Along with the gestalt-orientation factor, two additional aspects of theoretical orientation merit attention. At least at the 1-month follow-up, client-rated outcome in TUT *but not in TLT* seemed to favor therapists who were able to admit to feelings of insecurity, discomfort, and nonunderstanding in their work, and who viewed therapy as involving a close personal relationship (as opposed to impersonal learning). These two therapist factors are often presented in clinical and at times research literature as important to outcome (Singer & Luborsky, 1977; Mitchell, Bozarth, & Krauft, 1977). Yet while they were so for TUT, they were unrelated to TLT outcomes. It may be that in brief TLT not enough time is allowed for such factors to "take hold." Alternatively, beyond some minimum, therapist openness to insecurity and attention to the nuances of the relationship may be inappropriate, if not impossible, in very brief work. Attention may need to be devoted to the most readily changeable and pressing client issues, and in successful TLT this may require a focus on concrete, immediate problems.

Do Therapist Attitudes and Experience Really Matter?

As Lambert (1979) points out, the general variable, "therapist experience" taps numerous qualities that may be assumed to increase with experience and age, confidence, security, integration, flexibility, knowledge, and so forth. One could assume, therefore, a strong relationship between experience and outcome. In fact, although the research on this topic does not demonstrate as potent a relationship as might be expected, the relationship does indeed exist (Auerbach & Johnson, 1977; Parloff, Waskow, & Wolfe, 1978). The present study provides additional support for the relationship between therapist experience and outcome, both in terms of client and therapist ratings, *but only when it is TUT with which we are concerned.* Amount of therapist experience does not seem to be a factor in TLT outcome, a finding that is contrary to clinical lore, which suggests that "Effective brief therapy requires a highly experienced therapist who can keep the therapeutic goals in sight and not get bogged down in content that is irrelevant to agreed-upon goals." (Butcher & Koss, 1978)

These findings relating experience and outcome are not surprising when one considers that experience among the group of therapists in the study actually means experience in time-unlimited approaches. It seems likely that any relationship between experience and TLT outcome that might have occurred was neutralized by this fact. Inspection of the literature of brief and time-limited approaches suggests that these treatments require therapist operations very different from those used in open-ended approaches (see, for example, Mann, 1973; Sifneos, 1972; Bellak & Small, 1965). Thus, in acquiring experience, the present therapists (like most therapists) may have been learning clinical skills that were to some extent nonfunctional or even harmful in brief TLT.

While it is unsurprising that experience in general was unrelated to TLT outcome, it is surprising that amount of experience in either TLT or structured short-term therapy prior to the project was also unrelated to TLT outcomes, both from therapists' and clients' vantage points. It is possible that this finding reflects a measurement problem, since experience in TLT and short-term therapy was assessed by asking therapists to rate themselves relative to other therapists they knew. Such self-reports may not really tap actual amount of experience since relative experience is very difficult to measure. At the same time, it is probably safe to say that *none* of the therapists in the study had received anything like formal training in TLT prior to the project. None had received supervision or coursework explicitly in TLT, and certainly none had done extensive reading in TLT before the project. It may well be that, for experience to affect outcomes positively, it must be the "right kind" of experience and include some formal training.

Attitudes toward TLT before and after participating in the project and amount of learning since beginning in the project tended to have modest but positive relationships to the therapist-rated outcome indices; they were unrelated to client-rated outcome. It should be noted that little variability existed on these items, with the large majority of therapists exhibiting a kind of guarded optimism about the efficacy of TLT before the project, and greater positiveness afterwards. Nearly all therapists felt they had learned a moderate amount about TLT during their participation. It seems likely that if these variables, attitudes toward and amount of learning about TLT, are to relate to client-judged outcomes, greater variability would need to exist.

The Usefulness of Therapists' Judgments After One Counseling Session

Up to this point in the discussion we have been examining essentially negative results about the relationship of our predictors to TLT outcomes. The positive results thus far have mostly occurred for TUT. Thus, we have examined why expected relationships such as that of therapist experience level and outcome emerged for TUT but not for TLT. While such analyses are necessary and useful, they still leave us with a sense of empty-handedness with respect to the correlates of success and failure in TLT. As indicated in the Results section, however, some notably positive results emerged when the predictors reflected therapists' judgments after the initial interview.

Before discussing these results, we want to remind the reader that all clients in the study participated in an intake interview with a staff member. Following the intake session, the interviewer wrote a summary that usually described the client's presenting problem, more general issues with the client, prognosis, and treatment suggestions. The therapist to whom the client was later assigned had access to these intake evaluations. Thus the ratings that were made after the first counseling session were probably derived from the counselor's actual clinical impressions in conjunction with those reported by the intake interviewer.

Four variables rated after the initial counseling interview seem especially useful in predicting outcomes, especially for TLT but in some cases for both TLT and TUT. The correlations between a therapist's ratings of these variables after the initial counseling session and both the client and therapist-rated outcomes were surprisingly high given that (a) some of the correlations were between therapist ratings and *client-judged* outcome (surprising because the relationship among ratings made by different criterion sources, for example, counselor and client, tend to be low in most studies), and (b) some of the relationships are among therapist-rated phenomena after the first session and client-rated outcomes *18 months after treatment!*

The extent to which the client is seen as motivated for counseling appears to be an equal factor in success in TLT and TUT. Butcher and Koss (1978) have noted that initial motivation is viewed as an important criterion for success in brief therapy. Our findings confirm that, but suggest that initial motivation, as judged by the therapist, is an equally influential factor in TUT.

Three factors seem especially relevant to success in brief TLT: clients' initial willingness to change (as rated by the therapist), therapists' confidence that the client will profit from the treatment being offered, and therapists' predictions about the extent to which they will enjoy working with the client. Why do these factors seem especially influential in brief TLT, for example, versus TUT? It seems almost plausible that the brief amount of time allotted to treatment in 8-session TLT does not permit modification of the initial tendencies reflected in these three items. For example, if a client is seen as unwilling to change, brief TLT may not allow enough time to counter these initial resistances. A similar point might be made for therapists' expectations about the extent to which they will enjoy working with their clients. More generally, "expected enjoyment" probably has a heavy component of the therapists "liking" of the client, and both research and theory suggest that such liking is an important factor in outcome (Ehrlich & Bauer, 1967; Mills & Abeles, 1965; Garfield & Affleck, 1961; Kell & Burow,

1970; Stoler, 1963). Our research found predicted enjoyment to be related to outcome in brief TLT, but not in TUT. It may be that the initial reaction of the therapist as often as not is modified as she or he spends greater amounts of therapeutic time with the client, as in TUT. In brief TLT, however, not enough time is allowed for such a modification.

The same argument would appear to be applicable to the "therapist confidence" factor as well. Additionally, the finding of therapists' confidence that the client will profit from the treatment is positively related to TLT outcome may relate importantly to our discussion in Chapter 2 of the role of therapist expectancy in brief TLT. There we noted that therapists had relatively low success expectancies in brief TLT with the initially more poorly adjusted client. We wondered if such expectancies played a role in the less successful outcomes with that subgroup. The present findings do seem to support such a hypothesis. At a minimum, it seems clear that when therapists lack confidence that brief TLT will be helpful, the probability is moderately high that their expectations will be realized (especially when clients' 18-month follow-up evaluations are the criterion). Of course, we do not know if the phenomenon is due primarily to either (a) therapists accurately detecting something in the client, or (b) therapists' low expectations regarding the potential of brief TLT irrespective of the client. We suspect that both factors contribute.

Therapists' ratings of the degree of disturbance of psychopathology (pervasiveness of pathology rather than problem acuteness) related only to therapists' outcome rating of personality change due to counseling and only for TUT clients. The *more* initially disturbed the clients, the *greater* is the personality change. None of the clients' outcome ratings were associated with this initial judgment of disturbance. These findings further underscore the complexity of the role of what might be called "initial maladjustment." Garfield (1978), for example, notes that this factor is more complex than was earlier assumed. Lambert (1979) points out that initial maladjustment is a complex and multidimensional factor that must be carefully defined before it can be expected to correlate with *some* change measures; the direction of that correlation, however, will depend on the type as well as the time of measurement. Most central to our purposes, and clearly contradictory to clinical lore, therapists' initial judgments of pervasiveness of psychopathology do not appear to be a factor in the success or failure of brief TLT. Inventoried initial adjustment, however, as noted in Chapter 2, does appear to be important. In other words, at the very least, quick first impressions by the therapist of the client's pathology do not appear to predict success or failure in subsequent TLT while tested initial adjustment does. It is not clear from the current data whether these initial impressions are modified as the treatment progresses and do become adequate predictors. However, it must be noted that the very nature of TLT does not allow much time for such modification (or much time for such modification to have any practical value).

A final point pertains to the sleeper effect in the relationship of post-initial interview ratings with client-judged outcome. This effect seemed most prominent in brief TLT. In the 1-month follow-up, 4 of 15 possible correlations attained statistical significance, whereas 10 of the 15 did so at 18 months for the 8-session TLT group. Apparently these are factors whose influence gradually emerges— after clients' reactions shortly following termination have been put into perspective. This of course further supports the many calls for long-term follow-ups in therapy outcome research.

Summary and Conclusions

In attempting to highlight the findings that appear most notable regarding the factors influencing TLT outcomes and TLT versus TUT differentially, we provide the following summary statements: (a) Among a group of relatively experienced therapists, we found no support for the notion that some would be especially good at TLT, while others might be relatively more effective in TUT; (b) general theoretical orientation tended to be unrelated to outcomes, although some exceptions to this statement emerged and were discussed; (c) contrary to expectations, the aspect of theoretical orientation labeled therapist directiveness was unrelated to client-judged outcomes; it was, however, correlated with therapists' outcome evaluations; (d) amount of therapist experience was modestly related to TUT but not TLT outcome; Self-reported experience in TLT and structured short-term therapy was not a factor in TLT outcomes; (e) contrary to clinical lore, initial degree of disturbance, defined as pervasiveness of psychopathology, was unrelated to client-rated outcomes, but it was *positively* related to therapists' ratings of personality change due to counseling; (f) therapists' initial judgments of clients' motivation for counseling was a factor in TUT and TLT outcomes from the vantage points of both the therapist and the client.

Finally, therapists' ratings (after an initial counseling session) of clients' willingness to change, therapists' confidence that the treatment they could offer would be helpful, and therapists' expected enjoyment in working with the client were especially associated with brief TLT outcomes. Since 8-session TLT is, by definition, brief, there is apparently too little time for the client's qualities tapped by these therapists' initial reactions to become modified. Such modification, however, does often occur in TUT. The three "influencers" appear to be especially promising initial predictors of outcome, both shortly after counseling and some months later. In Chapter 5 we examine factors that emerge in treatment that are conducive to continued change after counseling termination.

REFERENCES

AUERBACH, A. H., & JOHNSON, M. Research on the therapist's level of experience. In A. Gurman and A. Razin (Eds.), *Effective psychotherapy: A handbook of research*. New York: Pergamon, 1977.

BELLAK, L., & SMALL, L. *Emergency psychotherapy and brief psychotherapy.* New York: Grune & Stratton, 1965.

BERGIN, A. E., & LAMBERT, M. J. The evaluation of therapeutic outcomes. In S. L. Garfield and A. R. Bergin (Eds.), *Handbook of psychotherapy and behavior change* (2nd ed.). New York: Wiley, 1978.

BUTCHER, J. N., & KOSS, M. P. Research on brief and crisis-oriented psychotherapies. In S. L. Garfield and A. E. Bergin (Eds.), *Handbook of psychotherapy and behavior change* (2nd ed.). New York: Wiley, 1978.

DOLLIVER, R. H. Some limitations of Perls' gestalt therapy. *Psychotherapy: Theory, Research, and Practice,* 1981, *18,* 35–45.

DOLLIVER, R. H., WILLIAMS, E. L., & GOLD, D. C. The art of gestalt therapy or what are you doing with your feet now? *Psychotherapy: Theory, Research, and Practice,* 1980, *17,* 136–142.

EHRLICH, H. J., & BAUER, M. L. Therapists' feelings toward patients and patient treatment outcome. *Social Science and Medicine,* 1967, *1,* 283–292.

GARFIELD, S. L. Research on client variables in psychotherapy. In S. L. Garfield and A. E. Bergin (Eds.), *Handbook of psychotherapy and behavior change* (2nd ed.). New York: Wiley, 1978.

GARFIELD, S. L., AFFLECK, D. C. Therapists' judgments concerning patients considered for psychotherapy. *Journal of Consulting Psychology,* 1961, *25,* 505–509.

GELSO, C. J. Research in counseling: Methodological and professional issues. *The Counseling Psychologist,* 1979, *8,* 7–36. (a)

GELSO, C. J. Research in counseling: Clarifications, elaborations, defenses, and admissions. *The Counseling Psychologist,* 1979, *8,* 61–67. (b)

HOWARD, K. I., ORLINSKY, D. C., & TRATTNER, J. H. Therapist orientation and patient experience in psychotherapy. *Journal of Counseling Psychology,* 1970, *17,* 263–270.

KELL, B., & BUROW, J. *Developmental counseling and therapy.* Boston: Houghton Mifflin, 1970.

KRUMBOLTZ, J. D. (Ed.). *Revolution in counseling: Implications of behavioral science.* Boston: Houghton Mifflin, 1966.

LAMBERT, M. J. *The effects of psychotherapy* (Vol. 1). Montreal, Quebec: Eden Press, 1979.

LUBORSKY, L., CHANDLER, M., AUERBACH, A., COHEN, J., & BACHRACH, H. Factors influencing the outcome of psychotherapy: A review of quantitative research. *Psychological Bulletin,* 1971, *75,* 145–185.

LIEBERMAN, M., YALOM, I., & MILES, M. *Encounter groups: First facts.* New York: Basic Books, 1973.

MANN, J. *Time-limited psychotherapy.* Cambridge: Harvard University Press, 1973.

MILLS, D., & ABELES, N. Counselor needs for nurturance and affiliation as related to liking for clients and counseling process. *Journal of Counseling Psychology,* 1965, *12,* 353–358.

MITCHELL, K., BOZARTH, J., & KRAUFT, C. A reappraisal of the therapeutic effectiveness of accurate empathy, nonpossessive warmth and genuineness. In A. Gurman and A.

Razin (Eds.), *Effective psychotherapy: A handbook of research*. New York: Pergamon, 1977.

PARLOFF, M., WASKOW, I., & WOLFE, B. Research on therapist variables in relation to process and outcome. In S. Garfield and A. Bergin (Eds.), *Handbook of psychotherapy and behavior change* (2nd ed.). New York: Wiley, 1978.

PEABODY, A., & GELSO, C. Counselors' theoretical orientations at the Counseling Center. College Park: University of Maryland Counseling Center Research Report #2–77, 1977.

SIFNEOS, P. E. Short-term psychotherapy and emotional crisis. Cambridge: Harvard University Press, 1972.

SINGER, B., & LUBORSKY, L. Countertransference: The status of clinical quantitative research. In A. Gurman and A. Razin (Eds.), *Effective psychotherapy: A handbook of research*. New York: Pergamon, 1977.

SMITH, M. L., & GLASS, G. V. Meta-analysis of psychotherapy outcome studies. *American Psychologist,* 1977, *32,* 752–760.

STOLER, N. Client likeability: A variable in the study of psychotherapy. *Journal of Consulting Psychology,* 1963, *27,* 175–178.

SUNDLAND, D. M. *Therapist Orientation Questionnaire, Up-to-Date.* Paper presented at the Third Annual Meeting of the Society for Psychotherapy Research, Nashville, June, 1972.

SUNDLAND, D. M., & BARKER, E. N. The orientation of psychotherapists. *Journal of Consulting Psychology,* 1962, *26,* 201–212.

5

Client Change Factors Predictive of Continued Growth After Brief, Time-Limited Counseling

Diane M. Adelstein, Charles J. Gelso, James R. Haws,
Kathryn G. Reed, and Sharon Baron Spiegel

In Part One of this book we presented evidence from three studies suggesting that the changes accruing in brief TLT persist well beyond the end of counseling. Most central to the current chapter, we noted in Chapter 3 that TLT appears to be effective in setting into motion a change process that, in the eyes of the recipients of counseling, continues at least up to a year (the follow-up point) after termination. As a part of that study, we interviewed a small number of former clients who reported continued growth after counseling. A central goal was to acquire some beginning understanding of what goes on during TLT that underlies or facilitates continued growth after termination. The data in this chapter are aimed at furthering this beginning understanding. Specifically, the question we addressed was *"Are there developments that emerge in the client and/or the treatment situation during TLT that are at once detectable by the therapist and predictive of continued growth after treatment ends?"*

As part of the study reported in Chapter 3, the authors, four of whom had at least three years of clinical experience in conducting 12-session TLT, developed a therapist-completed questionnaire that we hoped might capture important changes occurring during psychotherapy. We focused on changes that theoretically should

The order of authorship is alphabetical and does not reflect our relative contributions to the project, which we feel were approximately equal.

auger well for continued client growth after termination, and this chapter reports the results. Thus, the question was not simply what predicts improvement in therapy; rather it was what predicts improvement during therapy and after therapy, as well.

Method

Details of the methodology for this study have been presented in Chapter 3. To summarize, the subjects were 38 students who had completed a minimum of 8 sessions of TLT (with usually a 12-session duration limit) a year prior to the follow-up. At the time of the client follow-up, the therapists were given their clients' case folders to help stimulate their recall. Folders contained all available information about the client, for example, intake evaluation, case notes, test results, termination summary. After reexamining the folder the therapist was asked to complete two inventories with respect to his or her recollections of the client's progress in counseling. One of the inventories, the *Counseling Change Measure,* was reported on in Chapter 3 (see Appendix I). The second, the *Client Change Inventory,* (CCI) formed the basis for the analyses in this chapter.

The Client Change Inventory

We devised the CCI for the present study to develop a therapist-completed form containing items that might be predictive of both change during treatment and continued growth following counseling termination.

The CCI (see Appendix J) contains 30 items reflecting important areas of therapeutic improvement, therapeutic process, and psychological health. It is divided into eight subscales that represent important domains of client adjustment that we hypothesized might be predictive of continued change after therapy. These subscales are obviously not orthogonal, nor was any effort made to refine them in that way for the sake of psychometric purity. Thus, we were less concerned with devising a new instrument and more interested in generating the kinds of questions that would be of heuristic value. In fact, the correlations among subscales ranged from .54 to .90, with median correlation of .71.

Therapists complete the CCI by indicating degree of agreement-disagreement with each item on a 7-point Likert scale. The subscales and definitions are as follows:

I.   *Life Adjustment* (4 items): Assesses improvement in life situations (vs. intrapsychic change) and selected problem areas. It assesses symptom relief during treatment, and the ability to obtain satisfactions from school and work.

II.   *Self-concept* (4 items): Measures comfort with self, self-esteem, and realism of self-image.

III. *Communication Skills* (4 items): Measures ability to assert self, express feelings and needs, and also understand others' point of view.

IV. *Interpersonal Relationships* (3 items): Assesses motivation for improved relationships, maturity of relationships, and capacity for intimacy.

V. *Attitudes Toward Therapy* (4 items): Assesses attitudes/evaluations toward current treatment and openness to future therapy. Also measures the client's capacity to carry on the work of therapy independently.

VI. *Client-therapist Relationship* (4 items): Assesses concordance of client's and therapist's views of the client's problems, and the changes occurring during counseling. Also assesses the importance of therapy to the client as well as the client's tendency to avoid thinking about the work between sessions.

VII. *Client Insight* (4 items): Assesses client understanding of his or her problems, the factors underlying them, and the client's ability to integrate feelings and intellect.

VIII. *Time-limited Therapy* (3 items): Assesses client and therapist comfort with time limits by the end of the work, and the establishment and maintenance of a central focus in the work.

In order to get an elementary and preliminary picture of the reliability of the CCI, the instrument was given to 24 therapists not otherwise involved in the study. They were instructed to complete the CCI with respect to a client with whom they had recently completed a course of 8–16-session therapy. It was then administered again 2–3 weeks later. (See Chapter 3 for further details of the administration.) The retest reliability coefficients (Pearson r's) for the total score was .94, and for the subscales as follow: Life Adjustment, .86; Self-Concept, .70; Communication Skills, .81; Interpersonal Relationships, .89; Attitudes Toward Therapy, .91; Client-Therapist Relationship, .92; Client Insight, .94; Time-Limited Therapy, .71.

Procedure and Analysis

Clients' evaluation of changes in feelings, behavior, and self-understanding during therapy and between termination and the 1-year follow-up were gathered for all 38 clients. These evaluations were obtained through the Client-Rated Counseling Outcome form (Appendix H), as described in Chapter 3. Suffice it to say that this form asks clients to rate the three dimensions just noted. Ratings were made at the time of follow-up, but clients were asked to rate changes occurring during counseling and after termination, again on the three change dimensions.

Completed CCI's were gathered from the 21 therapists of these clients. The CCI's were completed at the same time (one year after termination) as the client change ratings.

The data analysis proceeded in two steps. The first step entailed computation of Pearson correlation coefficients between the eight CCI subscales and the total score on the one hand and the clients' self-ratings of feeling, behavior, and self-understanding change on the other; the CCI scales were correlated with (a) clients' ratings of change between termination and follow-up (again, made at the point of follow-up), and (b) a measure of cumulative client change. The latter was simply the sum of clients' self-ratings of change during treatment and between termination and follow-up.

The analyses in the first step were simple, univariate correlations between single subscales and the total score on the CCI and criterion items. The second step in the analysis consisted of step-wise regression analyses, with CCI subscales as predictors and client self-ratings of change (as in "a", and "b" in the preceding paragraph) as criteria. The aim of employing multiple correlational procedures (stepwise regression analyses) was to determine if a complex configuration of CCI assessments could better predict client growth after termination than could simple univariate correlations. We reasoned that the multiple regression analyses indeed would result in improved prediction, since what was being predicted was a highly complex and difficult-to-predict criterion, that is, clients' reports of change, both one year after termination and a combination of during- and after-therapy change. The complexity of the predictive tasks becomes further illuminated when one considers that we are predicting *client* changes at the above points from *therapists'* ratings.

Results and Discussion

Before presenting and discussing the main analyses of this chapter, and in an effort to set the stage for those analyses, let us remind the reader of some pertinent findings from Chapter 3. First, therapists' and clients' assessments of changes during therapy in what we have labeled feeling improvement, behavior change, and self-understanding improvement are at least modestly interrelated (see Table 3–2 in Chapter 3). Thus, to a point at least beyond chance, therapists and their clients are judging client during-therapy growth in similar ways. On the other hand, therapists' and clients' judgments of during-therapy change on these three change dimensions are largely unrelated to clients' assessments of change between termination and follow-up (see Table 3–6 in Chapter 3). In other words, although clients and therapists show some agreement on during-therapy change, and although clients do report positive change both during and after counseling, neither therapist nor client assessment of during-therapy growth is predictive of later client-perceived growth. With these findings as a backdrop, let us now look at how therapists' evaluations of their former clients relate to client-reported growth after termination in terms of feeling improvement, behavior change, and self-understanding improvement.

The Prediction of Post-Therapy Change

In Tables 5–1, 5–2, and 5–3 we present (a) simple Pearson correlations (*r*'s) of the CCI subscales with client-rated change between termination and follow-up one year later on the dimensions of feeling improvement, behavior change, and self-understanding improvement; and (b) multiple correlation coefficients (*R*'s) from step-wise regression analyses, with the CCI scales as the predictors and the three client ratings as the criteria. Note that the "Shrunken *R*" is the multiple correlations adjusted to take into account the fact that multiple correlations are almost always *overestimates* of the relationships among variables. The Shrunken *R* gives an estimate of what the true relationship would be upon cross-validation (see Guilford, 1965, pp. 400–402). The shrunken R^2 gives the proportion of variance in the criterion accounted for by the combination of predictors, again correcting statistically for the overestimate inherent in *R*.

The first noteworthy feature of Tables 5–1, 5–2, and 5–3 pertains to the simple *r*'s given in the left-hand column. It can be seen that *in no case is a simple, univariate correlation between CCI scales and the criteria significant.* That is, therapists' evaluations of their clients were not related to clients' ratings of improvement between termination and follow-up. This finding holds equally for

Table 5–1. **Stepwise Regression Analysis with Subscales of the** *Client Change Inventory* **as Predictors and** **Client-Rated** *Feeling Improvement* **Between** **Termination and Follow-Up as the Criterion**

Scale	Simple *r*	*R*	Shrunken *R*	Shrunken R^2
Attitude toward therapy	− .24	.24	.24	.06
Interpersonal relationships	.12	.34	.30	.09
Communication skills	− .22	.48*	.44	.19
Self-concept	− .19	.51*	.45	.20
Client insight	− .07	.55*	.48	.23
Client-therapist relationship	− .11	.56	.48	.23
TLT	− .07	.56	.47	.22
Life adjustment	− .05	.56	.47	.22
Total score	− .08			

* = $p < .05$, ** = $p < .01$

Table 5–2.   Stepwise Regression Analyses with Subscales of the
***Client Change Inventory* as Predictors and**
Client-Rated *Behavior Change* Between
Termination and Follow-Up as the Criterion

Subscale	Simple r	R	Shrunken R	Shrunken R^2
Interpersonal relationships	.23	.23	.23	.05
Communication skills	– .13	.44*	.42*	.18
Client insight	.17	.49*	.44*	.19
Self-concept	.03	.53*	.47	.22
TLT	.14	.55*	.47	.22
Life adjustment	.12	.55	.46	.21
Attitudes toward therapy	.10	.55	.44	.19
Client-therapist relationship	.08	.55	.42	.18
Total score	.10			

* = $p < .05$, ** = $p < .01$

the criteria of feeling improvement (Table 5–1), behavior change (Table 5–2), and self-understanding improvement (Table 5–3). The lack of a significant relationship of single predictors and the criteria is consistent with the finding noted at the beginning of the Results section that clients' and therapists' ratings of during-counseling change were unrelated to clients' ratings of change between termination and follow-up. Those relationships, too, were assessed through simple r's.

The results presented above make very clear that growth after termination is not predictable from simple univariate procedures. But, at a statistical level, we suspected that a true relationship between the CCI scales and our three criteria for change after termination might be masked or suppressed by subjects' reported growth *during* therapy. To examine this, we statistically held constant during-therapy change reported by clients and by therapists on the three dimensions (i.e., we partialed them out of the relationship of CCI to ratings of change between termination and follow-up). The resulting partial correlation coefficients were still nonsignificant. Thus, *the lack of a relationship between therapists' ratings of client growth during counseling on the CCI and clients' posttherapy growth occurs regardless of the extent or type of client growth during treatment.*

The stepwise regression analysis begins by yielding the variable that correlates highest with the criterion, for example, Attitudes Toward Therapy in Table

Table 5–3.   Stepwise Regression Analysis with Subscales of the
**   *Client Change Inventory* as Predictors and Client-**
**   Rated *Self-Understanding Improvement* Between**
**   Termination and Follow-Up as the Criterion**

Subscale	Simple r	R	Shrunken R	Shrunken R^2
Self-concept	– .20	.20	.20	.04
Life adjustment	.13	.47*	.45*	.20
Client insight	.07	.52**	.48*	.23
Communication skills	– .06	.54*	.49*	.24
Attitude toward therapy	– .11	.58*	.51	.26
TLT	– .00	.59*	.51	.26
Interpersonal relationship	.05	.59	.50	.25
Client-therapist relationship	.06	.59	.50	.25
Total score	.07			

* = $p < .05$, ** = $p < .01$

5–1. It then gives in descending order the variable that independently adds the most to the correlation with the criterion. The relationship of the combined predictors at any point with the criterion is expressed as R, the multiple correlation coefficient. The form of R that is most pertinent for this research is the shrunken R (and shrunken R^2) for reasons discussed earlier.

Tables 5–1, 5–2, and 5–3 present the hierarchical ordering of CCI scales and the multiple correlation coefficients between the appropriate combinations of CCI scales and the criteria. The dotted line in each table indicates conservatively the point at which adding variables becomes unreliable. We used the following conservative criteria for determining the reliability of the added variable: (a) the shrunken R itself was statistically significant ($p < .05$); (b) the addition of the predictor yielded a shrunken R^2 at least .02 greater than yielded by the prior predictor (thus the added variable accounted for at least 2% more of the variance in the criterion than did the predictor to which it was added); and (c) the new variable was a statistically significant addition.

The central question in these regression analyses was this: While single CCI scales do not correlate significantly with our criteria, do combinations of these scales so correlate? In response to this question, it can be seen that two of the three criteria (behavior change, Table 5–2; and self-understanding improvement, Table

5–3) are indeed predictable from a multivariate combination of the CCI scales. Note also, however, that while we can make reliable (beyond chance) predictions of behavior change and self-understanding improvement during the year following termination, the predictions are not all that powerful. Thus, when we optimally combine predictors, we still cannot account for more than about a quarter of the variation in our criteria.

Finally, it should be noted that the CCI scales that appear to add the most to our predictive power are *Client Insight, Communication Skills,* and *Self-concept.* More than the others, these three scales appear at or around the top of the hierarchical orderings in the three tables, and they tend to yield statistically significant *R*'s or shrunken *R*'s when added to other variables. On the other hand, the scales *TLT* and *Client-Therapist Relationship* do not add to the prediction in any instance. These findings are discussed more fully in the Conclusion section.

The Prediction of Change in Motion

The data in Tables 5–1, 5–2, and 5–3 show the relationship of our CCI predictors with client-estimated change between termination and follow-up. The "change-in-motion" hypothesis predicts that TLT is effective in beginning or

Table 5–4. Stepwise Regression Analysis with Subscales of the
Client Change Inventory as Predictors and
Cumulative Index of _Feeling Improvement_
as the Criterion

Scale	Simple r	R	Shrunken R	Shrunken R^2
Communication skills	− .16	.16	.16	.03
Client insight	.12	.42*	.39*	.15
Attitude toward therapy	− .02	.47*	.42	.18
Life adjustment	− .01	.49*	.43	.18
Client-therapist relationship	.01	.49	.40	.16
TLT	.02	.50	.41	.17
Interpersonal relationship	.09	.50	.39	.15
Self-concept	.04	.50	.37	.14
Total score	.02			

* = p < .05, ** = p < .01

setting into motion (during therapy) a process that continues and sometimes accelerates following termination. Thus, to determine if one could predict the change-in-motion process, the predictors must be correlated with a criterion that combines client change during and after treatment.

Tables 5–4, 5–5, and 5–6 present the stepwise regression analyses where the CCI scales are the predictors and a cumulative index of feeling improvement (Table 5–4), behavior change (Table 5–5), and self-understanding improvement (Table 5–6) are the criteria. The cumulative index was arrived at simply by adding client-rated changes during therapy (Items 1, 2, and 3 of the *Client-Rated Counseling Outcome Questionnaire*, Appendix H) to changes after therapy (Items 5, 6, and 7 of the same questionnaire).

The results reported in Tables 5–4, 5–5, and 5–6 are similar to those on client change between termination and follow-up (Tables 5–1, 5–2, and 5–3), although there are some differences. The simple, univariate correlations between the CCI scales and the criteria are predominantly nonsignificant. (Note the two exceptions in Table 5–5.) Thus, we generally cannot predict the change-in-motion phenomenon through the use of single predictors. On the other hand, we do obtain reliable predictions of feeling improvement and behavior change (Tables 5–4 and 5–5) with multiple correlational devices. This predictive efficacy is most notable in Table 5–5, where client-rated behavior change is being predicted. Here a

Table 5–5. Stepwise Regression Analysis with Subscales of the *Client Change Inventory* as Predictors and Cumulative Index of *Behavior Change* as the Criterion

Scale	Simple r	R	Shrunken R	Shrunken R^2
Client insight	.35*	.35*	.35	.12
Communication skills	– .04	.58**	.56**	.31
Self-concept	.23	.61**	.58**	.34
Client-therapist relationship	.26	.62**	.58**	.34
TLT	.20	.62**	.55*	.30
Interpersonal relationship	.21	.62*	.55	.30
Attitude toward therapy	.34*	.62*	.53	.28
Life adjustment	.25	.62*	.51	
Total score	.30			

$* = p < .05, ** = p < .01$

Table 5–6. **Stepwise Regression Analysis with Subscales of the**
***Client Change Inventory* as Predictors and**
Cumulative Index of *Self-Understanding*
***Improvement* as the Criterion**

Scale	Simple r	R	Shrunken R	Shrunken R^2
Life adjustment	.20	.20	.20	.04
Interpersonal relationship	– .07	.35	.32	.10
Client insight	.16	.38	.33	.11
Communication skills	– .06	.46	.39	.15
Attitude toward therapy	.03	.52	.42	.18
Self-concept	– .02	.55	.43	.18
Client-therapist relationship	– .01	.56	.43	.18
TLT	.03	.57	.43	.18
Total score	.06			

* = $p < .05$, ** = $p < .01$

combination of Client Insight, Communication Skills, and Self-concept accounts for over a third of the variance in client-rated behavior change. As was the case with the predictions in Tables 5–1, 5–2, and 5–3 (not surprising in light of the overlap in the criteria), the predictors just noted—Client Insight, Communication Skills, and Self-concept—appear to be the most useful ones, while TLT and Client-Therapist Relationship do not add to the predictive efficiency in any case.

Conclusions

We return now to the primary question of this investigation: *"Are there developments that emerge in the client and/or the treatment situation during TLT that are at once detectable by the therapist and predictive of continued growth after treatment ends?"* Our tentative answer is that three factors or developments, in combination with each other or with additional factors, seem most predictive. Thus, factors we have labeled *Client Insight, Communication Skills,* and *Self-concept* may form a constellation of indices that lend themselves to long-term change. Taken singly, it does not appear that any of these three may be enough to facilitate durable counseling changes. But if therapists see their clients developing appropriately and positively in the area of self-concept, exhibiting the development of insight, *and* expressing themselves more effectively with others during TLT, the chances are good that these clients will report very durable changes. This finding is supported by our limited interview data presented in chapter 3. There we noted that clients who exhibited significant posttherapy growth that they attributed to their therapy generally reported increased insight, more appropriate expressiveness/assertiveness, guilt reduction (not measured by the CCI), and enhanced self-concept. The similarity of these phenomena to those emerging on the CCI analysis is striking. It must be remembered here that the four clients whose semistructured interviews were discussed in chapter 3 were from the *same sample* as those in this chapter. The significant finding, however, appears to be that these very different methods yield such similar results.

Discovering which factors are not related to continued growth is as important as determining which ones are. That is especially so because the predictors in this study (the CCI scales) were ones that the research team felt would relate to the criteria. Most notably, the scale labeled Time-Limited Therapy (TLT) in no instance related to the criteria, either alone or in combination with other predictors. Thus, whether or not the counselor and client feel comfortable with the duration limit, even by the end of counseling, does not seem to be a factor in benefit from TLT, at least when it is the therapists who are rating comfort. Even more surprising, and in contrast to clinical theory in TLT (Mann, 1973), the early establishment and maintenance of a central focus in TLT seems inconsequential to durable change as a result of that treatment. Conversely, it appears that TLT in which the participants do not focus on one central issue (presumably because of some clinical decision that such a focus is not called for) may be just as effective as TLT that employs a central focus. In retrospect, this outcome makes clinical sense to us, particularly in light of our experientially derived impression that a therapist virtually cannot force a central focus on a client. Such a focus must emerge naturally from the material of the case, although of course it may be facilitated by the therapist.

Along with the TLT scale, it was found that the CCI scale labeled Client-Therapist Relationship was unrelated to continued growth, either alone or in combination with any other CCI scale. This was especially surprising because one of the four items assessed the extent to which the client avoided thinking about what was discussed in the therapy between sessions. Our semistructured interview data (chapter 3) suggested that clients who show positive long-term change that they attribute to TLT appear to think about the work a great deal between sessions. It may well be that therapists' views of how much their clients think about the work (CCI) and clients' views of this are very different. If this is so, it appears that the clients' views are what matter vis-à-vis continued growth after termination, at least in terms of clients' perceptions of such growth. Relatedly, it might be helpful if therapists made a point to check with their clients on this matter during the treatment. It may be that therapists simply do not usually know or find out in TLT how much their clients are thinking about the work.

We conclude this chapter by pointing out what we see as the limitations and the merits of this particular study. Of course, the use of client-self reports as the exclusive criterion source is a limitation. As indicated at several points in the book, results obtained from such reports should not be generalized to those obtained from other criterion sources (e.g., observer or test data). At the same time, the client represents one crucial outcome source, and we offer that clients' judgments are vital to our gaining an understanding of the factors involved in successful TLT. A second, and probably more central limitation, is that we cannot determine from these data if the findings are peculiar to TLT or equally applicable to TLT and TUT. From a practical point of view, for example, in terms of agency application, it may suffice to know that this or that variable is predictive of continued growth following TLT. From the vantage point of scientific understanding of counseling/psychotherapy, however, it would be quite important to discover if factors predictive of outcome in one treatment also apply to another. Finally, the fact that therapists' ratings were made approximately one year after termination must be noted as a limitation. Despite the fact that therapists were given all available case materials to help stimulate their recall, much of the aliveness of their cases must have been lost. Future studies would do well to obtain such ratings soon after termination.

We suggest that the major contribution of the study, perhaps more than its substantive findings, resides in a methodological feature. That is, we found that variables that were not predictive of outcome when taken individually were indeed predictive when combined in a linear fashion through the use of multiple correlational procedures. This suggests that when we are studying highly complex multidimensional criteria, simple univariate methods may often not suffice. Yet more complex procedures such as multiple regression are all to infrequently employed in counseling and psychotherapy research, and the present findings argue strongly for their usage.

REFERENCES

GUILFORD, J. P. *Fundamental statistics in psychology and education* New York: McGraw-Hill, 1965.

MANN, J. *Time-limited psychotherapy*. Cambridge: Harvard University Press, 1973.

PART THREE

Expectancies and Process of Time-Limited Therapy

Introduction to Part Three

Parts One and Two of this book described investigations of the effectiveness of TLT—that is, does TLT work, and how well and for whom does it work. In Part Three we turn our attention to initial expectancies, goals, and the process of TLT. Our questions here concern how TLT works, rather than whether it works. Once we had completed the earlier studies of the end points of TLT, it seemed important to refine further our understanding of this therapy mode by studying the beginning and middle of the process.

The first two chapters of this part used the laboratory setting to control more rigorously variables potentially affecting the initial impact of time limits on clients and counselors. Daniel McKitrick and Charles Gelso focused their study on the effect of time limits on clients' initial expectancies of therapy outcome. Since the analogue setting allowed manipulation of client problem chronicity, the authors were able to use this variable as a carefully controlled moderator of clients' reactions to TLT versus TUT. Different rationales for using time limits were also studied in relation to clients' outcome expectancies.

The results of McKitrick and Gelso were extended by Deborah Hazel Johnson's chapter into the domain of therapists' expectancies. Again using an analogue setting, her study held client variables constant in order to examine the impact of TLT versus TUT on therapists' goals and outcome expectancies. In addition, theoretical orientation was used as a potential moderator variable of the therapists' differential reactions to TLT and TUT.

With expectancies having been studied rather thoroughly in laboratory experiments, it was then time to put expectancies to the test with actual clients and therapists. In the third chapter in this part, Janet Cornfeld, Deborah Hazel Johnson, Sharon Spiegel, Jean Whittaker, Daniel Wasserman, and Charles Gelso did an exploratory study focusing on clients' expectancies. The interest of these authors was on client's expectancies of duration, since the essence of TLT is the focus on length. The field setting of this study allowed a linkage of initial expectancies with clients' initial adjustment levels and with the subsequent outcome of counseling.

The final chapter in this section looked at the actual ongoing process of TLT. James Mann (1973), the major theorist regarding TLT, has postulated that the way a client reacts to the time limits is shown by in-therapy behavior and its predictable changes over time. Jacque Moss Miller, Christine Courtois, Judy Pelham, Elayne Riddle, Sharon Baron Spiegel, Charles Gelso, and Deborah Hazel Johnson empirically validated Mann's theory in their Chapter 9 study. By obtaining data regarding such client behavior as defensiveness, lateness, and goal orientation in each TLT session, these investigators contrasted characteristics of earlier TLT sessions with later ones.

After presenting these process studies, the empirical core of the book is complete. We conclude after this part with a final summary chapter that integrates the findings of the various studies.

6

Initial Client Expectancies in Time-Limited Therapy

Daniel S. McKitrick and Charles J. Gelso

The previous chapters in this book have presented experimental and correlational studies of the outcomes of TLT, and the client and therapist factors associated with outcome. These investigations were of actual counseling, and were done in the natural settings in which counseling occurs. The present chapter represents the first attempt in our program to examine TLT in a laboratory situation. As such, the study contains some of the frequently discussed advantages and disadvantages of counseling or psychotherapy analogue research (Gelso, 1979; Kazdin, 1978; Munley, 1974; Strong, 1971). We moved our research into the laboratory and away from the natural field setting for two reasons. First, the laboratory setting permitted us to study with greater precision some of the variables we were already looking at in the field setting. Second, we could study some factors in the lab that, for one reason or another, could not be experimentally manipulated in actual counseling.

To begin with, we felt it important to investigate how clients might react *initially* to the idea of time limits. In what ways does the establishment of time limits at the beginning of counseling affect the client's expectations of how she or

This chapter is an extended version of an article appearing in the *Journal of Counseling Psychology*, 1978, *25*, 246–249, Initial client expectancies in time-limited counseling. Adapted by permission of the publisher and author. Copyright © 1978 by the American Psychological Association.

he and the therapist will behave in the treatment, and of the outcomes of that treatment? Clinical literature and lore suggest that time limits create higher degrees of client activity and responsibility-taking, as well as greater therapist activity (Hoch, 1972; Munroe, 1955; Rank, 1945; Sifneos, 1972; Taft, 1933). Would such effects on the counseling *process* emerge right from the beginning of the work, that is, in terms of clients' expectations of their role and the therapist's role?

Along with studying the effects of time limits on the client process expectancies, we sought to assess the effects of time limits (on expected counseling *outcome*) in conjunction with two variables that earlier field research led us to believe were important. Thus, we examined the impact on client initial outcome expectations of (a) TLT versus TUT when the client's problem was either chronic or acute, and (b) the rationale for the time limit given to the client by the therapist.

Research presented in previous chapters indicates that qualities within the client mediate the effects of time limits. Problem chronicity (vs. acuteness) would appear to be one such quality and, indeed, clinical literature does suggest that clients with chronic problems would not do well or expect to do well in brief TLT (Gottschalk, Mayerson, & Gottlieb, 1967; McGuire, 1965), or at least not as well as they would in TUT. McGuire suggests that clients who view their problems with a historical perspective tend to react to the use of time limits with pessimism and humiliation. Thus, we would suspect that clients with chronic difficulties would hold more negative expectancies about the therapist, or the relationship she or he offers, as well as the outcomes of TLT.

Another possible influence on initial client expectancies is the rationale for the time limits used by the counselor. The rationale seems particularly important because the client may misinterpret the time limits as reflecting a negative attitude on the therapist's part, such as rejection, or consideration of the client's problems as trivial. In fact, Henry and Shlien (1958), in one of the few TLT studies that reported the rationale given clients, inferred that their rationale of a long waiting list for therapy caused clients to feel abandoned, deserted, and resentful after therapy.

Recognizing the potential influence of rationales, Gelso, Spiegel, and Mills (Chapter 2) suggested that therapists using TLT should not employ a long waiting list as the sole rationale for time limits. Rather, counselors were encouraged to identify with the treatment, and let clients know that at least part of the rationale for time limits was the belief that TLT would be helpful. Thus, the therapist would convey that the individual client was a concern of the therapist; that is, she or he was not just interested in reducing the waiting list. Additionally, the therapist's expressed confidence in both therapeutic approach and the outcome of therapy, it was expected, should have a positive effect on the clients' expectations of therapist relationship attitudes (empathic understanding, positive regard for the client, and so forth) and of successful therapy outcome.

Given the above discussion and research on the rationale for time limits, we would expect that clients would feel better about the therapist's attitudes toward him/her (the client) and the outcome of treatment if the rationale were that the therapist felt that TLT would work versus that TLT was being used because of a long waiting list. We sought to compare the effects of these two rationales for time limits on clients' expectations of (a) the effects of TLT and (b) the extent to which the therapist would be empathically understanding, positively regarding of the client, and genuine in the counseling. These latter variables have been viewed as constituents of a good therapeutic relationship (Rogers, 1957; Truax & Carkhuff, 1967).

The formulations examined above led to three specific hypotheses in the present investigation: (a) The use of time limits will increase client-subjects' expectations for client activity and responsibility-taking, as well as for therapist activity; (b) client-subjects given the rationale for time limits that such limits are effective will have more positive outcome and therapist-client relationship expectancies than will client-subjects given the rationale of a long waiting list; (c) time limits and client problem chronicity will interact such that client-subjects will have more positive relationship and outcome expectancies in TUT than in TLT when the client is seen as having a chronic problem. When the client is seen as having an acute problem, on the other hand, client-subjects will have more favorable relationship and outcome expectancies in TLT than in TUT. The latter part of this interaction hypothesis was based on the findings in Chapter 2 that the initially better adjusted clients seemed to do *at least as well* in TLT as in TUT.

Method

Subjects

The subjects were 80 females enrolled in an introductory psychology course at the University of Maryland-College Park. Subjects received extra course credit for participation. The modal subject was 18 years old (range 18–24) and a freshman (50%). The subject sign-up sheet in no way identified the nature of the experiment.

Stimulus Material

The stimulus material consisted of a 10-minute videotape of a simulated first interview between a female counselor (26-year-old PhD counseling psychologist) and a female confederate client (22-year-old senior). The client confederate familiarized herself with a list of symptoms (depression, anxiety, low self-esteem, and submissive-deferential reactions to others) and then role-played a client with those symptoms. The counselor's style might best be characterized as client-centered/reflective. No cues were given in the videotape regarding length of treatment or the chronicity of the client's problem.

Procedure

The experiment contained three independent variables: time limits (12-session limit vs. no time limits), chronicity of problem (chronic vs. acute) and rationale for time limits (effectiveness/appropriateness of limits vs. long waiting list). Subjects were run in groups of 5–10, and the treatment-combination cell to which they were assigned was determined by the content of written material they were required to read before and after the tape. Assignment was made on a random basis.

Upon arrival for the experiment, the experimenter introduced the videotape as "an early part of the first session between a therapist and client." It was stressed here that subjects should put themselves into the client's place when viewing the session. Under the guise of further familiarizing subjects with the interview session, subjects read written materials before and after viewing the tape. The pretape material manipulated the chronicity variable. Subjects in the acute condition read that the client's problem had essentially a one-week history and onset, while those in the chronic condition read that the filmed client's problem had a several-year history, although its precipitant occurred one week previously. In both conditions the precipitant for seeking counseling was a crisis generated by a breakup with a boyfriend. In the chronic condition, subjects read that the client suffered from depression, a sense of inferiority, and low self-esteem for "a long, long time," and for several years was on the verge of seeing a therapist. In the acute condition, subjects read that the client had these same feelings but that they just began about a week ago.

It should be noted that, although the length of the problem's history was the variable of interest, subjects are apt to view a chronic problem as both lasting longer and being more severe than an acute problem. To hold perceived severity constant across conditions, the symptoms of the acute condition were made to sound more severe than these same symptoms in the chronic conditions; for example, in the acute condition the client indicated that she felt *deeply* depressed and uneasy, while in the chronic condition she felt depressed and uneasy.

After viewing the tape, subjects read materials that manipulated the time limit and rationale variables. Subjects in the time-limited counseling condition read that the therapist asked the client to agree to a 12-session limit, one hour per week. Those in the open-ended condition read only that counseling would be one hourly session per week. It should be noted that a 12-session limit was chosen on this study because it is a typical limit for various time-limited approaches (e.g., Mann, 1973; Patterson & O'Sullivan, 1974), because it complies fairly well with the length of a school semester, and because other studies in our research program, along with other investigations (e.g., Munro & Bach, 1975), have used limits in the vicinity of 12.

The rationale variable was manipulated by having subjects in the "waiting list" condition read that the therapist said she wanted to use a time limit because of a long waiting list of people wanting counseling. In the "time limits effective" condition, subjects read that the therapist told the client she wanted to set a time limit because she believed it was effective and appropriate.

Within this three-factor design, the factors of Time Limits (12-session limit vs. no limit) and Chronicity of Problem (chronic vs. acute) were completely crossed with each other. The Rationale for Time Limits factor, however, did not cross with Time Limits; that is, only subjects in the 12-session condition could be given a rationale for a time limit. Thus, 20 subjects were randomly assigned to each of the 4 Time Limits × Chronicity cells ($n = 80$). Then the 40 subjects who were given a time limit were randomly assigned to one of the two Rationale for Time Limits conditions (waiting list vs. time limits effective/appropriate).

Dependent Variables and Measures

After reading the prefilm material, viewing the videotape, and reading the posttape materials, clients completed a packet of instruments (order counter-balanced within each treatment combination cell). Subjects completed all instruments in terms of how they would expect to feel if *they* had been the client in the counseling situation just depicted and would continue for the duration of the session depicted, and for whatever other sessions they wanted to attend. Instruments are briefly described as follow:

RELATIONSHIP EXPECTANCIES. The Relationship Inventory (Barrett-Lennard, 1962) was modified to apply to initial expectancies. This is a widely used instrument (64 items) designed to measure the counselor attitudes of empathy, congruence, and level and unconditionality of regard. The Inventory was devised to tap clients' perceptions of the extent to which therapists possess Rogers's necessary and sufficient conditions.

ACTIVITY AND RESPONSIBILITY EXPECTANCIES. Subjects' expectancies for therapist and client activity during counseling were measured with semantic differentials in which subjects rated the concepts of expected client and therapist activity on five bipolar objective scales. Scales were developed by selecting from 25 objective pairs rated as pertinent to psychotherapy (Mills, 1970) those five pairs that three advanced counseling psychology graduate students judged most pertinent to therapist and client activity. For expected therapist activity, the scales were expressive-constricted, closed-open, relating-distant, mature-immature, and deep-shallow. For expected client activity, scales were constrained-free, relating-distant, closed-open, expressive-constricted, frustrated-content.

Expectancies for client responsibility were assessed by the degree of subject agreement with five statements reflecting how much the client takes responsibility (vs. depends on counselor) for making decisions and changes. Subjects responded to the statements on 7-point scales, with anchors ranging from "very much agree" to "very much disagree." This questionnaire was developed by first selecting from the Perception of Counseling Inventory (Volsky, Magoon, Norman, & Hoyt, 1965) 15 statements the authors felt reflected client responsibility. The five statements finally selected were those ranked by three advanced counseling psychology graduate students as most pertinent to client responsibility.

OUTCOME EXPECTANCIES.   Subjects completed the Self Acceptance Scale (Phillips, 1951) in terms of how they would expect to feel following counseling. The Scale contains 25 statements that purport to reflect self-acceptance, and subjects respond in terms of their degree of agreement with each statement (5-point scale). Robinson and Shaver (1974) list research reporting high reliability and validity for the Scale.

Subjects' expectancies (a) of satisfaction with length of counseling, (b) with being helped in a way they wanted or needed to be helped, and (c) of comfort with ending counseling were measured by three 7-point scales. The first two of these scales were patterned after those utilized by Gelso, Spiegel, and Mills in Chapter 2. The comfort-with-ending scale was specially devised for the present study, and asked students to rate on a 7-point scale (1 = very comfortable, 7 = very uncomfortable) "How comfortable are you expecting to be with ending therapy?"

Results

To determine if the independent variables were successfully manipulated, subjects responded to a feedback questionnaire following completion of the criterion measures. All but one subject were able to identify correctly whether they were in the time-limited condition and the rationale for time limits. Also, those in the chronic condition rated the client's problem as having a much longer history than those in the acute condition ($\overline{X}$'s for chronics and acutes = 5.33 vs. 2.93, respectively, where 7 = extremely long and 1 = extremely short history, $p <$ .001). As hoped for, however, subjects in the acute versus chronic condition did not approach differing significantly in their judgments of the severity of the client's problems ($\overline{X}$'s = 2.98 vs. 2.63 for the chronics and acutes, respectively). These data indicate with a high degree of certainty that the desired manipulations occurred. Finally, no subject was able to guess the purpose of the experiment.

For each dependent variable, two 2-way analyses of variances were performed, one being a Time Limits × Chronicity analysis, and the other a Chronicity × Rationale analysis. Our first hypothesis stated that *The use of time limits will increase client-subjects' initial expectancies for client activity and responsibility, and for counselor activity.* For the Time Limits × Chronicity analysis, the main effects of Time Limits on the 3 relevant scales (Client Activity, Client Responsibility, Counselor Activity) did not approach statistical significance. As can be seen in Table 6–1, the differences between subjects in the time-limited versus

Table 6–1.   **Means, Standard Deviations, and *F* Ratios for**
Activity and Responsibility Measures of the
Time-Limited vs. Time-Unlimited Conditions

	Time limits				
	Time-limited treatments (n = 40)		Time-unlimited treatment (n = 40)		
Measures	$\bar{X}$	SD	$\bar{X}$	SD	F
Client responsibility	24.7	4.6	25.4	4.5	.41
Client activity	23.4	6.8	23.5	7.3	.01
Counselor activity	26.6	5.9	26.4	5.9	.02

Note. All *F*'s are nonsignificant.

time-unlimited conditions are miniscule. Thus, client-subjects expected no more client or counselor activity or client responsibility in time-limited counseling as compared to time-unlimited counseling, in contrast to our hypothesis.

The second hypothesis indicates that *client-subjects given the rationale for time limits that they are effective/appropriate will have more positive relationship and outcome expectancies than will client-subjects given the rationale for a long waiting list.* The main effect of the Rationale factor from our Chronicity × Rationale ANOVA's is the effect relevant to this hypothesis. Table 6–2 presents the results of that analysis for each relevant dependent variable.

Table 6–2 indicates that the "time-limits-are-effective" rationale did not differ significantly from the "waiting list" rationale on any variable. The difference between these rationales, however, did approach significance on the Effect of Counseling scale, that is, "Are you expecting counseling to help you in the way you want or need to be helped?" That is, the time-limit rationale tended to influence client-subjects' outcome expectancies in a more positive way when the effectiveness rationale rather than the waiting list rationale was used.

The final hypothesis stated that *Time limits and chronicity will interact such that client-subjects will have more positive outcome* and *relationship expectancies in TUT than TLT when the client is seen as having a "chronic" problem; but client-subjects will have more favorable expectancies of TLT when the client has an acute problem.* The relevant analysis here was the interaction effects from our Time Limits × Chronicity ANOVA's on the outcome and relationship measures. Table 6–3 indicates that these interactions attain or approach significance on all relationship measures. Significance was also obtained on the Effect of Counseling scale ("Are you expecting counseling to help you in the way you want or need to be helped?") and was approached ($p < .10$) on the Length of Counseling scale ("Are

**Table 6–2.   Means, Standard Deviations, and *F* Ratios for
Relationship and Outcome Measures of the
Two Rationales for Time Limits**

| | Rationale for time limits | | | | |
| | Waiting list (n = 20) | | Effectiveness (n = 20) | | |
	$\bar{X}$	SD	$\bar{X}$	SD	F
Relationship Variables					
Level of regard	14.0	14.4	15.9	14.7	.24
Empathic under-standing	9.3	15.9	13.6	15.8	.97
Unconditionality of regard	1.3	11.1	4.6	13.6	.65
Congruence	11.4	15.5	9.8	15.6	.13
Outcome Variable[a]					
Self-acceptance	69.1	16.8	6.7	14.6	.14
Effect of counseling	2.7	1.4	2.0	.9	3.27*
Comfort with ending	2.5	1.3	2.7	1.6	.30
Length of counseling	2.6	1.7	2.9	1.2	.29

[a]The lower the score the more positive the expectancies
* = $p < .10$

you expecting counseling to last long enough to help you in the way you want or need to be helped?").

Newman-Keuls post hoc tests on the significant interactions indicated that in no case were differences between time-limited and unlimited conditions significant for subjects in the acute condition. In the chronic condition, however, subjects with the time-unlimited set obtained significantly higher expectancy scores than those in the time-limited condition on Level of Regard (.01), Empathic Understanding (.05), and Unconditionality (.05). While in the same direction, the comparison on the Effect of Counseling scale did not attain significance. Inspection of the means from our Time Limit × Chronicity interactions clearly reveals that, by and large, these effects were a function of the depressed scores of subjects in the Chronic condition given the time-limited set. Means in the three other conditions were approximately equivalent.

Table 6–3. Means, Standard Deviations, and *F* Ratios for Relationship and Outcome Measures on the Time Limits by Chronicity Interaction

| | Chronic | | | | Acute | | | | |
| | Time-limited (n = 20) | | Time-unlimited (n = 20) | | Time-limited (n = 20) | | Time-unlimited (n = 20) | | |
Measures	$\bar{X}$	SD	$\bar{X}$	SD	$\bar{X}$	SD	$\bar{X}$	SD	F
Relationship variables									
Level of regard	8.6	15.6	26.5	9.7	21.4	10.3	23.2	10.9	8.64***
Empathic understanding	5.8	16.6	19.0	11.6	17.2	13.1	16.5	11.4	5.08**
Unconditionality of regard	–1.0	10.9	11.3	14.4	6.8	12.9	5.8	11.4	5.31**
Congruence	5.7	19.4	16.9	10.9	15.4	12.4	15.4	12.3	3.39*
Outcome variables[a]									
Self-acceptance	71.0	14.0	71.6	20.1	65.3	16.8	62.8	11.2	.18
Effect of counseling	2.9	1.4	2.2	1.2	1.8	.7	2.2	1.4	4.03**
Comfort with ending	3.1	1.5	3.1	1.6	2.2	1.0	2.2	1.1	.00
Length of counseling	3.4	1.7	2.6	1.3	2.0	.8	2.2	1.7	3.58*

[a] The lower the score the more positive the expectancies

* = $p < .10$
** = $p < .05$
*** = $p < .01$

In addition to direct hypothesis tests, the analyses permitted examination of main and interaction effects of our three independent variables on all dependent variables. In summary, it was found that subjects in the time-unlimited condition had more positive relationship expectancies than those in the limited condition on Levels of Regard (.01), Empathic Understanding (.05), Unconditionality (.10), and Congruence (.10). These main effects of time limits are deceptive, however, since the interactions noted above indicate that these effects are accounted for by the fact that subjects in the Chronic (but not the Acute) condition possessed the negative expectancies regarding time-limited counseling.

Finally, on nearly all of our relationship and outcome measures, subjects in the Acute condition possessed more positive expectancies (attaining or approaching the .05 level) than those in the Chronic condition. None of the remaining comparisons (other than those noted above) attained statistical significance.

Discussion and Some Conclusions

As we discuss the findings and their implications, it should be kept in mind that this study was done in the laboratory, and did not employ actual clients receiving counseling. At the same time, we attempted to simulate actual counseling by asking our subjects to try to place themselves into the role of a client receiving a first interview. The generalizability of such findings probably are best interpreted in light of their connection to actual field research and to clinical theory and observation.

Activity and Responsibility in Time-Limited Counseling

Our first hypothesis was clearly unsupported. Thus, time limits in no way affected client-subjects' initial expectancies for client activity or responsibility or for therapist activity. This finding raises questions about why so many theorists consider these activity and responsibility variables so central to time-limited approaches. To the extent that such theory has any validity, a plausible revised hypothesis would be that it is the *counselor's* and not the client's initial expectations for activity and responsibility (and consequent behavior) that set in motion clients' *eventual* awareness of these factors, and the concomitant behaviors. It is the counselor, after all, who has the experience with and knowledge of how time limits operate in therapy. The counselor thus may need to instill these expectancies into the client, that is, for greater activity and responsibility-taking. The findings in Chapter 2 indicate that therapists do report being more active in TLT than TUT. So the use of time limits does seem to affect *therapist* activity level, and it makes intuitive sense that this effect would eventually alter clients' in-therapy behavior.

An alternative explanation for the above findings is that it simply takes some time for the client's activity level and responsibility-taking behavior to be affected by time limits (independent of the effect on the client mediated by the counselor's expectations). Thus, apart from the counselor's behavior, clients may well become more active and responsible in TLT only as the process unfolds—when they develop a better feeling for what TLT is going to be like, and when they perhaps become more aware that time is passing. Relatedly, at some point in the treatment, clients may realize a reality of the time limits, that if someone does not take some initiative, therapy could well end before anything is accomplished.

In sum, it seems clear that time limits do not initially cause clients to expect to be more active and responsible in counseling, or to expect their therapists to be more active. We have evidence that therapists are indeed more active in TLT (Chapter 2), and it may well be the counselor's expectancies and behavior in TLT that facilitate clients' learning to be more active and responsible (if, in fact, clients do become more active and responsible). At the same time, clients' eventual awareness of the meaning of a limit, for example, that counseling will soon end, also may increase activity and responsibility. These interpretations are consonant with our clinical experience and observations, but clearly more empirical research is needed on this topic of activity and responsibility in TLT if we are to have firm answers.

What Should We Present to Clients as the Rationale for Time Limits?

Client-subjects' relationship and outcome expectancies did not differ according to the rationale for time limits. Thus, although some trends in the expected direction did emerge it did not seem to matter appreciably whether the therapist identified with the efficacy of TLT as a rationale for its use (effectiveness/appropriateness rationale) or used the waiting list as the rationale. While the most parsimonious explanation for this surprising finding is simply that the rationale is unimportant, an alternative explanation is suggested by Henry and Shlien (1958) and seems worth noting. Briefly, these researchers suggested that the detrimental effects of a "waiting list" rationale in their study were not evident until after the development of the client-therapist relationship, when the formerly impersonal rationale became personal. Since the rationale for time limits is still likely to be impersonal after an initial session, the potential negative effects may not have been evident in the current study.

A related explanation for the apparent irrelevance of the rationale for time limits is that the dependent measures in the present experiment were insensitive to the actual effects that do occur initially. Our measures pertained to the expected relationship (therapist empathy, regard, and congruence) and the effects of therapy. It is possible that initially clients do not react negatively to these criteria when given a waiting list rationale, but, rather, react more critically to impersonal targets such as the time limits themselves.

Support for the above explanation is derived from our client-subjects' reactions to a postexperiment feedback questionnaire we administered after completion of other measures but before experimental debriefing. The final three items of this form were designed to secure subjects' free comments on their expectancies and guesses of the purposes of the experiment. Several subjects, however, chose to use these questions as means to comment on other aspects of the study. Most germane to the present discussion, 8 of 20 subjects in the "waiting list" condition made some form of derogatory statement about their experience and the counseling. Typical comments were that subjects felt constricted or "turned off" by the time limits. In contrast, only 1 of the 20 subjects in the "TLT works" condition made similarly derogatory remarks (χ^2 for the difference betwen 8/20 and 1/20 = 7.03, $p < .01$). In fact, one subject commented that the time limit should allow ample time for her problem to be resolved.

While the data just reported are obviously post hoc and thus must be interpreted cautiously, they suggest that the two rationales we used may produce subtly different effects on clients' expectations. Do the findings about rationale, when taken together, offer any guidance for the practice of TLT? We suggest that they do. Combining our results with Henry and Shlien's inferences, we suggest that as a counselor it would be wise to align one's self with the efficacy of TLT as part of the rationale given to clients. Of course therapists must not deceive their clients. They should not be positive if they do not feel positive. At the same time, reflection on clinical practice suggests to us that it is usually possible to make some positive observation to the client, even if attached to a "waiting list" rationale. For example, a kind of statement we have found easy to make, honest, and positive in clients' eyes is that "We use a time limit because of the large number of students seeking service, and because we find that most students profit quite a bit from 12-session TLT, although of course it will not solve all their problems." Then, if the therapist can honestly state this, we will add something to the effect that "From what we have discussed, I expect that TLT should be very helpful for you."

The Role of Chronicity in Time-Limited Therapy

A portion of our third hypothesis received clear and strong support. In essence, when the client was seen as having a chronic problem, client-subjects' relationship and outcome expectancies for TLT were clearly deflated. On the other hand, contrary to prediction, TLT and TUT were seen in an equally positive light when the client presented an acute problem.

It will be remembered that we attempted to manipulate perceived chronicity, while holding constant severity of disturbance. The manipulation check suggested that this effort was successful. Thus, it appears that, regardless of severity of disturbance, the level of chronicity (vs. acuteness) of the client's problem may be an important determinant of how she or he "receives" the idea of a time limit. When the problem is seen as chronic, it appears that the client will not react favorably to a time limit, assuming of course that the time permitted for therapy is experienced as brief relative to that problem. This suggests that if brief TLT is to be employed with clients who see their concerns as long-standing, the counselor may well need to institute special procedures early to allay the negative relationship and outcome expectancies that will emerge. If the problem has a largely acute flavor, on the other hand, TUT and TLT will be received in an equally positive way.

When combined with the field research presented in Chapters 2 and 4, it appears that "problem chronicity versus acuteness" may well be part of a constellation of client qualities that serves as an indicator of receptivity to and success in TLT. Thus, clients who are better adjusted initially, whose problems are acute, and who are seen in an initial interview as motivated for counseling, willing to change, and enjoyable to work with may be highly suited to brief TLT. They will expect to do well in it right from the beginning, and in fact they will grow from the treatment. To boot, the time limit will result in much saving of agency time with this group. Conversely, clients with chronic problems will initially react negatively to the time limit. Additionally, if these clients are in the lower range of measured adjustment, and are seen initially as less motivated for counseling, less willing to change, and less enjoyable to work with, the probability seems high that brief TLT will not be helpful. It remains to be seen if procedures can be developed that will enhance the likelihood that such clients will profit from brief and/or time-limited interventions. It seems to us that this is an important and potentially fruitful direction for TLT research to take.

REFERENCES

BARRETT-LENNARD, G. Dimensions of therapist response and causal factors in therapeutic change. *Psychological Monographs,* 1962, *76* (43, Whole No. 562).

GELSO, C. J. Research in counseling: Methodological and professional issues. *The Counseling Psychologist,* 1979, *8,* 7–36.

GOTTSCHALK, L. A., MAYERSON, P., & GOTTLIEB, A. A prediction and evaluation of outcome in an emergency brief psychotherapy clinic. *Journal of Nervous and Mental Disease,* 1967, *144,* 77–96.

HENRY, W. E., & SHLIEN, J. Affective complexity and psychotherapy: Some comparisons of time-limited and unlimited treatment. *Journal of Projective Techniques,* 1958, *22,* 153–162.

HOCH, P. H. *Differential diagnosis in clinical psychology.* (Ed. posthumously by M. O. Strahl & N. D. C. Lewis) New York: Science House, 1972.

KAZDIN, A. E. Evaluating the generality of findings in analogue therapy research. *Journal of Consulting and Clinical Psychology,* 1978, *46,* 686–693.

McGUIRE, M. T. The process of short-term insight psychotherapy. *Journal of Nervous and Mental Disease,* 1965, *141,* 219–230.

MANN, J. *Time-limited psychotherapy*. Cambridge, Massachusetts: Harvard University Press, 1973.

MILLS, D. H. Adjectives pertinent to psychotherapy for use with the semantic differential: An heuristic note. *Psychological Reports*, 1970, *26*, 211–213.

MUNLEY, P. N. A review of counseling analogue research methods. *Journal of Counseling Psychology*, 1974, *21*, 320–330.

MUNRO, J. H., & BACH, T. R. Effect of time-limited counseling on client change. *Journal of Counseling Psychology*, 1975, *22*, 395–398.

MUNROE, R. *Schools of psychoanalytic thought*. New York: Henry Holt & Company, 1955.

PATTERSON, V., & O'SULLIVAN, M. Three perspectives on brief psychotherapy. *American Journal of Psychotherapy*, 1974, (Apr.), 265–277.

PHILLIPS, E. L. Attitudes toward self and others: A brief questionnaire report. *Journal of Consulting Psychology*, 1951, *15*, 79–81.

RANK, O. *Will therapy and truth and reality*. New York: Knoff, 1945.

ROBINSON, J. & SHAVER, P. (Eds.) *Measures of social psychological attitudes*. Ann Arbor, Michigan: Institute for Social Research, 1974.

ROGERS, C. R. The necessary and sufficient conditions of therapeutic personality change. *Journal of Consulting Psychology*, 1957, *21*, 95–103.

SIFNEOS, P. E. *Short-term psychotherapy and emotional crisis*. Cambridge, Massachusetts: Harvard University Press, 1972.

STRONG, S. Experimental laboratory research in counseling. *Journal of Counseling Psychology*, 1971, *18*, 106–110.

TAFT, J. *The dynamics of therapy in a controlled relationship*. New York: Macmillan Company, 1933.

TRUAX, C. B., & CARKHUFF, R. R. *Toward effective counseling and psychotherapy*. Chicago: Aldine, 1967.

VOLSKY, T., MAGOON, T. M., NORMAN, W. T., & HOYT, D. P. *The outcomes of counseling and psychotherapy*. Minneapolis: University of Minnesota Press, 1965.

7

Counselor Expectancies and Goals in Time-Limited and Time-Unlimited Counseling

Deborah Hazel Johnson

In focusing on clients' initial reactions to time limits, McKitrick and Gelso's Chapter 6 study stimulated our thinking about the process of TLT. If some clients have such differing expectancies of TLT and TUT from the very beginning of counseling, might counselors not also have such expectancy sets? Particularly since it is often thought that counselors may set the stage for making TLT optimally effective (Butcher & Koss, 1978), it would seem crucial to determine whether counselors approach TLT and TUT with different initial expectancies of outcome.

A further impetus to study counselors' expectancies came from a review of outcome literature on counseling duration and TLT (Johnson & Gelso, 1980). Consistent with the widely cited review by Luborsky and his colleagues (Luborsky, Chandler, Auerbach, Cohen, & Bachrach, 1971), most studies in the Johnson and Gelso review found longer therapy to be more effective than shorter therapy. However, the conclusion is quite different when the *source* of criterion measure is considered: 89% of the studies using counselor ratings found longer therapy more effective, while only 50% of those using client ratings demonstrated such a trend. Similarly, comparing outcomes of TLT with those of TUT, studies using client ratings have tended to favor TLT highly, while studies using counselor ratings are more mixed. Two possible interpretations of these findings are that counselors are biased in favor of longer counseling and/or that counselors and clients may have very different goals for the counseling process. Might these differences in out-

145

come ratings arise from initial expectancy sets regarding the relative efficacy of TLT and TUT? This question, together with our interest in following the McKitrick and Gelso study with another expectancy study focusing on counselors, led us to plan the study reported in this chapter.

In addition to studying counselors' expectancies for TLT and TUT, we were also interested in exploring counselors' goals for the two counseling structures. This interest in goals arose from a problem in TLT versus TUT outcome studies, labeled by Johnson and Gelso (1980) the "different criterion" hypothesis. That is, many comparative outcome studies used satisfaction rating scales, so counselors' and clients' internal criteria for satisfactory outcome could have differed from one another and for TLT as opposed to TUT. A common criterion for the client may be a sense of well-being, whereas for the counselor it may be personality change (Strupp & Hadley, 1977). We would suspect, then, that such differing criteria would, indeed, lead to different conclusions as to the relative effectiveness of TLT and TUT, depending on whose criteria were being used.

As Strupp and Hadley (1977) so aptly note, with the increasing number of third-party payments and the greater need for accountability, we need to use multiple criteria to judge the effectiveness of counseling. This point is particularly well taken when we compare shorter to longer therapy: goals and outcomes appropriate to one may not suit the other. Furthermore, goals appropriate for a publicly funded agency may need to reflect society's and clients' goals, whereas private practitioners may more appropriately incorporate counselors' criteria to gauge their progress. Do counselors, however, actually make such differentiation?

Using McKitrick and Gelso's idea of the importance of initial expectancies on subsequent counseling, we planned the present study to compare counselors' initial goals and expectancies for TLT with those for TUT. Such a comparison is important both clinically, to further understand the respective processes of each type of counseling, and methodologically, to demonstrate possible problems in comparing outcome ratings of TLT and TUT.

We again chose a laboratory setting for the study, since the nature of our questions required the rigorous control allowed by such a setting. While a comparison of counselors' goals and expectancies for clients in TLT versus TUT in a natural setting would have had to be across groups of clients, in the laboratory we could use the same client in both conditions. Similarly, since we were also interested in counselors' reactions to two different types of clients, our analogue experiment permitted such a comparison while simultaneously controlling for such extraneous variables as severity of disturbance and attractiveness.

The main purpose of this study was to determine whether and in what ways counselors initially approach TLT and TUT with different *goals, outcome expectancies,* and *role expectancies.* Secondarily, we explored some client and therapist variables that might moderate the relationship between counseling structure and counselors' goals and expectancies.

In general, we hypothesized that counselors would perceive TLT as a less extensive treatment modality than TUT. This perception might influence counselors' goals in both a quantitative and a qualitative way, such that TLT would be characterized by fewer and more delimited types of goals. Similarly, regarding expectancies of outcome, we suspected that such expectancies might be equivalent for TLT and TUT when the more delimited types of client change were being considered (e.g., change in clients' feelings), but that outcome expectancies would be greater for TUT for more extensive types of client change (e.g., personality change). In addition to types of outcomes expected, we chose to study the time at which client change is judged, since there is some evidence that change may continue past termination (see Chapter 3).

Role expectancies were included in this study to provide a test of the hypothesis raised by McKitrick and Gelso. When those authors found no effect of time limits on clients' expectancies of their own or of their counselors' activity levels, it was hypothesized that it is *counselors'* initial (precounseling) expectancies that bring about clients' subsequent more active role. Since Chapter 2 had found counselors reporting more activity in TLT than in TUT, it seemed likely that counselors from the beginning of TLT would expect themselves and their clients to be more active than in TUT.

Finally, to investigate potential moderators, we chose a client variable and a counselor variable that theorists have postulated to be important in TLT. Some theorists, such as Mann (1973) and Sifneos (1972), have suggested that some client problem types are more appropriate for TLT than others; in particular, dependency and ability to form interpersonal relationships have been suggested as core issues determining a client's appropriateness for TLT. Accordingly, the client variable investigated in this study was client problem type, in terms of dependency/independence conflicts. The counselor variable studied was counselors' general active-directiveness, because it has generally been thought that the more active, directive counselor orientations are especially appropriate for TLT (Butcher & Koss, 1978).

Method

Subjects

Subjects were 32 (20 female, 12 male) counselors currently engaged in counseling. Eighteen of the counselors were counseling center senior staff members or associates who averaged 7 years postdoctoral counseling experience; the remaining 14 were fourth-year clinical or counseling psychology graduate students or predoctoral interns, all of whom had at least 3 years of counseling experience. All subjects had experience in doing both TLT and TUT, having worked at least 6 months in the Counseling Center, where approximately three-fourths of all clients were seen on a time-limited basis.

Measures

THERAPIST ORIENTATION QUESTIONNAIRE (TOQ).   To measure counselors' philosophies and professed strategies in their approaches to counseling, we used the TOQ (Sundland, 1972; Appendix E), as was used and described previously by Gelso, Spiegel, and Mills in Chapter 2. Although many subscales of the TOQ have been derived through factor analysis (Howard, Orlinsky, & Trattner, 1970; Sundland & Barker, 1962), none provided a satisfactory measure of the combination of activity and directiveness, the variable we wished to use. Therefore, we derived an active-directiveness subscale through a face-validity approach based on experts' judgments. Three experienced doctoral-level counselors rated the TOQ items on a 7-point Likert scale measuring the extent to which each item characterized an active, directive counselor. Items that were rated by all three raters as either "Quite characteristic" (6 or 7 on the 7-point scale) or "Quite uncharacteristic" (1 or 2) were chosen to comprise the active-directiveness subscale. The scale thus derived had 14 items, and is presented in Appendix M.

GOAL STATEMENT INVENTORY (GSI).   The GSI (McNair & Lorr, 1964; Appendix N) is a 30-item instrument that provides a method for measuring and classifying counseling goals according to three empirically independent factors (Appendix O): Reconstructive Goals (personality and behavior change), Stabilization Goals (maintenance of current functioning level), and Situational Adjustment Goals (coping with the presenting situation). In addition to the subscale scores, an overall goal score (composite) was obtained as a measure of the total number of goals checked.

COUNSELORS' EXPECTANCIES QUESTIONNAIRE.   Expectancies scales based on the scales developed by Gelso et al. (Chapter 2) were used to measure counselors' role and outcome expectancies. For role expectancies, we used two 7-point Likert scales regarding the activity levels that counselors expected of themselves and of the client, in comparison to the general activity level in that counselor's counseling sessions. Our outcome expectancies measure focused on outcomes at two different times and in five different change areas, as discussed previously. Expectancies as to improvement (a) at termination and (b) two years after termination of counseling were rated on 7-point Likert scales for each of the following five change areas: presenting problem, client feelings, client behavior, overall personality change, and change in general functioning. In addition to scores for each of these ten types of outcome expectancies, two composite scores were obtained, one the sum of expectancies of all types of outcomes at termination, and the other at the two-year follow-up.

Stimulus Materials

Two sets of written intake notes and two five-minute videotapes simulating a client talking at the beginning of an initial counseling session were developed to portray the two different client problems: Problem A, fear of intimacy, and

Problem B, unhealthy dependency. The materials described clients who need some counseling, could conceivably benefit from TUT, and have enough ego strength to benefit from TLT. Notes and scripts were matched for both problem types in terms of length, number of affect words, number of self-referents, and amount of history disclosed.

To insure that the scripts and intake notes presented the two problem types as similar on most variables except type of problem, we did a check on the written stimulus materials before proceeding to videotape. Three experienced doctoral-level counselors, naive regarding the purpose of the study, rated the intake notes and scripts on 5-point Likert scales for problem chronicity, amount of history disclosed, problem severity, likeability of client, realness of presentation of problem, extent to which client could benefit from more than 12 sessions, extent of unhealthy dependency, and extent of fear of intimacy. The problem types were intended to be similar on all dimensions except the last two. The ratings indicated that the written materials fulfilled preset criteria of acceptability on all scales; that is, the materials were similar on all dimensions except the problem types, which were significantly different.

We decided to have the clients portrayed by white females, since such characteristics represent the modal client seen in our center. Two white female undergraduate theater majors memorized and practiced both scripts until their portrayals were similar. To insure similarity of presentation across actresses and problem types, three master's-level counseling graduate students read the intake notes and then rated each of the four videotapes on the ten 5-point Likert scales used for the previous ratings of the written materials. Again criteria for acceptability were achieved, confirming that the two client presentations differed only on problem type and that the actresses were comparable in portraying each problem type.

Procedure

Counselors first took the TOQ, at their convenience. (Those counselors who had several years previously taken the TOQ for the Chapter 2 study were retested, to insure current results.) Using a median split, counselors were categorized as high active-directive or low active-directive on the basis of their TOQ active-directiveness scores.

The experimental design consisted of two between-subjects variables (TOQ active-directiveness and type of counseling structure) and one within-subjects variable (client problem type). Counselors were grouped according to TOQ active-directiveness (high, low) scores, and then were randomly assigned to type of counseling structure (TLT, TUT). In addition, to control for any possible actress and problem presentation variance, counselors were further randomly assigned to actresses playing each part (Actress 1 playing Problem A and Actress 2 playing Problem B, or Actress 2 playing Problem A and Actress 1 playing Problem B) and presentation order (Problem A followed by Problem B, or Problem B followed by Problem A), so that all possible actress/order combinations occurred within each TOQ/counseling structure cell. Thus, each counselor saw both client problem types within one type of counseling structure (TLT or TUT).

Counselors, tested individually, first read the intake notes for the first client. Both the intake notes and the experimenter stressed the counseling structure (TLT or TUT) to which the client was assigned. Counselors were then instructed to watch the videotape, thinking of it as the beginning of the first counseling session. After the videotape, counselors reacted to the client under the given counseling structure by responding to the GSI and the Counselors' Expectancies Questionnaire. The procedure was then repeated for the second client presentation, followed by a questionnaire that served as a manipulation check for client problem type and counseling structure.

Results

To be sure that we had manipulated our independent variables in the intended way, we prefaced our analyses of the experimental questions with an analysis of the counselors' responses to the manipulation check questionaire. All counselors were able to identify correctly the counseling structure (TLT or TUT) and the client problem types (fear of intimacy or unhealthy dependency).

Preliminary to addressing the main research questions, we computed an intercorrelation matrix to determine the relationship of all dependent variables to one another. Since a large number of such variables was used in the study, we wanted to make sure that we were measuring distinctly different concepts with each variable, rather than merely obtaining a more global response set. Indeed, as Table 7–1 shows, most measures were statistically independent. The only significant correlations ($p < .05$) occurred (a) between each of the goals subscales and the goals composite, due to the composite having been derived by summing the subscales, and (b) between the composites of expectancies of change and at follow-up. The latter correlation was unsurprising since client change at termination usually is, in fact, correlated with change at follow-up. Thus, our attempt to measure a number of unrelated variables seems largely to have been successful.

To examine the research questions, $2 \times 2 \times 2$ analyses of variance (ANOVA's) for repeated measures were carried out, with the independent variables being counselor active-directiveness (high vs. low), counseling structure (TLT vs. TUT), and client types (the repeated variable: Problem A, fear of intimacy, vs. Problem B, unhealthy dependency). These ANOVA's were done for each of the various dependent measures: goals, role expectancies, and outcome expectancies. Because a relatively large number of measures (18) was used, we wanted to be cautious not to place too much confidence in isolated significant effects that might have been due to chance. Toward this purpose, we first formed a composite measure for each type or group of dependent variables by summing the scores

Table 7-1. Intercorrelation Matrix for Main Dependent Variables

		Reconstructive goals	Stabilization goals	Situational goals	Counselor activity	Client activity	Composite of goals	Composite expectancies at termination	Composite of follow-up expectancies
Reconstructive goals	TL[a]		.44	.49	.20	.01	.80***	.21	−.10
	TU[b]		−.08	.25	−.34	.49	.69**	−.02	−.10
	Both[c]		.19	.31	−.23	.34*	.77***	.38*	.19
Stabilization goals	TL			.73***	.26	.10	.86***	.16	.09
	TU			.21	.00	.12	.56*	.30	.16
	Both			.47**	.13	.11	.71***	.19	.12
Situational goals	TL				.40	.17	.83***	.17	−.07
	TU				−.17	.06	.67**	−.47	−.59*
	Both				.10	.10	.70***	−.11	−.27
Counselor activity	TL					−.18	.33	.46	.29
	TU					−.45	−.28	−.26	.07
	Both					−.38*	−.05	−.10	−.02
Client activity	TL						.09	−.50*	−.22
	TU						.40	.22	.16
	Both						.29	.03	.09
Composite of goals	TL							.22	−.02
	TU							−.04	−.22
	Both							.28	.09
Composite at termination	TL								.52*
	TU								.81***
	Both								.74***

[a]"TL" indicates scores for time-limited counseling structure; $n = 16$.
[b]"TU" indicates scores for time-unlimited counseling structure; $n = 16$.
[c]"Both" indicates scores for both time-limited and time-unlimited counseling structures together; $n = 32$.

* $p < .05$
** $p < .01$
*** $p < .001$

of those variables (goals, role expectancies, outcome expectancies at termination, and outcome expectancies at two-year follow-up), and did ANOVA's on these composite variables. We then did the individual ANOVA's on each individual dependent variable. The results of these analyses are given in Table 7–2, according to groups of dependent variables. Only those results concerning main or interactive effects of counseling structure (TLT vs. TUT) are discussed here, since it is those effects that are the focus of this book. All results reported are below the $p < .05$ significance level.

Goals

We had hypothesized that goals for TLT would be fewer in number and less extensive in type than the goals for TUT. The results indicated that there were, indeed, differences in *types* of goals for TLT and TUT, although our hypothesis that there would be differences in *numbers* of goals was not statistically borne out. While the mean total number of goals for TLT ($M = 12.78$) was, as hypothesized, somewhat less than for TUT ($M = 15.12$), this was not a statistically significant difference.

Regarding types of goals, TLT and TUT did not differ regarding the less extensive types of goals: Stabilization Goals and Situational Adjustment Goals. For these more modest goals, counselors did not distinguish between TLT and TUT. They did, however, have fewer of the more extensive Reconstructive Goals for TLT ($M = 7.72$) than for TUT ($M = 9.97$). It was only, then, in the most extreme case of attempting personality reconstruction that the counselors approached TLT with lessened objectives as compared to those for TUT. Thus, the difference between TLT and TUT in terms of goals appears to be more qualitative than quantitative.

While the above analyses considered the general effect of counseling structure on goals, we had also hypothesized that this relationship would depend on the type of counselor. A counselor whose general theoretical orientation is more active and directive might have quite similar goals for TLT and TUT, while a less active counselor might lessen the goals for TLT. Thus, we hypothesized that counseling structure would have an interactive effect with counselor orientation on the dependent measure of counseling goals. Results, however, showed no such interaction on either overall number of goals, Situational Adjustment Goals, or Reconstructive Goals. On these three measures, high active-directive counselors and low active-directive counselors shared similar approaches to TLT and TUT. In contrast, Stabilization Goals did show an interaction, but in a somewhat different way from that anticipated. High active-directive counselors had more Stabilization Goals in TUT ($M = 3.87$) than in TLT ($M = 2.31$), rather than the hypothesized equal number in TUT and TLT. In accordance with the hypothesis, low active-directive counselors had the opposite pattern: they had more Stabilization Goals for TLT ($M = 3.87$) than for TUT ($M = 2.50$).

Table 7-2. Analyses of Variance: F Ratios for the Effects of Counseling Structure, Counselor Active-Directiveness (TOQ), and Client Type on Counselor Goals, Role Expectancies, and Outcome Expectancies

Measure	Structure (A)[a]	TOQ (B)[a]	Client type (c)[a]	(A × B)[a]	(A × C)[a]	(B × C)[a]	(A × B × C)[a]
Goals							
Composite	3.629	0.016	0.088	2.726	1.555	0.088	0.173
Reconstructive	10.897**	0.681	3.794	0.034	0.949	0.607	3.073
Stabilization	0.027	0.027	0.351	6.738*	1.697	1.697	0.126
Situational	0.000	1.796	1.659	3.395	0.000	1.062	3.251
Role Expectancies							
Counselor Activity	4.049	0.450	0.432	0.162	0.847	0.155	2.091
Client Activity	1.777	1.137	8.383**	0.284	3.018	0.084	2.096
Outcome Expectancies							
At Termination							
Composite	15.663**	1.457	1.783	0.177	4.089	0.770	0.525
Presenting Problem	11.541**	0.615	3.338	0.000	4.543*	0.834	0.371
Client Feelings	6.886*	1.423	0.863	0.057	0.863	0.096	0.863
Client Behavior	12.077**	0.314	0.019	0.314	6.923*	0.019	0.019
Personality	11.839**	3.581	6.095*	0.030	1.524	0.857	0.095
General Functioning	13.552**	0.000	0.000	2.800	1.223	2.175	1.223
At Two-year Follow-up							
Composite	9.941**	0.126	15.035**	0.597	1.879	0.676	0.014
Presenting Problem	9.133**	0.000	12.259***	2.022	0.072	1.161	0.290
Client Feelings	6.712*	0.000	7.368***	0.419	1.179	1.179	0.000
Client Behavior	4.729*	0.006	9.464***	0.318	3.172	0.236	0.236
Personality	12.309***	3.569	12.302***	0.073	1.884	0.023	0.209
General Functioning	10.845**	0.270	13.031***	0.270	2.692	0.969	0.108

[a]$F_c(1,28) = 4.20, p < .05$; $F_c(1,28) = 7.64, p < .01$.   *p < .05.   **p < .01.

No interaction of counseling structure with client problem type was hypothesized for the goals measure, and none was demonstrated by the ANOVA's; nor
was there a 3-way interaction.

Role Expectancies

We hypothesized that in TLT counselors in general would have expectancies
of greater client activity and counselor activity than in TUT. Furthermore, we
expected that high active-directive counselors would have more similar counselor
role expectancies for TLT and TUT, while low active-directive counselors would
expect themselves to be less active in TUT than in TLT.

Analyses, however, revealed no effect of counseling structure on counselors'
role expectancies, as either a main effect or in interaction with active-
directiveness. These results were rather surprising, particularly since counselor
and client roles have been shown in several cases (e.g., Gelso et al., Chapter 2;
Wattie, 1973; Reid and Shyne, 1969) to be rather different in TLT from those in
TUT. We examine these findings further in the Discussion section; suffice it for
now to say that counselors, regardless of orientation, do not expect their own or
their clients' role to change between TLT and TUT.

Outcome Expectancies: At Termination

Our hypotheses here differentiated among different types of client change
expected to occur by the time of counseling termination. For the more extensive
types of change (change in behavior, personality, and general functioning), we
hypothesized that counselors would expect more such change in TUT as opposed
to TLT. The more delimited change areas (change in presenting problem and client
feelings), we believed, would produce equal counselor expectancies for TUT and
TLT.

ANOVA results supported some but not all of these hypotheses. The composite measure (total of all five types of change) showed counselors having lower
expectancies of overall change in TLT than in TUT; at termination, similarly,
there were lower expectancies for change in behavior, personality, and general
functioning in TLT than in TUT. However, in contrast to our hypothesis, counselors did not make major differentiations according to type of client change. Their
lowered expectancies for TLT in the more extensive types of change extended also
to the more delimited change areas, that is, presenting problem and client feelings.
*Thus, for all measured types of client change, counselors expected TLT to be less
effective than TUT.*

As with the goals measures, we hypothesized that counselor active-
directiveness would moderate the effects of counseling structure on counselors'
expectancies of outcome at termination. Because we believed that high active-
directive counselors probably approach TLT similarly to the way they approach

TUT, we hypothesized that these counselors would have equal outcome expectancies for TLT and TUT at termination, while the low active-directive counselors would expect more change of all types in TUT than in TLT. The analyses, however, showed no such significant interactions on any of the scales of outcome expectancies at termination. Both low and high active-directive counselors expected less extensive change of all types for TLT than for TUT.

Considering the two client problem types, we hypothesized that there would be no interactions with counseling structure on expectancies of improvement in the more delimited areas of feelings and presenting problem at termination, but that the Problem A client (fear of intimacy) would be associated with lower expectancies of improvement in the more deep-seated areas of behavior, personality, and general functioning than the Problem B client (unhealthy dependency) in TLT but not in TUT. ANOVA's revealed no interactive effect of client type and counseling structure on the composite for outcome expectancies or on the expectancies subscale of general functioning. As hypothesized, the more specific expectancies of improvement in feelings at termination of TLT and TUT were not affected by client problem type. However, such interactive effects did occur on expectancies of improvement in presenting problem (not hypothesized) and in client behavior (hypothesized). On expectancies of change in presenting problem at termination, analyses showed that Problem A (fear of intimacy) was associated with greater expected improvement in TUT ($M = 5.50$) than in TLT ($M = 4.25$), while Problem B (unhealthy dependency) was seen as doing about as well in TLT ($M = 4.31$) as in TUT ($M = 4.69$). Similarly, on expectancies of change in client behavior at termination, Problem A was associated with higher expectancies in TUT ($M = 5.62$) than in TLT ($M = 4.06$), while there were no such differences for Problem B (TUT, $M = 5.00$; TLT, $M = 4.62$). In summary, then, while dependency and intimacy conflicts were both expected by counselors to show more improvement in TUT than in TLT in the areas of client feelings, general functioning, and personality change, only the client with unhealthy dependency was expected to make equal changes in presenting problem and behavior in TLT and TUT, at termination.

Outcome Expectancies: At Two-Year Follow-Up

Because informal evidence led us to believe that many counselors see TLT as having only short-term effects, we examined expectancies of both short- and long-term client change. The questions in this section, then, focused on counselors' initial expectancies of the extent and types of client change two years after termination.

As hypothesized, counselors had higher expectancies for client change in TUT than in TLT, at two-year follow-up. All types of client change (change in feelings, presenting problem behavior, personality, and general functioning) showed this effect. These differences in expectancies for TLT and TUT at two-year follow-up were thus similar to those at termination.

Again, as for the termination expectancies, we anticipated that counselor active-directiveness and client problem type would differentially influence two-year outcome expectancies. For this two-year time period, however, no such interactions occurred. Counseling structure (TLT or TUT) alone affected counselors' long-term expectancies, and neither counselor nor client type influenced the general pattern of TLT clients being expected to have made less change than TUT clients.

Time of Outcome Measurement

Since there is evidence (Johnson & Gelso, 1980; Gelso et al., Chapter 3) that TLT may begin a change process that does not reach full fruition until some time after termination, we were interested in whether counselors incorporated such a change process into their expectancies. To investigate this question, we added time of outcome measurement (termination vs. follow-up) to the design as an independent variable. Here, it was the interaction of time of outcome measurement with counseling structure that was of primary interest, with the three-way interactions of these variables with counselor type or problem type of secondary interest.

Our analyses showed that, beyond the general trend for both TLT and TUT clients to be expected to retain less improvement at two-year follow-up than at termination and the already-discussed higher expectancies for TUT outcome than for TLT outcome at both times of outcome measurement, no such interactions occurred. TLT and TUT clients alike were expected to exhibit less improvement at two-year follow-up than at termination. At both times of outcome measurement, there were higher expectancies for TUT outcome than for TLT outcome; and the amount of decrease in improvement between termination and two-year follow-up was no different for TLT clients than for TUT clients. Apparently counselors do not see either TLT or TUT as beginning a change process that extends beyond termination.

Neither counselor type nor client type had an effect on the above relationship.

Discussion

As in Chapter 6, we begin our discussion of the implications of our results with the note that our findings occurred in a laboratory setting, and therefore we must exercise caution in generalizing to the actual counseling setting. However, unlike the Chapter 6 subjects who were not actually counseling participants, the subjects in this study were actual counselors involved in doing both TLT and TUT. Our caution thus is concerned with the possible artificiality of reacting to a videotaped "client," rather than an actual client in person. We do have some informal evidence to support the generalizability of our findings; comments of study participants after the experiment often centered on the realness of the client presentation and the consequent stimulation of counselors' feelings in reaction to our "clients."

Goals

Our interest in counselors' goals came from two sources: (a) the often-reported theoretical axiom that goals must be more delimited in TLT, and (b) the frequently lower outcome ratings of counselors as compared to clients, as we discussed in the Introduction. We had anticipated that counselors would have lower goals for TLT than for TUT, but were particularly interested in exploring the nuances of these differences.

Much of the theoretical literature (e.g., Wright, Gabriel, & Haimowitz 1961; Posin 1969) suggests that TLT is characterized by a less extensive number and more delimited types of goals than TUT, such that TLT focuses more on supporting existing defenses (overcoming situational problems by drawing on client strengths) while TUT works toward uncovering defenses and changing the personality structure. The present study showed counselors largely having viewpoints consistent with this conceptualization.

In contrast to these findings and the cited theoretical views, there is evidence that TLT need not exclude personality change as a goal. The empirical literature demonstrates that when differences in personality change have been found between the two therapy structures, the TLT structure is favored (Johnson & Gelso, 1980). Similarly, Sifneos (1967) takes the view that TLT can appropriately be anxiety-provoking, working to change personality dynamics rather than just supporting existing defenses. While further evidence is needed to confirm the capabilities of TLT to influence personality reconstruction, it would seem that our counselors may be a bit too pessimistic in their goals for TLT. It may be particularly true in agencies such as ours, whose average TUT duration (20–25 sessions) was of length such that the implementation of a time-limited policy was needed, that counselors may tend to underestimate the changes possible through TLT. (However, we do not want to overemphasize this point, since the difference in Reconstructive Goals for TLT and TUT was significant but not huge, indicating that counselors do attempt some personality change in TLT.)

As a moderator of goals, counselor active-directiveness was not nearly so potent as might have been hypothesized based on the literature emphasizing the necessity for an active, directive counselor role in TLT (Butcher & Koss, 1978). This lack of effect is reminiscent of the Gelso, Mills, & Spiegel (Chapter 4) finding that the TOQ directiveness scale (not the same as that used in the current study) was unrelated to client- and counselor-judged outcomes. The current study adds confirmatory evidence to the hypothesis of Gelso et al. that general theoretical beliefs may not extend to behavior enough to differentially effect TLT and TUT. The TOQ, used in both this chapter and Chapter 4 to measure orientation, tends to focus on counselors' beliefs and tolerances for various practices, rather than on their actual behavior. It would be useful in future research to attempt to behaviorally differentiate between counselors who are more effective in TLT and those more effective in TUT.

The above notwithstanding, we did find orientation affecting Stabilization Goals (supporting client's defenses) differentially in TLT and TUT. The finding that high active-directive counselors subscribed to Stabilization Goals more for TUT than for TLT could indicate that these counselors felt that TUT opens up more emotionally charged issues for clients, necessitating more covering work. Some support for this conjecture may be found in the incidental finding that these same counselors liked doing TLT significantly more than did the less active-directive ones; perhaps the more active counselors feel less need to do "covering" work in TLT and thus appreciate TLT's limitations.

Role Expectancies

McKitrick and Gelso (Chapter 6) followed their null results on clients' expectancies for different roles in TLT and TUT with the hypothesis that it may be counselors rather than clients who have such differing expectancies. In contrast, though, the present study found that counselors expected similar activity levels for both themselves and their clients in TLT and TUT.

How can we interpret this finding, particularly given the fact that the Chapter 2 study, which used many of these same counselors, found counselors actually reporting more activity in TLT? We tentatively suggest that the differences in these findings may be due to the differences in time of measurement. This explanation is consistent with McKitrick and Gelso's alternative idea that it may take counseling participants time in counseling to be affected by the time limits. Neither the client-subjects in Chapter 6 nor the counselors in this chapter antici-pated role shifts when asked their expectancies before counseling began. The Chapter 2 counselors, though, in retrospect acknowledged more activity in TLT. Accordingly, TLT may stimulate either or both participants into greater activity once they are involved in the sessions; perhaps only the reality of the ever closer time limits affects role differences. We would suggest, then, that TLT may be characterized by more activity closer to termination, but that there may be less difference in TLT and TUT earlier in the therapeutic contact. It remains to be answered why counselors experienced in TLT still do not expect more activity from the beginning of new client contacts.

An alternative hypothesis might question whether in fact there *is* greater activity in TLT. Since the Chapter 2 data are based on therapists' retrospective self-reports, therapists may *feel* that they have been more active due to the compressed number of sessions or more active thought processes, but their behavior may not indicate such activity. Clearly, we need data extending self-report to more behavioral measures. Further empirical investigations of these hypotheses will be crucial to better understanding the process of TLT, pinpointing which process aspects of TLT bring about greater effectiveness, and training therapists to do TLT.

Outcome Expectancies

A major finding of this study was that counselors have lower outcome expectancies for TLT than for TUT, with little differentiation regarding types of client change and no belief in time as a curative factor. While the counselors did see TLT as an equally effective treatment in helping an overly dependent client make changes in presenting problem and in behavior, the overall direction of expectancies for TLT is rather pessimistic. The results are particularly striking given the research findings that TLT has generally been found to produce at least as highly positive changes as does TUT in delimited areas of client change. What implication does this discrepancy between counselor expectancies and empirical realities have for clinical practice and for research?

First, since expectancies are so often considered a major part of the effectiveness of TLT (Butcher & Koss, 1978), low outcome expectancies may in fact precipitate a self-fulfilling prophecy: the less effective a counselor believes TLT will be, the less impressive the outcome, thus the less impressed the counselor will be with TLT. Based on the evidence in previous chapters that TLT *can* be a quite effective counseling modality, it would seem incumbent upon us to bring this empirical knowledge to bear upon clinical practice. Convincing counselors that TLT can have as great an impact on at least some areas of client change as does TUT would seem to be crucial for agencies implementing a TLT policy. To do such convincing, it would be helpful to further determine the source of counselors' biases. From the outcome evidence in Parts I and II, it is clear that these counselors are being effective in TLT with or without their biases; however, it is possible that further benefits could be reaped if biases were reduced.

The counselors' lack of differentiation regarding times of outcome ratings suggests one reason some counselors may have difficulty accepting TLT. In contrast to TUT, counselors often do not have a chance to see the full effects of TLT, because the clients leave before they have finished accomplishing the changes which counseling has begun (see Chapter 3). To avoid counselor frustration with a time-limit policy, it may be helpful to both counselor and client to add a follow-up assessment to the TLT process, done by the counselor. Such a session would allow both to observe the fruits of their labor after intervening time has gelled some of the changes.

Counselors' lower expectancies for TLT may also create methodological problems in comparative outcome studies, as counselor ratings of outcome may partially reflect counselors' expectancies of change. This hypothesis is in accordance with the tendency for counselors' outcome ratings to be lower for brief counseling than are other sources of outcome measurements (Johnson & Gelso, 1980). Multiple measures of outcomes and behaviorally anchored counselor rating scales are suggested to minimize this problem.

We must add to the above points the possibility that there may be some reality to the counselors' low expectancies. That is, counselors may see nuances in client change not perceived by other sources of outcome measurement. In this regard, we are reminded of Strupp and Hadley's (1977) notion of differing definitions of therapy outcome: counselors', clients', and society's definitions may be different from one another, but none is the "correct" viewpoint. TLT could indeed be less effective than TUT according to counselors' definitions but not according to others'. Perhaps it is precisely this point that needs to be addressed in changing an agency to a TLT policy, since such changes are usually made due to external rather than internal pressures. Even if a counselor believes TLT to be less effective, if a policy of TLT is the way to be of best service to clients and to society, perhaps counselors' definitions of counseling effectiveness are less important to such an agency than are the others' definitions. Decisions made on this basis, however, put responsibility on the decision-makers to help counselors deal with their own feelings of incompleteness in achieving their own counseling goals.

THE EFFECT OF A CLIENT MODERATOR VARIABLE.   Although the counselors did not make major differentiations in expectancies for an overly dependent client and one with intimacy difficulties, they did see the overly dependent client as doing equally well in TLT and TUT on several change dimensions. The client with intimacy difficulties, in contrast, was seen as doing better on all change dimensions through undergoing TUT rather than TLT.

Apparently the counselors subscribed to some extent to Mann's (1973) notion that TLT is an effective modality for clients with separation/dependency conflicts. However, the counselors also seemed to believe that the choice of TLT or TUT for various client types may depend somewhat on what types of outcomes are desired.

These results once again point to the need for an agency to delineate the types of goals that it wants to help its clients achieve. Is it more important that a client make improvement in the presenting problem, or that the client goes beyond the situational to the point of making personality change? Furthermore, our current results suggest that for some clients and types of outcomes, TLT may be at least equivalent to TUT, whereas for others there may be large differences between TLT and TUT. Combining these results with those of Chapters 2, 3, 4, and 6, we tentatively suggest that chronically disturbed clients and the more socially isolated clients may do best in TUT, while less chronic clients who have interpersonal or identity difficulties but who can readily "hook into" a relationship may benefit on many dimensions from either TLT or TUT.

In conclusion, we have explored the ways in which counselors approach TLT and TUT, and found that the two counseling structures elicit different attitudinal sets in counselors from the very beginning. Since Chapter 6 found that clients also react early to the idea of a time limit, we conclude that time limits indeed create a rather different counseling process from open-ended counseling. In Chapter 8, we will examine the ways in which initial psychological sets influence the results of TLT.

REFERENCES

BUTCHER, J. N., & KOSS, M. P. Research on brief and crisis-oriented therapies. In S. Garfield & A. Bergin (Eds.), *Handbook of psychotherapy and behavior change* (Rev. ed.). New York: Wiley, 1978.

HOWARD, K. I., ORLINSKY, D. E., & TRATTNER, J. H. Therapist orientation and patient experience in psychotherapy. *Journal of Counseling Psychology*, 1970, *17*, 263–270.

JOHNSON, D. H., & GELSO, C. J. The effectiveness of time limits in counseling and psychotherapy: A critical review. *The Counseling Psychologist*, 1980, *9*, 70–83.

LUBORSKY, L., CHANDLER, M., AUERBACH, A. H., COHEN, J., & BACHRACH, H. M. Factors influencing the outcome of psychotherapy: A review of quantitative literature. *Psychological Bulletin*, 1971, *75*, 145–185.

MANN, J. *Time-limited psychotherapy*. Cambridge, Massachusetts: Harvard University Press, 1973.

McNAIR, D. M., & LORR, M. Three kinds of psychotherapy goals. *Journal of Clinical Psychology*, 1964, *20*, 390–393.

POSIN, H. I. Approaches to brief psychotherapy in a university health service. *Seminars in Psychiatry*, 1969, *1*, 399–404.

REID, W. J., & SHYNE, A. W. *Brief and extended casework*. New York: Columbia University Press, 1969.

SIFNEOS, P. E. Two different kinds of psychotherapy of short duration. *American Journal of Psychiatry*, 1967, *123*, 1069–1074.

SIFNEOS, P. E. *Short-term psychotherapy and emotional crisis*. Cambridge: Harvard University Press, 1972.

STRUPP, H. H., & HADLEY, S. W. A tripartite model of mental health and therapeutic outcomes. *American Psychologist*, 1977, *32*, 187–196.

Sundland, D. M., & Barker, E. N. The orientation of psychotherapists. *Journal of Consulting Psychology*, 1962, *26*, 201–212.

WATTIE, B. Evaluating short term casework in a family agency. *Social Casework*, 1973, *54*, 609–616.

WRIGHT, K., GABRIEL, E., & HAIMOWITZ, N. Time-limited psychotherapy: Advantages, problems, outcomes. *Psychological Reports*, 1961, *9*, 187–190.

8

Duration Expectancies and Client Satisfaction with Time-Limited Counseling

**Janet Lynn Cornfeld, Deborah Hazel Johnson,
Sharon Baron Spiegel, Jean P. Whittaker,
Daniel Wasserman, and Charles J. Gelso**

After several studies in our research program on TLT had explored outcomes of TLT (Part One), McKitrick and Gelso (Chapter 6) and Johnson (Chapter 7) took a rather different focus and investigated participants' initial expectancies of TLT outcome in analogue settings. From these studies we learned that TLT sets in motion a quite different set of outcome expectancies from the very beginning of the therapeutic contact. The present chapter discusses a study that extended the results of the two previous studies in several important ways: (a) It examined initial expectancies of duration, a variable of particular relevance to TLT; (b) it used the natural counseling setting rather than a laboratory; and (c) it linked initial expectancies to counseling outcome measures.

The idea for the present study arose from our realization that part of the thinking regarding TLT carried some unchecked basic assumptions. When we concerned ourselves with the traditional outcome questions such as whether 12-session TLT is as good as longer TUT, our assumption seemed to be that a greater number of sessions is more desirable. When a staff member in our agency questioned whether our time limit may discourage prospective clients from coming to the Counseling Center, the assumption was that many clients want more than 12 sessions. These assumptions may stem from the fact that many counselors trained in a more traditional model of counseling seem to believe that the time limit restricts rather than enhances good counseling, and that clients as well as counselors desire something quite different. In fact, we realized that we had no data about how many sessions clients do want or expect, and we had no information linking such expectancies to actual outcome of counseling. This study, then, was designed to find out more about clients' expectancies of duration.

In the McKitrick and Gelso study (Chapter 6) the investigators asked students to put themselves in the place of a client on a videotape and then to project their expectancies of the outcome of TLT versus TUT. The analogue setting of that study allowed the investigators to manipulate experimentally the chronicity of clients' problems, with the result that the more chronically troubled client was expected by the students to improve more through TUT than through TLT, whereas the less chronically troubled client was expected to improve equally through TLT and TUT. Since that study used a controlled laboratory setting, we thought it crucial for the next step to determine whether these findings extended to the actual counseling setting. Do clients' (as distinct from McKitrick and Gelso's student nonclients) initial adjustment levels influence their expectancies for TLT? We decided in this study to alter the question somewhat from that of McKitrick and Gelso, to explore duration expectancies rather than outcome expectancies, since so many of our assumptions about TLT focus on its duration.

Once we began thinking about clients' initial duration expectancies, we wondered how stable these expectancies are. Even if a client originally wants a very few sessions, does the client really have enough information on which to make this judgment? Once counseling has begun, it may become clearer to the client that a "quick fix" is not possible, or material might arise that the client would wish to pursue. In such cases a client might at termination be dissatisfied with the time limits, even though having originally wanted only a few counseling sessions. Thus, the importance of linking initial duration expectacies with outcome satisfaction measures added a second dimension to our study.

A final avenue for exploration in the current study was to examine the relationships between outcome measures of different dimensions and sources. First, we were interested in seeing whether a client's satisfaction with counseling in general was necessarily linked to final satisfaction with the time limits. A client might feel frustrated with the time limit (as Mann [1973] suggested) and yet be able to make very satisfactory progress in counseling. Furthermore, a client might feel satisfied with counseling but also want to pursue further counseling: recidivism, as Gelso, Spiegel and Mills (Chapter 2) pointed out, need not be viewed as condemning TLT. We thus investigated the relationships among several types of outcome satisfaction measures.

Along with looking at different types of outcomes, we were interested in determining the correlation between clients' and counselors' views of the outcome of TLT. Are clients and counselors equally satisfied/dissatisfied with time limits? Is a counselor's perceptions of a client's likelihood of seeking further help similar to the client's perception? Because a review by Johnson and Gelso (1980) concluded that counselors often do perceive TLT as less effective than do clients, we suspected that our various outcome measures might show differences between clients and counselors (as was found by Gelso et al. in Chapter 2). Since we began this study with the hypothesis that clients may expect fewer sessions than do counselors, it was of particular importance to relate clients' initial duration expectancies not only with their own perceptions of outcome but also with those of their counselors.

Our investigation, then, had five major questions for study. First, we simply asked how many counseling sessions clients initially want or think they need. Second, is there a relationship between client initial adjustment and client initial and ultimate reactions to the time limit? Third, are clients' initial feelings about the time limit related to their postcounseling satisfaction? Fourth, are general satisfaction with counseling, satisfaction with the time limit, and likelihood of seeking further counseling significantly interrelated measures? And fifth, do client and counselor perceptions of outcome differ?

In exploring these questions in the natural counseling setting, we traded the control and rigor of the analogue studies in Chapters 6 and 7 for the genuineness and complexity of the field setting. Since our questions for exploration were concerned with real clients, a field study was clearly the setting of choice. With such a choice, however, came the difficulties and weaknesses of doing research in an applied setting (see Gelso [1979] for a more extensive discussion of these issues). Sample sizes often cannot be rigidly predetermined, measures may need to be chosen for their availability and practicality rather than their psychometric characteristics, and control or comparison groups may be unavailable. We found these difficulties impinging on our design, and were ultimately unable to make as strong conclusions as we had hoped. The study does, however, suggest some provocative concepts, and it does yield sound basic data. It is with these issues in mind that we describe its design and its findings.

Method

Subjects

Subjects for this study were University of Maryland-College Park students who were seen in intake appointments at the Counseling Center during a 5-week period early in the spring semester of 1978. All were voluntarily seeking help for personal-social concerns, and all subsequently became Counseling Center clients in 12-session TLT. While the n's differ for different analyses, a total of 93 clients served as subjects.

Procedure

For the expectancies part of the data collection, students with intake appointments were randomly assigned to one of two conditions. One group of students completed brief questionnaires both pre- and post-intake, while a second group completed only the post-intake questionnaire. These two conditions were used in order to obtain the desired information but also to control for sensitizing clients to the time limit before their completion of the expectancies questionnaire.

The pre-intake questionnaire consisted of one question: "About how long (at one session per week) do you feel you need or want counseling in order to deal adequately with your concerns?" The post-intake questionnaire consisted of three items: "(1) Had you heard before you came to the Counseling Center that there is usually a time limit for counseling? (2) Do you think you will be able to deal adequately with your concerns in up to 12 sessions? (3) If not, how many additional sessions do you think you would need or want?" Clients' responses to these questionnaires were collected by the receptionist, and were not seen by their counselors.

As part of standard procedure, intake counselors rated clients on a 5-point Likert scale of adjustment. The reliability of this scale was judged to be quite satisfactory based on a finding of 79% interjudge agreement on a very similar scale (Counseling Center staff, 1966). After intake, students in both groups were randomly assigned to counselors via the usual agency procedure, and counseling then proceeded as usual.

The follow-up phase of the data collection consisted of obtaining outcome assessments from clients and counselors after terminating counseling. Such assessments were possible only for those clients who had begun counseling more than 12 weeks before the end of the semester, so that they could have completed their 12-session limit during the semester. We contacted these clients by telephone and their counselors by mail within 4 weeks after counseling termination and asked them to respond to a follow-up questionnaire. There were four questions on the follow-up questionnaire: three 5-point Likert scales for rating general satisfaction with counseling, the extent to which the respondent felt the number of counseling sessions was sufficient, and the perceived likelihood of the client's seeking further counseling during the next year, and one open-ended question, for those who thought the number of sessions was insufficient, regarding how many more sessions they would have wanted.

Usable pre-intake questionnaires (i.e., those on which clients put a numeric estimate of desired duration) were obtained from 54 students and post-intake questionnaires from 50 students (2 students returned unusable pre-intake questionnaires, on which they put a question mark for the number of sessions expected). However, only 34 of these students met our criterion of having begun counseling early enough that they could have completed all 12 sessions by the end of the semester. Follow-up data were received from counselors for all 34 students. Due to summer vacations and moves, we were able to contact by telephone only 23 of these clients for follow-up, all of whom responded to the follow-up questionnaire. Thus, our findings must be viewed with some caution, since client satisfaction data were only available for 68% of the clients.

Results

Results of the statistical analyses follow, grouped by the five main hypothetical questions that were discussed in the Introduction. Because of the small number of subjects, each analysis was done using all subjects for whom we had that particular set of data. The number of subjects shifts depending on the research question, since the research design precluded all subjects receiving both the pre-intake and post-intake questionnaires.

1. *How much counseling do clients really want or think they need?* Before intake, 87% of the clients polled (total $n = 54$) responded that they wanted or needed fewer than 12 sessions. The modal response was 3 sessions, indicating that most clients had very modest expectancies of duration. It is also noteworthy that the mean number of sessions wanted, 8.8, was affected by one person desiring as many as 78 sessions, and another wanting 52 sessions (excluding those two people, the mean was 6.6). Our data revealed, then, that most clients initially expected to receive only a few sessions, although a very few clients may come to the Center wanting much more extensive counseling.

After intake, during which clients were told of the 12-session limit, 30% of the clients (total $n = 48$) said they had previously known about the time limit. Of all clients responding to the post-intake questionnaire, 83% believed that 12 sessions would be enough.

Thus, in answer to the above hypothetical question, a large majority of the clients believed before beginning counseling that they wanted or needed far fewer than 12 sessions. Very few clients came to the Center expecting even relatively long-term counseling or therapy. These expectancies could not be explained solely by clients already knowing about the time limits, as only a minority had known of the limits before intake.

Because it is conceivable that prospective clients who already knew about the time limits but wanted long-term therapy chose not to come to the Center at all, we also decided to analyze the effect of pre-intake knowledge of time limits on the post-intake belief that 12 sessions would be enough. We reasoned that if the above idea regarding knowledgeable long-term clients were true, more of the clients who had heard of the time limits, as compared to those who had not heard, would believe 12 sessions would be adequate. Those who knew of the limit but did not believe 12 sessions would be enough would, in such a case, have sought help elsewhere or not at all.

Of the 15 clients who had heard of the time limit, only 1 thought the time would not be enough to deal adequately with the client's concerns; 33 clients had *not* heard of the time limit, 7 of whom believed that the time would not be adequate. A chi-square analysis ($\chi^2 = .70$, $df = 1$, $p > .05$) indicated that these proportions did not differ more than would have been expected by chance. Thus, while the numbers alone might cause us not to reject the hypothesis regarding long-term clients staying away from the Center, the analysis provides at least statistical evidence that there is not a sound quantitative basis for this hypothesis.

2. *Is there a relationship between client adjustment and client reactions to the time limit?*

First, we were interested in determining whether the number of sessions a client initially wanted was influenced by the client's level of adjustment (as judged by the intake counselor). Using the Pearson product-moment correlation, we found that there was no relationship between these variables ($r = .02$, $df = 26$, $p > .05$). Apparently initial adjustment, as rated by intake counselor, is of little or no consequence in terms of the amount of counseling wanted or needed.

Next, we examined the relationship between initial adjustment level and satisfaction with outcome ($n = 23$). Regarding clients' feelings at follow-up, initial adjustment level was not related to general satisfaction with counseling ($r = -.26$, $df = 21$, $p > .05$), satisfaction with the time limit ($r = -.23$, $df = 21$, $p > .05$), or perceptions of the client's likelihood of seeking further counseling ($r = .35$, $df = 21$, $p > .05$).

Similarly, adjustment level was not related to any of the counselors' outcome judgments: counselors' general satisfaction ($r = .05$, $df = 21$, $p > .05$), satisfaction with the time limits ($r = -.01$, $df = 21$, $p > .05$), or perceptions of the client's likelihood of seeking further counseling ($r = .35$, $df = 21$, $p > .05$).

Regarding our question, then, intake counselors' ratings of client adjustment level seemed to have no consistent effect on client expectancies of duration or on any of the outcome measures (as judged by clients or by ongoing counselors).

3. *Are clients' pre-counseling feelings about the time limit related to their post-counseling satisfaction?*

This question was oriented toward determining whether clients who were initially unperturbed by the time limits later felt disturbed by the brevity of their counseling. Thus, to answer the question, Pearson product-moment correlations were done, relating clients' pre-intake expectancies of counseling duration with various post-counseling measures of satisfaction.

First, we examined the relationship of clients' duration expectancies to their post-counseling satisfaction with the time limits; these variables were found to be unrelated ($r = .33$, $df = 8$, $p > .05$). Next, we were interested in seeing whether clients' post-counseling perceptions about whether they would seek more counseling were related to their initial duration expectancies, since it was possible that clients with initial desires for more counseling may have expected to seek more after TLT. The analysis, however, showed no such relationship ($r = -.06$, $df = 8$, $p > .05$). Thus, at least for this quite limited sample, clients' initial expectancies of duration gave no indication of how they would later feel about the time limit or about whether they wanted more counseling beyond that limit.

We then expanded the question to see whether clients' pre-counseling feelings about the time limit were related to their *counselors'* post-counseling perceptions. Pearson correlation coefficients were calculated to investigate each possible relationship of variables. As was true for clients' satisfaction with the time limits, counselors' satisfaction with the time limits seemed not to be related to clients' initial duration expectancies ($r = -.34$, $df = 13$, $p > .05$). However, unlike clients' perceptions of their likelihood of seeking further counseling, counselors' perceptions of that likelihood were significantly related to clients' precounseling expectancies of duration ($r = -.62$, $df = 13$, $p > .05$). Thus, the *smaller* the number of sessions the client originally expected, the *more* probable it was that the counselor believed the client would seek more counseling.

In answer to our hypothetical question, then, clients' initial feelings about the time limit were not related to their post-counseling satisfaction with duration or with counseling. A mixed picture is presented when considering whether clients' initial feelings about the time limit related to counselors' post-counseling satisfaction with duration.

4. *Are different indices of client satisfaction interrelated? Are different indices of counselor satisfaction interrelated?*

Here, our interest was in the relationships among the three outcome measures for both clients and counselors. Pearson correlations were calculated to determine the relationship between general satisfaction with counseling, satisfaction with the time limits, and likelihood of seeking further counseling.

For clients, none of these relationships was significant. That is, clients' general satisfaction with counseling was not related to their satisfaction with the time limit ($r = .25$, $df = 22$, $p > .05$) or to their perceived likelihood of seeking further counseling ($r = -.17$, $df = 22$, $p > .05$). Interestingly, then, we find that being satisfied or dissatisfied with one aspect of counseling is not predictive of clients' responses to other outcome indices.

Similarly, the counselor outcome measures were not related to each other. There was no significant relationship between counselors' general satisfaction with the counseling and their satisfaction with the time limit ($r = -.07$, $df = 33$, $p > .05$) or between counselors' general satisfaction and counselors' perceptions of the clients' likelihood of seeking further counseling ($r = .30$, $df = 33$, $p > .05$). Counselors' satisfaction with the time limit also did not relate to their perceptions of the clients' likelihood of seeking further counseling ($r = .28$, $df = 33$, $p > .05$).

In sum, an individual's (whether client or counselor) judgments about the outcome of counseling were not unitary or interrelated: general satisfaction, satisfaction with time limits, and likelihood of seeking further counseling seemed to be independently formed opinions, for both clients and counselors.

5. *Do client and counselor perceptions of outcome differ?*

Because we suspected that clients and counselors might have very different outcome criteria, we examined the relationship of clients' outcome judgments to counselors'. Specifically, we investigated whether clients and counselors differed in general satisfaction, satisfaction with the time limit, client's likelihood of seeking further counseling, and the number of more sessions that would have been desired (if dissatisfied with the time limit).

Three of these measures showed no significant difference between clients and counselors. The participants were similar in their general satisfaction (on a 5-point Likert scale, with 5 = very satisfied, Client M = 4.13, Counselor M = 3.65; t = 1.66, df = 22, p > .05) and in their perceptions of the client's likelihood of seeking further counseling (on a 5-point Likert scale, with 5 = very likely, Client M = 3.13, Counselor M = 3.39; t = .47, df = 22, p > .05). On a 5-point Likert scale, with 5 = "time limit was very sufficient," clients (M = 3.17) did not differ significantly on satisfaction with the time limit from counselors (M = 2.30, t = 1.66, df = 22, p > .05), although a possible trend may be noted (at the p < .10 level) toward clients being more satisfied than counselors.

In contrast, clients and counselors did differ significantly on the fourth measure. Fewer clients (n = 7) than counselors (n = 20) were dissatisfied with the time limit and, when dissatisfied, clients would have desired fewer additional sessions beyond the time limit (M = 12.43 sessions) than dissatisfied counselors would have wanted (M = 38.95, t = 2.27, df = 25, p < .05).

In answer to the question, then, there were few statistically different perceptions of outcome when comparing clients and counselors. We suspect, however, that our small sample may have obscured possible differences; of the four types of outcome scales, three showed clients being more satisifed by at least ½ point on the 5-point Likert scale. While such evidence is only suggestive, it does fit with the significant result of clients wanting fewer additional sessions than did counselors when dissatisfied with the time limit.

Discussion

The complexity of issues raised in a study of this nature is highlighted in our results by their lack of conclusive support of our hypotheses. Yet, we found some potentially important and suggestive ideas that in some cases were quite unexpected. To evaluate the results most cogently, we discuss them as they relate to each of our initial research questions.

1. How much counseling do clients really want or need?

The great majority of our clients believed before beginning counseling that they wanted or needed fewer than 12 sessions, and very few after being informed of the time limit believed that 12 sessions would be inadequate. These findings are congruent with those of Garfield and Wolpin (1963), who found that 70% of their patients in an outpatient psychiatric clinic expected 10 or fewer therapy sessions. As Hoffman and Remmel (1975) noted, most clients do not want long-term therapy.

Our concern that our clients may be dismayed at the time limit appear to arise more from our own projections than from any evidence from our clients. Nationwide surveys have found typical outpatient therapy length to be quite brief, about

5–6 sessions (Bloom, 1981), and Gurman (1981) noted that the notion of longer therapy is due to "therapists' traditional and idealized standards regarding treatment length" (p. 417), rather than because of the actualities. Indeed, clients may have more realistic duration expectancies than do their therapists (Garfield, 1978).

Accordingly, we see it as very important to focus on the clients' perceptions of counseling, rather than our own. Instead of assuming that a time limit is perceived negatively by clients, we must acknowledge the reality that most (although not all) clients would not see such a limit as restrictive. We found no evidence that prior knowledge of the time limit discouraged potential clients from seeking counseling; indeed, we might hypothesize that a limit might meet with relief from some potential clients who would otherwise fear becoming involved in long-term therapy.

2. Is there a relationship between client adjustment and client reaction to the time limit?

In essence, here we were inquiring whether clients expecting a longer duration were more or less disturbed than others. Rather surprisingly, we found no such relationship, in contrast to the findings of two other studies (Chapters 2 and 6) that did find a relationship between adjustment and satisfaction with and appropriateness of TLT. In light of these two studies, why would our findings be so discrepant? We believe the discrepancy may be at least partially due to the concept labeled "felt disturbance" (Truax and Carkhuff, 1967), as distinct from overt disturbance preceivable by others. Felt disturbance, or internally experienced maladjustment, was the concept used by McKitrick and Gelso (Chapter 6) and by Gelso et al. (Chapter 2), while the current study operationalized adjustment as the judgment of the intake counselor. Thus, in this study, clients' awareness of their adjustment levels may or may not have been consistent with the counselor ratings. Similarly, when post-first-interview counselor ratings of adjustment were used in Chapter 4, disturbance level was unrelated to outcome in TLT. We are suggesting, then, that the *client's* awareness of emotional difficulties may be more important in determining TLT appropriateness and effectiveness than is a more objective (or, at least, more distant) measure of adjustment. As summarized by Garfield (1978), the literature indicates that clients who experience anxiety early in therapy may have the best prognosis. We suspect that therapists' early perceptions of client adjustment are not necessarily correlated with felt disturbance, and thus that clients' duration expectancies may be more related to felt disturbance than to therapist-judged adjustment level. While this speculation is as yet untested, we do know that there is no relationship between clients' duration expectancies and their counselors' initial perceptions of the clients' adjustment levels.

Two other explanations are also postulated as reasons for our lack of significant results. First, it is possible that the less adjusted clients made an effort to appear healthier, manifested perhaps in lowered duration expectancies. If this conjecture were true, then less adjusted clients would have duration expectancies similar to those of better adjusted clients, but for different reasons. Another interpretation rests on measurement method; in this study, adjustment was rated on a scale with little range. If adjustment is indeed related to clients' duration expectancies, this scale may have been too homogenous to pick up true differences.

3. *Were clients' pre-counseling feelings about the time limit related to their post-counseling satisfaction?*

Initial duration expectancies were found to be unrelated to clients' and counselors' overall satisfaction with counseling and to clients' (but not counselors') satisfaction with the time limit. The only post-counseling variable that was related to these pre-counseling expectancies was counselors' perceptions of clients' likelihood of seeking further counseling; students who initially expected just a few counseling sessions were judged by their counselors to be more likely to seek additional counseling after termination than those students who initially expected the greater number of sessions.

Why did clients' initial expectancies have so little impact on outcome ratings? And why was the one rating that did relate to expectancies this particular variable? The answer to the first question may be addressed by looking at other literature investigating these variables. In a review of such studies, Garfield (1978) concluded that the results are quite mixed as to whether clients' expectancies relate to outcome; our results, then, are not surprising given the general inconclusiveness in this area. To attempt to make sense of this lack of cohesive findings, Perotti and Hopewell (1976) speculated that after undertaking treatment ongoing beliefs, not initial expectancies, may be the more relevant factor in determining outcome. As mentioned in the introduction to this chapter, before treatment begins a client may have inadequate information on which to base expectancies. It may be only during the therapy process that the client begins to have well-formed expectancies about duration. Thus, clients may not initially be "turned off" by the time limits, but later they may or may not find that the time limit is constricting.

The fact that clients' duration expectancies were inversely related to their counselors' perceptions of their likelihood of obtaining more counseling may indicate that some of those clients with low duration expectancies may have had a tendency to minimize their own needs, perhaps defensively. That is, some of those who had low estimates might have initially been more psychologically naive, and thus their counselors (but not they themselves) believed they would get further help. We do not want to make too much of this one relationship, since it is the only one out of six in this section of the analyses that was significant. At this point we can only conclude that clients' pre-counseling duration expectancies seem to matter very little to the outcome of TLT.

4. *Are different indices of client satisfaction interrelated? Are different indices of counselor satisfaction interrelated?*

Our findings indicated that none of the three outcome measures in our study related to one another for clients or for counselors. These results are probably most attributable to individual differences. For instance, we had subjects who reported being satisfied with the time limit and also satisfied with counseling; while others, satisifed with the time limit, expressed dissatisfaction with the counseling. Similar variability was found for each of the three outcome measures, resulting in a canceling out of effects.

This finding is a particularly interesting one, since we would have expected a global "halo" (or "anti-halo") effect of counseling that causes clients to rate various aspects of the counseling similarly. Our results suggest that the issue of time limits may influence feelings in a way quite independent from the influence of general satisfaction, and that neither of these variables necessarily indicates whether further counseling is probable. A vivid illustration of this point was the comment of one client who, although quite satisfied with the counseling in general, was dissatisfied with the time limit because, he said, it was like "learning how to drive and then running out of gas." We must be careful, then, not to automatically assume counseling is dissatisfying if clients dislike the time limits, or that pursuing further counseling necessarily means that clients were dissatisfied with the time limits. Further research on TLT should carefully distinguish among these variables. Part of this problem may also be due to the generality of satisfaction questions; perhaps using outcome measures that specifically relate to the client's presenting problem may yield better outcome data in TLT. Asking a client to rate satisfaction with counseling outcomes regarding the presenting problem may be more appropriate to TLT than asking for general satisfaction.

5. Do client and counselor perceptions of outcome differ?

Clients and counselors were similarly satisfied with counseling in general and had similar perceptions of the clients' likelihood of seeking further counseling. However, clients tended to be more satisfied with the time limit and wanted significantly fewer additional sessions when dissatisfied than did the counselors.

As we discussed at the beginning of this chapter, we as counselors have often made the assumption that because we tend to dislike time limits our clients also will. This result, particularly viewed in conjunction with several of our other results, sheds doubt on that assumption. Our clients seemed neither to initially desire a larger number of sessions than the time limit allowed nor to ultimately experience major frustration with the time limit. We suspect that the counselors' goals may have been more extensive than those of the clients, so that more time would have been necessary for the counselors to work in the way that many desired. (It may be noted in this regard that Johnson [Chapter 7] did find counselors having fairly extensive goals for TLT.) This difference between clients and counselors may also be related to counselors' clinical experience and expertise affording them a superior view of their clients' therapeutic needs in order for real lasting change to occur. There must be a balance, however difficult, between choosing therapies in accordance with our clients' (the consumers') wishes and choosing therapies in accordance with professionals' knowledge. This balance, we believe, is the challenge that TLT presents to us.

Limitations and Implications

Results of this study were far less dramatic than we had anticipated, and due to small sample sizes are at times difficult to interpret. We found significant results in 3 out of 16 instances with all other results nonsignificant. Since by chance alone nearly this many of the analyses could have been significant (Sakoda, Cohen, and Beall, 1954), we must consider our results only suggestive, needing to be further confirmed. As we mentioned earlier, the applied and evaluative nature of our research questions prohibits laboratory conditions and thus greatly reduces the amount of control possible. We found that we endured imperfect measures, a smaller than desirable sample, and less precise statistics than we would have liked. Nonetheless, the findings give some good basic information against which to check our assumptions about therapy and about TLT in particular.

How can our findings be applied to counseling agencies considering the merits or liabilities of implementing TLT? First, the reluctance of some agencies to use a time limit has revolved around concern that fewer clients will use the counseling services and will be disappointed with the limit. In fact, our results show clients initially expecting even fewer sessions than the limit of 12, and being quite satisfied by their TLT at the end. Furthermore, it was the *counselors* who were more dissatisfied with the time limit than the clients. Thus, agency reluctance about using a time limit may revolve around counselor attitudes about TLT—quite a different story. Since this group of counselors had undergone rather extensive in-service training about using TLT and had actively made the choice that the agency should implement a TLT policy, we suggest that further investigation into the source of counselors' ambivalent attitudes should take place. Perhaps counselors hold the belief that clients are not satisfied with TLT, and would alter their attitudes if this belief were shown to be untrue. We suspect, however, that part of this attitude may be due to the perception that TLT is more superficial and less inherently interesting to do, an attitude that is undoubtedly harder for an agency to combat.

We have mentioned the need to replicate this study, particularly to increase the number of subjects in the final sample. Other research studies suggested by the current one include exploring the nature of concerns and subsequent counseling for those clients who initially expect relatively long-term work. Such investigation would aid in identifying those clients for whom referral out of intake is recommended, and perhaps circumvent some counselor discomfort with TLT. We suspect that, in the final analysis, as in so many other areas, it will be found that TLT works well for many (but not all) clients with many concerns and with many counselors, and that a partial TLT policy is more sensible than either a completely open-ended TUT policy or an absolute TLT policy for everyone (as noted in the Addendum to Chapter 2). Until the time when we can more clearly delineate the boundary conditions for such policies, however, we need to keep in mind the differences between counselors' feelings and clients' feelings about TLT.

REFERENCES

BLOOM, B. L. Focused single-session therapy: Initial development and evaluation. In S. H. Budman (Ed.), *Forms of brief therapy*. New York: Guilford Press, 1981.

COUNSELING CENTER STAFF. Inter-judge agreement on the use of counseling categories. *Journal of College Student Personnel*, 1966, *7*, 213–217.

GARFIELD, S. L. Research on client variables in psychotherapy. In S. L. Garfield and A. E. Bergin (Eds.), *Handbook of psychotherapy and behavior change: An empirical analysis*. New York: Wiley, 1978.

GARFIELD, S. L., & WOLPIN. M. Expectancies regarding psychotherapy. *Journal of Nervous and Mental Disease*, 1963, *137*, 353–362.

GELSO, C. J. Methodological and professional issues. *The Counseling Psychologist*, 1979, *8*, 7–36.

GURMAN, A. S. Integrative marital therapy: Toward the development of an interpersonal approach. In S. H. Budman (Ed.), *Forms of brief therapy*. New York: Guilford Press, 1981.

HOFFMAN, D. L., & REMMEL, M. L. Uncovering the precipitant in crisis intervention. *Social Casework*, 1975, *56*, 259–267.

JOHNSON, D. H., & GELSO, C. J. The effectiveness of time limits in counseling and psychotherapy: A critical review. *The Counseling Psychologist*, 1980, *9*, 70–83.

MANN, J. *Time-limited psychotherapy*. Cambridge: Harvard University Press, 1973.

PEROTTI, L. P., & HOPEWELL, C. A. *Expectancy effects in psychotherapy and systematic desensitization: A review*. Paper presented at the Seventh Annual Meeting of the Society for Psychotherapy Research, June 18, 1976, San Diego, California.

SAKODA, J. M., COHEN, B. H., & BEALL, G. Test of significance for a series of statistical tests. *Psychological Reports*, 1954, *31*, 172–175.

TRUAX, C. B., & CARKHUFF, R. R. *Toward effective counseling and psychotherapy*. Chicago: Aldine, 1967.

9

The Process of Time-Limited Therapy

Jacque Moss Miller, Christine A. Courtois,
Judy P. Pelham, Phyliss Elayne Riddle,
Sharon Baron Spiegel, Charles J. Gelso,
and Deborah Hazel Johnson

In the preceding chapters, TLT was explored through examining various pre- and post-therapy variables. Due to those studies, we had a much better idea of how TLT affects our clients, but found ourselves lacking adequate knowledge of what actually occurs *during* TLT. Conceptually, major review articles (Butcher & Koss, 1978; Johnson & Gelso, 1980) suggested that the TLT process seems to be qualitatively different from TUT; no empirical study, however, had actually examined the nature of TLT. The present study, then, was designed to investigate client behavior throughout the course of TLT.

Toward this end, we chose to investigate the predominant conceptual model of TLT used in our Counseling Center, that of James Mann (1973). Mann's model provides a comprehensive approach to TLT based on his clinical observations, but has not been researched in an empirical fashion. Our study was designed to test Mann's model as well as to generally examine the process of TLT. Rather than manipulating any variables, our interest was to observe TLT as it occurs naturally.

According to Mann's model, TLT should be conducted within a 12-session limit (a number that he reports was selected arbitrarily). The 12-session model includes time limitation as an important process variable along with other factors that have been found in his clinical work to be essential for the success of therapy. These other factors include limited, specified goals, counselor directiveness and optimism, client expectancies of improvement, and selection of clients who are not severely depressed or acutely psychotic. Mann's model is a process model in which he describes TLT as a "sequence of dynamic events" that include the proscription of time, the definition of a focal problem, and distinct stages or phases of therapy, each with its significant issues and client behaviors.

Mann's theoretical stages set the framework for our study. During the first three or four sessions, a client experiences rapid symptomatic improvement in the presenting problems. While the client may bring up many issues, the therapist is urged to focus on the central issue of the therapy. The time limit is discussed directly by the therapist, but the client is so elated by beginning the process that the early sessions are characterized more by client positiveness than by dissatisfaction with the time limit. Soon, however, the therapists' insistence on discussing only the central issue causes the client to feel disappointment at initial magical expectations not being fulfilled. The client's disappointment leads to resistance by the seventh or eighth session, manifested by in-session behavior, negative transference, or scheduling problems. After struggling with these reactions, the client comes to accept the reality of limitations, and termination issues take precedence in the last three or four sessions. During the last portion of therapy, there is real progress. In these stages and issues, there are slight individual client variations, but, according to Mann, the stages are remarkably equal for different clients and therapists.

Thus, according to Mann's psychoanalytic model, clients in TLT go through a series of distinct and predictable stages. As described previously (Chapter 2), therapists in our agency had received in-service training on TLT using the Mann model, but their general theoretical orientations were diverse as a group. The present study was developed as a preliminary test of the extent to which Mann's model is valid for a general group of therapists. Are Mann's stages true of TLT in general, or are they valid only for psychoanalytically oriented TLT? The purpose of the study, then, was to empirically test the model in three ways. First, we hoped to determine if stages or phases do exist during TLT, with special attention to the question of whether there are differences in client behavior in various segments of counseling. Second, the study sought a beginning understanding of how regularly these stages occur, that is, their pervasiveness with different clients and therapists. Finally, we sought to find out if the ordering of stages across counseling was consistent with Mann's clinical theory on this matter.

Method

Subjects

Six senior staff therapists (three males and three females) of various theoretical orientations participated in the study. Each agreed to complete a questionnaire following each counseling session for a small number of their TLT clients. Therapists were permitted to select which of their clients to include, but were cautioned to select those who would be likely to complete TLT by the end of the present study (16 weeks after the beginning of the study). Two therapists each had three clients in the study; others had one or two clients.

As in the preceding chapters, clients were university students seeking help for personal-social concerns. In this chapter, data are reported for clients who met the following criteria: (a) They were in time-limited counseling, (b) had completed therapy by the end of the present study, (c) had attended at least eight sessions, and (d) had attended at least 80% of their therapy sessions or had questionnaires completed on at least 80% of their therapy sessions. (Note: Due to staff's occasional use of flexible contracting with TLT, a few time-limited clients may receive 13 or 14 sessions rather than 12.) Twelve clients met all four criteria.

Instrument

A questionnaire (Appendix P) was developed to gather information pertinent to the testing of Mann's model. The questionnaire was a 51-item inventory, with 4 Likert items and 47 items to be checked by the therapist if applicable for a given session. The following demographic information was requested: client's name or pseudonym, session and week numbers, and type of therapy contract (i.e., TUT, 12-session TLT, or TLT more than 12 sessions). The questionnaire was divided into seven sections: (a) scheduling, (b) mention of time limits, (c) counseling goals, (d) satisfaction/dissatisfaction, (e) resistance, (f) termination, and (g) miscellaneous items to address other issues. For 47 of the items, therapists were asked to check those items corresponding to client behavior or dynamics that had been observed during the particular session being rated. On 4 of the items, therapists were asked to indicate, on a 9-point Likert scale, how specific the client's goals were, how satisfied the client was with the therapists and the therapy session, and how resistant the client was during the session.

Procedure

The study was an observational one, with no manipulation of variables. The six therapists, unaware of the purpose of the study, completed one questionnaire for each of their clients following every scheduled appointment, regardless of whether the client actually attended. If the client failed to keep the appointment, the therapists were instructed to complete only the requested demographic and scheduling sections of the questionnaire.

The longitudinal data for each client were then divided into fourths corresponding to each fourth or quarter of therapy. This division was judged to be most theoretically similar to Mann's formulations, since he alludes to certain behaviors being more likely to occur during the first three sessions, other occurrences being more frequent in sessions 4, 5, and 6, and so on. Thus, dividing the data according to quarters of therapy facilitated comparison and contrast with Mann's model.

Results

A series of one-way analyses of variance (ANOVA's) for repeated measures was done to investigate the effect of quarter of therapy (first, second, third, or fourth quarter) on the various dependent variables. First, the ANOVA's for observed in-session behavior are discussed; later, we present results of the Likert scales. To obtain scores for the observed behavior variables, percentages of items checked were summed for each category (percentages rather than frequencies were used to allow within-quarter, between-item comparison). These percentages are presented for each item, by quarter of therapy, in Table 9–1. The questionnaire items were clustered by categories, so that the dependent variables were scheduling, time limits, goal setting, resistance, and termination. Following all statistically significant ANOVA's, we used Tukey's Honestly Significant Difference test (HSD; Winer, 1971) to determine where the differences between means occurred.

For the sake of clarity, we discuss the results according to categories. Subsequently, we provide a more integrated summary of these results. The alpha level was set at .05.

Scheduling

Mann hypothesized that clients are disappointed in mid-therapy after the rapid symptomatic improvement seen in the first quarter of TLT. He noted that clients may act out this disappointment through not attending sessions, arriving late, leaving early, and so on. Thus, we expected to find more scheduling difficulties in the second and perhaps third quarters of TLT.

Table 9–1.   Mean Percentages of Items Checked, by Quarter of Therapy

	Quarter of therapy				
	1	2	3	4	
Item	*M*	*M*	*M*	*M*	*F ratio*
Scheduling	2.92	19.17	3.75	2.42	24.43***
Time limits	21.25	8.75	5.75	28.83	24.41***
Goals	16.00	25.67	28.33	29.83	9.72***
Resistance	9.67	12.25	30.00	11.75	32.66***
Termination	1.92	4.25	5.08	32.83	50.45***

*** $p < .0001$

Indeed, there were differences in the number of scheduling issues across the different quarters of TLT. Following the significant ANOVA that demonstrated such overall differences, we calculated Tukey's HSD to determine which therapy quarters had more scheduling issues than others. The second quarter of therapy (usually around sessions 4–6) had many more scheduling issues than any other quarter. As shown in Table 9–1, the mean for the second quarter was much higher than the means for all other quarters ($p < .01$), and the first, third and fourth quarters were quite similar to one another in discussion of scheduling issues.

Time Limits

Mann noted that clients would discuss time limits initially and toward the end of therapy, since it is at the beginning and at the end that the limits become most salient. We hypothesized, then, that discussion of time limits would occur more in the first and last quarters of TLT than in the middle.

Our results confirmed this hypothesis. The ANOVA, as shown in Table 9–1, found overall differences among the therapy quarters in the discussion of time limits. According to Tukey's HSD test, the first quarter had more such discussion than did the second and third quarters, and the last quarter also was concerned with time limits more than were the second and third quarters ($p < .01$).

Discussion of Counseling Goals

Mann particularly emphasizes the importance of discussing goals early in TLT. Thus, it was anticipated that counseling goals would be discussed more often in the first quarter than in any of the later quarters.

Again the hypothesis was confirmed by the results. Following a significant ANOVA, which showed that differences exist across the therapy quarters, Tukey's HSD test indicated that these differences occurred between the first quarter and each of the other quarters ($p < .01$). Clients and counselors did deal with goals as a more central issue initially as compared to later in TLT.

Resistance

In Mann's model, protective symptoms and manifestations of negative transference occur at about the seventh or eighth session of TLT. In the present study, we hypothesized that resistance in general would be more predominant in the third quarter.

The findings were consistent with this hypothesis. A significant ANOVA found differences among the quarters, with the third quarter having more client resistance than the other quarters, as demonstrated by Tukey's HSD ($p < .01$).

Termination

Termination is a particularly important point of TLT, according to Mann's conceptualization. Mann stated that clients and counselors do (and should) spend much of their last few sessions discussing termination and dealing with its related issues. Accordingly it was expected that the last quarter of TLT would be more characterized by discussion of termination than would the preceding quarters.

Again, the results were confirmatory of the hypothesis. Following a significant ANOVA that showed an effect of quarter of therapy, we did Tukey's HSD to determine which quarters differed from the others. Clients dealt most frequently with termination issues during the fourth quarter of therapy, compared with the other three quarters ($p < .01$). While the HSD detected a significant heightening of termination discussion in the last quarter, examination of the data reveals that as TLT got closer to the end there was a trend toward discussing termination more frequently. Thus, the second quarter had slightly (but nonsignificantly) more termination discussion than did the first; such discussions also increased from the second to the third quarters, but in a nonsignificant way; but then there was a large and statistically significant increase in termination discussions from the third to the fourth quarters.

The above results are based on those parts of the questionnaire on which therapists checked client behaviors that occurred in the sessions. In addition to these checklists, therapists were also asked to rate on 9-point Likert scales the specificity of goals, the extent of client satisfaction with the session and with the therapist, and the amount of resistance during the session. In contrast to the previous analyses, which examined whether the *occurrence* of certain behaviors was influenced by therapy quarter, these analyses investigated the effect of therapy quarter on the *extent* to which the various dimensions were characteristic of the session. Table 9–2 presents the results of the ANOVA's performed on each of these Likert scales.

Table 9–2.   Analyses of Variance for the Four Likert-Scale Items
by Quarter of Therapy

Item	MS	F	p
Specificity of goals	684.03	2.28	.092
Client satisfaction with session	52.58	.40	.751
Client satisfaction with therapist	18.75	.14	.936
Amount of resistance	3,061.08	15.01	.0001

Specificity of Goals

No hypothesis had been made regarding the effect of therapy quarter on goal specificity, since Mann does not suggest that this variable changes over the course of TLT. Indeed, according to the therapists' ratings, goals were no more and no less specific in any one quarter of TLT than in the others.

Client Satisfaction with the Sessions

Mann's theory indicates that clients become more dissatisfied with TLT during the third quarter, but overcome this feeling in the final quarter. Accordingly, it was anticipated that there would be an effect of therapy quarter on client satisfaction with the sessions, so that satisfaction scores would be lowest in the third quarter. In contrast to this hypothesis, the ANOVA demonstrated no differences among therapy quarters in therapists' perceptions of client satisfaction with the session.

Client Satisfaction with the Therapist

Similar to the above conceptualization, a hypothesis based on Mann's model would suggest that clients would display less satisfaction with their therapists during the third quarter. As in the previous results, we found no such difference across therapy quarters on therapists' perceptions of their clients' satisfaction with them.

Amount of Resistance

Mann saw the third quarter of TLT as a time of client resistance, often manifested by negative reactions and protective symptoms. The consequent hypothesis in this study stated that resistance scores would be higher in the third quarter. Indeed, as shown in Table 9–2, there was a significant difference in resistance across therapy quarters. Using Tukey's HSD to find where this difference occurred, we found that therapists saw more client resistance ($p < .05$) during the third quarter ($M = 7.5$ on a 9-point scale) than in any of the other quarters (first quarter $M = 4.1$; second quarter $M = 5.0$; fourth quarter $M = 4.1$). Thus, the hypothesis based on Mann's model was confirmed regarding client resistance.

Summary of Results

Findings indicated that certain client behaviors do occur more regularly in particular TLT stages. In the first quarter of TLT, discussion of time limits and of counseling goals occur with high frequency. The second quarter is characterized by scheduling problems. In the third quarter, a high percentage of resistance behaviors in sessions occur, as well as therapists seeing the *extent* of resistance in each third-quarter session being quite high. However, client satisfaction with therapist and with sessions is *not* lower in the third quarter. Finally, time limits and termination issues are frequently discussed during the fourth quarter.

Discussion

Mann's model of the manner in which TLT unfolds was highly supported and validated in this study. Mann's model is presented fairly informally regarding the timing of the stages, so it was necessary for us to make several inferences in tightening the specificity of the stages. The model, however, was remarkably replicated in our study. In all but two cases, our results were identical to those hypothesized in his model. Both Mann's model and our results, then, demonstrate a developmental sequence of the TLT process. Initially, clients deal primarily with the structure of their projected course of therapy, focusing on time limits and counseling goals in a planful way (and, Mann would add, being rapidly relieved of their symptoms, although we did not obtain empirical evidence on this point). After about the third session of such planning, clients may become resentful of the time limit and act upon this feeling by raising scheduling problems. This resistance heightens by the sixth to ninth sessions, and during this stage may be shown more by the client's behavior within the sessions. After struggling with their annoyance at these limits, clients reach more acceptance of them by about the tenth session and are then ready to work through termination issues.

    Let us look at a few of our results in more depth, before sketching some implications of the results in general. Two variables that had results contrary to those hypothesized were (a) client satisfaction with the session and (b) client satisfaction with the therapist. According to Mann, client satisfaction would be lower during the third quarter of therapy than during other times. Our data, however, showed no such decrement of either type of satisfaction, with all quarters of therapy having about the same amount of satisfaction. At least insofar as client satisfaction can be perceived by the therapist, the fact that clients resist more in the third quarter of TLT does not indicate lessened satisfaction. It is quite possible that while clients behaviorally resist the limitations of TLT at this stage, on another level the clients are accepting of the necessity for such limitations. Resistance may be more a matter of fear of making changes or of going into greater depth on personal issues, rather than being indicative of discouragement or disappointment with the therapy.

    While the remainder of our results were statistically significant and supportive of Mann's model (with the possible exception of the goals specificity variables, not mentioned by Mann), it is interesting to note one piece of data hidden by our method of analysis. In examining therapy by quarters, we totaled data over several sessions. For the termination variable, we found that the fourth therapy quarter was characterized by much work on termination, as Mann suggested. Looking more specifically, however, at the number of sessions actually spent on termination, we find an average of only 1.3 sessions attending to termination, rather than the three or so mentioned by Mann; and even these 1.3 sessions may have only noted in passing, rather than focusing exclusively on, termination issues. Two possible explanations for this discrepancy occur to us. First, since the therapists were using their own clinical intuition in structuring the sessions, Mann may have overstated the number of sessions necessary for termination discussions. With such brief therapy, spending proportionately more of the time on the central focus and proportionately less on therapy issues such as termination may be most appropriate. This explanation assumes the therapists were right and Mann was wrong; an alternative explanation does just the opposite. Viewing as correct Mann's postulation that termination is the very essence of TLT, we could interpret the small amount of termination discussion as due to the therapists' own resistance to termination (an occurrence that Mann sees as normal). Thus, the therapists may have colluded with the clients in postponing dealing with termination. Since either of the above explanations assumes that there is one right way, before accepting either explanation we must acquire information linking termination discussion to TLT effectiveness. Does spending less time on termination fail to allow the client to learn to cope adequately with separation, as Mann would suggest, or does it instead offer a productively longer time to spend on the client's stated concerns and other problems, as our therapists seemed to think?

Stepping back from the specific results, let us conclude by taking a look at the overall implications of the results. The main purpose of the study was to investigate empirically the stages of TLT postulated by Mann, to see if these stages occur with eclectic rather than psychoanalytic therapists. What is the meaning of the fact that the Mann model was primarily confirmed?

The major importance of the results lies in the empirically demonstrated occurrence of the TLT stages across diverse types of therapists. While Mann's model assumes a psychoanalytic orientation, the TLT stages occurred in this study with therapists who were trained in doing TLT à la Mann but whose varying orientations meant that they did not necessarily do TLT according to the Mann model. Furthermore, the stages seemed to occur without the therapists making explicit efforts to produce them. Thus, there are certain predictable stages in TLT that, we suggest, may be more a function of the impact of the time limit than of a particular model of TLT or type of therapist.

A therapist beginning to do TLT would therefore be well-advised to know about and expect these distinct phases along with their salient issues. With such knowledge, a therapist can be more sensitized to the existence and meaning of certain client behaviors, and perspective could be provided for clients by telling them that their experiences as clients are part of the normal TLT process. Conversely, when a client fails to demonstrate some of the expected behavior, a therapist may be cued to see this lack as a diagnostic indicator (e.g., a client who does not exhibit some of the predicted behaviors may not be ego-involved in the therapy).

While this study explored and answered some of the basic questions about the process of TLT, several important unanswered questions remain to be studied. First, we do not yet know to what extent the stages in TLT are different from or similar to those in TUT. Could these same stages occur across the longer quarters of TUT, or might some of the stage behaviors characterize the initial dozen sessions of any type of therapy? It would seem probable that certain behaviors such as resistance to time limits are distinctive to TLT, and others, such as resistance to change, occur in both TLT and TUT; but further research is needed to investigate this hypothesis. Second, focusing on TLT alone, it will be important to determine whether the process of effective TLT differs from the process of ineffective TLT. For example, is progression through all four stages necessary for TLT to be successful? Finally, we wonder about moderating variables in the stages. Which client variables predict the rate of client progress through the various stages? Clearly we have only begun to understand what occurs during TLT; further understanding of this process and linkages of process to outcome can help us to better help our TLT clients.

REFERENCES

BUTCHER, J., & KOSS, M. Research on brief and crisis-oriented therapies. In S. Garfield & A. Bergin (Eds.), *Handbook of psychotherapy and behavior change*. New York: Wiley, 1978.

JOHNSON, D. H., & GELSO, C. J. The effectiveness of time limits in counseling and psychotherapy: A critical review. *The Counseling Psychologist*, 1980, *9*, 70–83.

MANN, J. *Time-limited psychotherapy*. Cambridge: Harvard University Press, 1973.

WINER, B. J. *Statistical principles in experimental design*. New York: McGraw-Hill, 1971.

PART FOUR

Conclusion

10

A Summing Up: Toward an Understanding of the Process and Outcomes of Time-Limited Therapy

As we learn so well when doing time-limited therapy, all things must come to an end. We have defined and circumscribed a problem area, explored many of its nuances, attempted to gain insight and answers (as well as raising more refined questions). Finally, we must cope with perhaps the most difficult task of all: to draw some conclusions, integrate our learnings, spell out future directions, and end, even in the knowledge that all is not nearly done. Accomplishing this task with this book is not unlike that with a time-limited client, and therein lies part of the intrigue of TLT. Endings and limits are crucial and critical components of nearly every aspect of life; yet few of us have mastered the task of dealing with them gracefully.

Again, as with TLT, our book ending will look both behind and ahead. In this chapter, we see some patterns in the diverse findings explored in more detail in the previous chapters. This chapter begins by sketching some aspects of effectiveness in TLT, initially comparing TLT with TUT very generally, and then filling in the details of client, counselor, and situational variables that allow TLT to be most effective. Next we discuss the TLT process—what *is* this treatment we have been studying? Finally, we look to the future by suggesting research directions that have yet to be explored.

Since empirical scrutiny of TLT is very recent indeed, the findings described in this book are but a beginning. To put our results in a more general context, and to test the validity and reliability to these findings, this chapter integrates our findings and clinical experience with existing literature. The early results in any field are inevitably amplified and modified by further research; we expect research on TLT to be no exception. Limitations of these studies and conclusions have been discussed in the preceding chapters. In this final summary chapter, despite the obviously preliminary nature of our findings, we have chosen to present them without constant qualification, since this more straightforward presentation style lends itself better to a conceptual understanding of the research results. The goal of early research is to provide answers, albeit tentative, to the most pressing questions of practitioners, to build a general theoretical scaffolding, and to clarify questions that need to be asked. Thus, we would encourage the reader to consider these results as stimuli rather than the final word.

A primary objective of this final chapter is to bridge the gap between science and practice. The mesh of our researcher and practitioner roles is clearly not only the impetus for this book, but also to a large extent the origin of the field of time-limited work. The often conflicting demands on current agency practitioners are many: the administrative demand of providing more service for less money and time; the clinical demand of going beyond Band-Aid treatment to the accomplishment of stable and meaningful results; the scientific demand of studying whether one method is better than another; and the personal demand of fulfilling our own needs for intellectual stimulation and narcissistic gratification. The answers regarding TLT can meaningfully come only from an integration of all these demands: to emphasize one at the neglect of others is to negate the complex and rich nature of the field. The history of TLT stems from both clinical and scientific foundations, and it is our hope that in this final chapter we can use our own diverse roles to make sense of our research findings.

Features of TLT Effectiveness

TLT versus TUT Effectiveness

As discussed by Wilson (1981), comparisons of different treatments must include "assessment of efficacy, various cost considerations . . . and consumer satisfaction" (p. 153). The studies in this book have spanned these diverse criteria in evaluating the usage of time limits in counseling. In summarizing the comparison of time-limited therapy and time-unlimited therapy, let us focus in turn on the various evaluation criteria and their meanings for agency policy and clinical practice. As we do so, it is important to remember the difference between agency and clinical considerations. If one were evaluating a type of therapy for clinical purposes, the major criterion would probably be its effectiveness in helping a client change. In contrast, agency considerations necessitate putting increased weight on various time and cost criteria, as well as using a different decision-making strategy. Thus, an agency might decide in favor of a TLT policy if TLT is not clinically contraindicated, in order to save time; while a clinician might require more positive indications (rather than the absence of contraindications). In discussing our findings, we distinguish between these two strategies, but emphasize the agency considerations since TLT is typically instituted for institutional as well as clinical reasons.

First, in terms of cost consideration, we have found that TLT indeed can save an agency time and thus cost per client. In both comparison studies (Chapters 1 and 2) the average counseling duration under TLT was less than that under TUT. Several other studies reported in the literature (Henry & Shlien, 1958; Reid & Shyne, 1969; Shlien, Mosak & Dreikurs, 1962) similarly indicated that the average number of TLT sessions was less than that of TUT sessions. Such savings, of course, necessarily require the time limit to be set at a number small enough to shorten typical duration, a calculation specific to each agency. Without such a savings, the implementation of a TLT policy would probably be pointless. Having found that TLT could accomplish the administrative purpose for which it was being considered, however, we next pursued additional questions of cost-effectiveness and quality assurance.

An early clinical concern was that although TLT might save time in the short run, it may be inappropriate over time if client recidivism rates are increased. Indeed, previous studies (Henry & Shlien, 1958; Phillips & Johnston, 1954; Reid & Shyne, 1969) gave rather contradictory evidence regarding recidivism, leading us to conclude in reviewing the literature (Johnson & Gelso, 1980) that better data on return rates were needed, including both number of clients receiving more therapy and number of additional therapy sessions received. The findings reported in Chapters 2 and 3 effectively quelled our clinical concerns. Although TLT clients did have a higher rate of seeking additional help than TUT clients, the subsequent treatment was more frequently briefer than TUT clients' later treatment; and the total number of sessions for TLT clients was smaller than that for TUT clients. Perhaps a client's initial experience in counseling serves as a model for the way in which counseling is subsequently used, with TLT clients having learned to think of their goals as circumscribed and termination as inevitable. For whatever reason, TLT does save an agency time, both on initial contacts and on overall number of contacts with a given client, including contacts not in the agency of initial contact. We conclude, then, that when using contact time as the criterion, TLT is a preferable treatment regarding cost effectiveness, as compared to TUT.

Most mental health agencies would not be content to base service policies on cost-effectiveness data alone. A second criterion is consumer satisfaction: does the client population feel better or less well served by one treatment rather than the other? Here we generally found that the time-savings of TLT occurs at little or no cost to many clients, at least in their own eyes. A month after counseling termination, TLT and TUT clients felt satisfied with their counseling, their counselors, and themselves (Chapter 2). There appear to be somewhat higher overall ratings in TUT than in TLT, particularly after 18 months (Chapter 2), a finding that could have led us to conclude that TLT was less satisfying in the long run. However, client moderator variables, to be discussed later, indicated that satisfaction is mostly a function of the type of client, and that as long as we selected our clientele for TLT, satisfaction would not need to be reduced. Since most of our clients come to us expecting far less than 12 sessions (Chapter 8), it is not surprising that the shorter length of TLT did not always lead to lessened satisfaction. Indeed, clients are most often unsure about whether their counseling lasted long enough (Chapter 2), regardless of how long it did last. Clients appear to focus much more on counseling factors other than length in determining their satisfaction. Since the TUT was generally in the 20-session vicinity and therefore not really long term, we were comparing relatively short-term counseling with time-limited treatment of even briefer duration. It is not surprising, then, that these clients made little distinction between TLT and TUT. With the very important caveat that TLT clients must be carefully screened, we can thus conclude that consumers of agency mental health services similar to ours appear to be quite satisfied with TLT. One could not draw much of a distinction between TLT and TUT based on consumer satisfaction alone, at least when the difference between TLT and TUT duration is not large.

The satisfaction of clients with briefer counseling appears to be a fairly well documented finding. Gurman (1981) notes that it is mental health professionals rather than consumers who hold the myth that brief counseling is anything new or different; he goes on to cite several studies that found that most therapy contacts last less than 12 sessions. In the same vein, our review of duration and TLT studies (Johnson & Gelso, 1980) concluded that client ratings of brief therapy are quite favorable, in contrast to the less favorable ratings by therapists. In the face of such striking differences between consumer expectancies and therapist beliefs, the importance of multifaceted evaluation of the feasibility of TLT becomes particularly apparent. Therapists and clients may have quite different evaluation criteria, and it is important to assess both sets of criteria.

Although administratively it seems obvious that decision-making should be based primarily on better meeting the agency objectives (here, a good delivery system for mental health), another important, but often more hidden, criterion is the counselors' reactions. Since counselors are hired on the basis of having good professional judgment, their professional reactions should clearly be used in evaluating a treatment. In this case, our evidence showed that TLT may not be so satisfying to many counselors as it is to clients. Our counselors were rather pessimistic about the possibility of helping clients change in TLT (Chapter 7); they were less satisfied with the time limits than were their clients (Chapter 8); and when dissatisfied with the time limits, counselors wanted more additional sessions than did clients (Chapter 8). While clearly these counselors were doing good work, apparently they found the time limits rather frustrating.

It is not surprising that there would be such adverse counselor reactions to TLT. Most counselors in our studies were highly trained during graduate and postgraduate work to do longer, unlimited treatment, but only recently became familiar with TLT, and then not because of their own professional interest but through agency pressures. (See our discussion later in this chapter for the effects of TLT experience.) In the earlier study (Chapter 1), the counselors mentioned their discomfort in working with time limits, the subsequent effect of which was the development of an in-service training program in TLT and permitting counselors to still treat some percentage of their clients with TUT (Addendum, Chapter 2). A similar discomfort was found by Muench (1965), who initially found counselors unwilling to conform to a fixed time policy. Only by allowing a range of possible time limits was Muench able to enlist the counselors' cooperation sufficiently to complete the study. While TLT seems to satisfy most evaluation criteria, the one regarding counselor discomfort clearly needs to be considered at an agency level before the adoption of a TLT policy. Counselor discomfort does not necessarily affect client-based measures of TLT outcome, but it does indicate that a TLT policy can make any agency function more poorly unless effort is made to satisfy counselors as well as clients.

Why would many counselors seem so uncomfortable and pessimistic about TLT? Besides their lack of familiarity with both briefer work and time limits, it seems quite plausible that counselors may notice treatment and outcome aspects of which clients are less aware. Counselors may hope to change a client's general coping style, for example, while the client may be satisfied with alleviating the situational complaint. TLT allows little room for integrating a number of seemingly unrelated characteristics into an overall understanding of personality dynamics and behavior patterns, but necessitates a much more focused approach. Consequently, TLT may force therapists to put aside the richness of their conceptualizations in favor of a less cognitively complex viewpoint, a switch that is often at least intellectually unsatisfying and at most neglectful of some therapeutic goals. The conflict between agency time demands and counselor reactions to TLT is a strong challenge to the priorities of any mental health institution, and one to which we have no definitive answers. Ultimately, the answer must lie in an agency's serious consideration of its values, objectives, and priorities.

Finally, we are left with the ultimate criteria: efficacy. Is TLT more or less effective than TUT? Clients' self- ideal-self discrepancy scores and counselor outcome ratings were used to measure efficacy, in addition to the clients' own outcome ratings. Once again, we found little difference between TLT and TUT with better adjusted clients. TLT and TUT clients both improved equally on self-ideal-self discrepancy, and both improved more than an untreated control group (Chapter 1). Counselor ratings of client change showed no significant differences between TLT and TUT (Chapter 2), although there was a modest overall trend in favor of TUT. In another study, the counselors seemed pessimistic about personality changes after TLT as compared to TUT, whereas TLT and TUT were viewed as perhaps somewhat more similar in inducing changes in client behavior and client feelings (Chapter 7). While we must qualify the above paragraph as not necessarily true for less adjusted clients, we can conclude that TLT generally appears about equal in efficacy to TUT, with the possible important exception of effecting personality change.

The question of differential efficacy of the two treatment types is clearly a complex one. Depending on which type of change, type of client, source of measurement, and time of measurement is being considered, rather different conclusions can be drawn. Since the methodological problems of these issues are delineated at length elsewhere (Johnson & Gelso, 1980), here we find it most useful to delve into the practical implications for agency policy, beginning with a discussion of agency decision-making. Clinical usage will be discussed in further detail in the subsequent section.

When doing the empirical research on the effectiveness of TLT versus TUT, we adopted the usual researchers' stance of concluding that differences existed if a predetermined probability level was reached in the data analyses. Such a stance allowed us to place confidence in the stability of our results: that differences are "real," rather than due to chance fluctuations. When it comes to agency policy-making, however, the word *significance* takes on a rather different meaning. Here it is necessary to distinguish between practical significance and statistical significance, since statistically stable differences may be less important than some minimal level of satisfaction and treatment efficacy. For example, on the rating scale regarding others' acting as though the client had changed, the TUT clients noted significantly more change than did the TLT clients; however, both types of counseling yielded ratings somewhere between "changed for the better" and "no change." While it might be ideal to implement the more highly rated counseling structure, it would also seem that satisfactory levels of performance are achieved by both. The difference, then, between statistical and agency decision-making strategies may be that agencies can be content with "good-enough treatment," rather than necessarily optimal treatment. In our TLT research, many measures found no differences between TLT and TUT. Those areas in which we did find differences are important to note as possible limitations to TLT, but in general we found TLT to achieve quite adequate results for most clients, with superior cost-effectiveness.

Further, we must question what it is that our agency is attempting to achieve. If TLT is indeed inferior to TUT in changing personality, is this issue important enough to our agency goals to warrant rejection of TLT policy? The answer will clearly depend upon the agency, but in our case and in the cases of many publicly funded agencies, the answer is determined by our charge to serve society at large, rather than a few individuals. As Strupp and Hadley (1977) noted, clients, therapists, and society have quite different criteria of mental health. Although therapists may value personality change, neither agency clients nor society may particularly desire such change, but certainly demand an increased sense of well-being and better adjustment. Since we find TLT doing a job generally equal to TUT in accomplishing these latter goals, it would seem that TLT with its greater cost-effectiveness would be the more accountable treatment modality, if not necessarily the more acceptable to mental health professionals. In contrast, a private agency with less social accountability pressure would most likely find TUT to be a choice more congruent with helping a few clients achieve in-depth understanding and change.

Treatment Factors within TLT

If indeed TLT can often be effective when compared to TUT, our next logical question concerns the conditions under which TLT is effective. Specifically, in this and the following section, we expand and qualify the above general findings, going from the overall question of efficacy to the oft-repeated "Who, what, when, where, why, and by whom" questions (Gelso, 1979; Paul, 1967). In particular, in the current section we focus on the factors within TLT that make for heightened effectiveness. Subsequently, we examine client and counselor factors that influence overall effectiveness.

LENGTH OF TIME LIMIT. A crucial question regarding TLT effectiveness is the optimal time limit. If the shortened TLT can be just as effective as longer TUT, can this finding be extended to the extreme to suggest that 5 minutes of counseling are equivalent to 5 years of therapy? While there is a body of literature indicating the efficacy of single-session counseling (e.g., Bloom, 1981), it would seem conceptually as well as clinically obvious that certain goals may be met in a very brief contact while others require more time. Evidence from our studies (Chapters 1 and 2) indicates that 16-session TLT may be more effective than 8-session TLT, and that (perhaps most notably) the oft-found positive correlation between duration and outcome is particularly true in 8-session TLT. Even though the 16-session TLT in Chapter 2 averaged only a few more sessions than the 8-session client contacts, there appeared to be a heightened sense of effectiveness under the longer time limit.

In searching the literature for related evidence about optimal time limits, we found only scant and indirect findings. Gass (1975), comparing various TLT lengths to TUT, concluded that 8-session TLT is somewhat better than 4-session TLT, with both superior to TUT. While we cannot know how 16-session TLT would have compared in that study, Gass's and our conclusions are rather similar in noting that a moderate amount of therapy may be better than a very small or very large amount. Such a conclusion was also reached by Butcher and Koss (1978), who noted their belief "that there is a lower limit on the amount of time a therapist can spend with a patient and demonstrate any therapeutic gain at all" (p.759). While we would acknowledge that there are certainly times that a very brief therapeutic contact can be highly effective (note Freud's well-known 1-session cure of Mahler), here the issue is more a general question of what limit can an agency effectively use for its services. Particularly since the return rate and subsequent additional agency time expenditure may be inversely proportional to the original time limit (Chapter 3), a limit of about 12 sessions seemed in our agency to offer optimal effectiveness with only a moderate recidivism rate. An optimal time limit must be individually determined by each agency, as we shall later discuss, since goals and typical durations vary so much across agencies.

TIME OF OUTCOME MEASUREMENT. The "when" of Paul's question is a crucial point in TLT evaluation. As Johnson and Gelso (1980) have noted, follow-up evaluations of TLT are particularly important, since the shorter duration of TLT may not allow all client changes to be apparent at termination, or at least fewer of the eventual changes than for the longer TUT may be seen at that time. Chapter 3 tested this idea, with the conclusion that change does seem to continue following TLT termination until at least one year afterward (the final measurement point), but the change is not dramatic. Instead, this postcounseling period may involve extension or consolidation of changes begun during TLT; we do not have evidence that qualitatively different changes occur during this period. Perhaps predictably, clients' initially high postcounseling feelings may diminish by a year later, while behavior change and self-understanding improve.

Based on the Chapter 3 evidence and that from other studies (Johnson & Gelso, 1980), we perceive part of the effectiveness of TLT to occur through its beginning a growth process that continues past termination with post-treatment time facilitating the consolidation of changes. Few TLT authors have explicitly spelled out such a "change-in-motion" process, although there appears to be implicit acceptance of its existence. In describing a developmental model of short-term group therapy, Budman, Bennett, and Wisneski (1981) note, "The final phase of the group concerns saying good-bye and leaving with hope. As in any other form of short-term treatment, there is an assumption that the work will continue" (p. 330). It seems quite congruent with the developmental approach often taken with TLT (e.g., Mann, 1973) that the therapy is meant to serve as stimulus (but not endpoint) for growth as well as removing obstacles to normalcy. Since, however, few therapists have been trained to work toward such goals (i.e., goals that at times even eliminate the possibility of the therapist seeing the full fruits of the labor), some retraining and some creative use of follow-ups by therapists appear to be strongly indicated.

NECESSITY OF INSIGHT. When we consider what aspects of counseling lead to continued client growth, we often consider insight to be very valuable. Our findings here indicate that although insight may indeed be a helpful factor in TLT (Chapter 5), it may not be necessary for a large amount of insight to occur. We found clients being more positive than their counselors about the amount of insight they had gained during counseling (Chapter 3); congruent with the counselors' rating, interviewers of some of these clients also perceived the clients' insight as "brittle" or shallow. Despite not having gained great insight, at least in mental health professionals' eyes, the clients had apparently made enough growth in insight to continue to improve generally past termination. We would suggest that some insight can be of great help, but that very deep insight may be unattainable in TLT, unimportant to the client and, indeed, unnecessary for satisfactory client growth. Accordingly, time in TLT may be best spent combining insight with behavioral and other interventions, as Butcher and Koss (1978) have also suggested.

DISCUSSION OF THE TIME LIMIT. Since some commonly noted factors in TLT effectiveness are the motivational force of the time limit and the confidence of the counselors in the results (Butcher & Koss, 1978), we had hypothesized that the rationale for the use of time limits would have a significant effect on TLT outcome. When we investigated the impact of initial rationale on clients' expectancies of outcome (Chapter 6), we found no difference between an effectiveness rationale and an agency time-savings rationale. The nonquantitative data from this study, however, led us to believe that the rationale may have a more subtle effect, not apparent on the usual objective measures: more clients seemed to react adversely to the time-saving rationale than to the effectiveness rationale. Since it may be that clients believe that agency concerns are part of the rationale even if effectiveness is given for the reason for the time-limit policy, it is recommended that the stated rationale include both reasons.

There is some evidence from the literature that the way in which time limits are integrated into the counseling is indeed highly influential to the outcome. Our comparison of TLT studies and duration studies (Johnson & Gelso, 1980) demonstrated that the use of explicit time limits may effect better outcomes than would be the case in equally brief counseling with no specific limit. Parad and Parad (1968) similarly determined that it was more effective to tell clients about the time limits rather than not mentioning limits. The way in which a therapist introduces the time limits may set the stage for a positive feeling about the use of limits, a feeling that is probably reinforced as the therapy proceeds if the therapist maintains confidence in the TLT process. Such overall confidence may be a potent factor in bringing about positive outcomes, since there is evidence that therapists' belief in the efficacy of TLT affects the results (Wattie, 1973). However, a good beginning rationale may get this process off to the best possible start, as well as possibly retaining more clients in therapy. Conversely, Henry and Shlien (1958) suggested that there may be a delayed negative effect of a time-saving rationale, such that the initially impersonal rationale becomes personalized only later when the client has developed a close relationship with the therapist. Combining these bits of empirical knowledge with our clinical intuition, we suggest that the technique of choice may be to present a combined rationale from the very beginning, emphasizing particularly a realistic confidence in the usefulness of TLT while also noting the need of the agency for such a policy.

MEANING OF DISSATISFACTION WITH TIME LIMITS. When trying to evaluate the effectiveness or sources of discomfort in TLT, we must be cautious not to mistake certain client dissatisfactions as condemning TLT. The presence of certain types of dissatisfaction is neither a negative nor a positive factor in the end results of TLT. Dissatisfaction with the time limit is not related to general dissatisfaction with counseling or to the client's perception of likelihood of seeking further counseling (Chapter 8). We also know that TUT clients at follow-up tend to ascribe more of their positive feelings to their time in counseling than do TLT clients (Chapter 2), perhaps due to the former's greater time expenditure and consequent resolution of cognitive dissonance. But again, such attribution does not necessarily indicate a more satisfied or healthy client. Client satisfactions and dissatisfactions may be *different* rather than unequal in TLT and TUT. Reid and Shyne (1969) found clients most dissatisfied with the duration, whereas TUT clients focused their dissatisfactions on the content of the interviews as being "nothing but talk." While the time limit is clearly an important factor in TLT, dissatisfaction with it is not antithetical to producing good results and may even be, as we shall see in a later section, a normal part of the process.

SUMMARY. To summarize, our results have allowed us to specify some treatment factors important to doing effective TLT. Setting the time limit at a moderate number of sessions can produce good results as well as save agency time. The specific time limit will depend on the individual agency and the agency goals; the optimum condition appears to be some blend of time-savings and goals, which could conceivably range from two sessions for some crisis centers to six months for some psychoanalytic agencies. An initial rationale for the time limit may fruitfully include both an effectiveness message and a note about agency time-savings. Using TLT as an agent for beginning ongoing change rather than as an end in itself appears to be a realistic use of this particular counseling structure. It may be useful to stimulate some insight during TLT, although an extensive amount of insight does not seem to be necessary. Finally, assuming that a client has been appropriately selected for TLT, client dissatisfaction with the time limit may be an integral part of the TLT process rather than being indicative of a more general dissatisfaction with treatment. While we would not want to cavalierly dismiss dissatisfaction with the time limit, such feelings can be used as grist for the TLT mill.

Client Moderators in TLT

Some of our major findings regarding TLT effectiveness have to do with the type of client with whom the work is done. Indeed, at times we found overall analyses comparing TLT and TUT telling us one thing, but when we used a client moderator we found quite a different conclusion. Even with the relatively intact, intelligent, motivated college student population, some clients performed better than others in TLT. An examination of moderators appears crucial to conclusion regarding the efficacy of time-limited policy; some client populations may benefit more from such a policy, while others may be receiving unsatisfactory services. Even within a given population, a global time-limited policy may ignore the variance in clients that appears to exist. Just as research on outcomes is optimally done using moderator variables, so do agency policies benefit from flexibility of approach depending on the specific client.

To synthesize our findings, we categorize client moderator variables into three groups: (a) *intrinsic client factors,* which are part of the client's ongoing personality dynamics; (b) *counselor-judged client factors,* which reflect the counselor's perceptions of the client's personality dynamics as well as the counselor's personal reactions to working with the client; and (c) *counseling-related client input variables,* which describe the client's specific reaction to the counseling situation. In making this categorization, we hope to be able to address the question of which types of client moderator/input variables are most relevant to TLT outcome. That is, which are more important, general personality or pathology variables, or the client's interpersonal behavior and impact on his or her individual counselor, or the client's feelings about various components of the counseling situation?

INTRINSIC CLIENT FACTORS. The studies reported in this book encompassed three general factors of this type: general adjustment, chronicity, and problem type (roughly comparable to diagnosis). Our research program began relatively conservatively, with the initial study (Chapter 1) using the MMPI to screen out clients in the most severely disturbed range. While the design of that study did not allow conclusions regarding the effect of client adjustment, it is noteworthy that when prescreening was used, 8-session TLT showed equal gains to TUT, at both termination and 2½-year follow-up.

Building on this preliminary demonstration of the efficacy of TLT, the subsequent study (Chapter 2) eliminated prescreening and used initial client adjustment as part of the research design. Here, client adjustment was defined as the discrepancy between client's self-ratings and ideal-self ratings (Bills Index of Adjustment and Values), and thus probably tapped the clients' internal awareness of their own adjustment. This variable turned out to be very important in differentially influencing outcomes of TLT and TUT: the highly adjusted clients did generally as well in TLT as compared to TUT, while the less adjusted clients clearly received more satisfactory treatment in TUT. These results, combined with those inferred from Chapter 1, allow a fairly strong conclusion that TLT may be both an effective and a time-saving treatment for clients perceiving themselves as fairly well adjusted, but that clients who experience themselves as more seriously troubled may do better with TUT.

From a conceptual viewpoint, it would seem likely that our remaining two intrinsic client variables, chronicity and problem type, are probably subcomponents of a more general adjustment variable. We wanted to determine specifically what aspect of clients' personality patterns led to the differential effectiveness of TLT and TUT, so we studied the next two variable types in very controlled settings, eliminating all factors except the specific variable of interest.

The pattern for chronicity (Chapter 6) was quite similar to that for adjustment (Chapter 2); acutely disturbed clients expected TLT and TUT to have about equal effects, while the chronic clients had higher expectancies of TUT than of TLT. Both the chronicity and the adjustment studies used moderator measures that indicated clients' self-perceptions. Accordingly, it may be concluded that self-perceptions of chronic problems or maladjustment are critical selection factors for TLT. Effective TLT can be done with the clients who perceive themselves as more acutely and moderately disturbed, whereas TUT may be a better choice for clients who perceive themselves as more chronically and seriously troubled.

Holding chronicity and maladjustment constant, we then proceeded to see whether client problem type influenced counselors' outcome expectancies (Chapter 7). While here we were not actually studying outcome, counselors' expectancies may give us some good clinical data on which to base selection. Counselors tended to see an overly dependent client as doing equally well in TLT and TUT regarding changes in presenting problem and behavior, while a client who feared intimacy was perceived as doing better in TUT (when both client types are of equal severity). These results are not quite so dramatic as those for adjustment and chronicity, but the pattern is somewhat similar: TLT may be as effective and result in greater agency time savings than TUT for clients with some personality features, while other types of clients may be better suited for TUT, regardless of time considerations.

COUNSELOR-JUDGED CLIENT FACTORS. How does this conclusion fit with that based on counselor judgments? Three of our studies used counselor judgments of client factors as moderators, factors quite similar to those intrinsic personality variables discussed above. Here the rating source of these variables was the counselor rather than the client. In contrast to the previous discussion of self-perceived adjustment, counselor-rated degree of disturbance was found *not* to be related to outcome in TLT (Chapters 4 and 8), although it was related to counselor-rated TUT outcome (Chapter 4). A combination of intrinsic client variables, as rated by counselors, did predict continued growth after TLT (Chapter 5): insight, self-concept, and communication skills, when occurring simultaneously, apparently helped the clients make optimal use of TLT by continuing to grow afterwards. These latter factors may be ratings of client characteristics related to high ego strength and good self-perception. Combining this interpretation with the null finding for counselor-rated degree of disturbance and the positive findings for self-perceived adjustment and chronicity, we find it plausible that clients' internal experience of their disturbance level rather than therapist perceptions of this variable may be a crucial moderator in influencing TLT outcome, perhaps more so than in TUT.

Several additional client moderators as judged by counselors were also found to affect TLT effectiveness. This group of moderators, in contrast to intrinsic personality characteristics, concerned the counselors' perceptions of what it would be like to work with that client and/or the client's approach to the counseling relationship. Here we find some particularly intriguing results: such variables seemed especially significant in affecting the outcome of 8-session TLT, even more so than 16-session TLT. We found that counselors' initial impressions of clients (on the dimensions of willingness to change, confidence that the client could profit from treatment, and predicted enjoyment in working with the client) were quite predictive of outcome in 8-session TLT—even 18 months after termination (Chapter 4)! A clear distinction, then, between the brief TLT and TUT or even the longer TLT is the importance of the quick formation of a good counselor-client relationship (Chapters 3 and 4) when the work is to be abbreviated. For TLT, relationship factors such as counselors' and/or clients' subjective experiences and impressions seem to be the most effective predictors of a good outcome, rather than such client personality factors as counselor-perceived disturbance level.

COUNSELING-RELATED FACTORS. Next we turn to counseling-related variables as experienced by the client. The two variables that we studied in this category were concerned specifically with the client's feelings about duration. Since a major concern about implementing a TLT policy was that clients would be disappointed, it was important to see if indeed clients' feelings about duration influenced TLT results. Since so few clients initially expected more than 12 sessions (Chapter 8), our original hypothesis that clients who wanted more would later be dissatisfied was clearly both untestable and irrelevant: there was no relationship of initial duration expectancies to outcome (either client- or counselor-rated; Chapter 8). Similarly, another study (Chapter 5) found that client's comfort with TLT duration was not predictive of change between termination and follow-up. At least based on this evidence, we have no reason to believe that clients' feelings are very negative about the time limits nor that early feelings about duration have much to do with outcome. Inferentially, it seems that feelings about duration may not necessarily indicate subjective level of need or disturbance.

SUMMARY. In summary, we found that TLT effectiveness depends a great deal on client type. Clients who perceived themselves as less troubled, who had been troubled for a shorter length of time, who were in a high state of readiness to change, and/or whose counselors found them good at relating early in the counseling relationship appeared to be the best candidates for TLT. If these findings are confirmed by further studies, such variables lend themselves well to differential client assignment, since they are amenable to rapid early measurement at the beginning of counseling. There are other variables that, perhaps surprisingly, are not predictive of TLT effectiveness: counselor ratings of client adjustment and client comfort with duration.

There is diversity of opinion in the literature regarding which clients are appropriate for TLT, but little good empirical evidence. Butcher and Koss (1978) noted that initial adjustment and acute onset are often considered good indicators of responsiveness to brief counseling, but that there is also evidence that more severely disturbed clients can benefit from brief work. Strupp (1981) concurs that severity of disturbance is a valid indicator, although he questions the importance of acute onset. Neither of these articles examined the source of rating for these client variables, while our findings indicate that source may be one of the most important components for accurate screening of clients for TLT. Strupp (1981) does discuss a somewhat similar notion: that good TLT clients may be those who are experiencing internal or intrapsychic pain but whose behavior does not appear to be particularly disturbed. To take his conceptualization one step closer to our own, we would expect that such clients are probably also fairly good at relating quickly to the counselor. This combination of internally experienced pain, good behavioral adjustment, and good ability to form a relationship with a counselor would seem to describe most accurately the client with whom TLT is most effective. Our findings suggest that clients' self-assessments of adjustment and counselors' first impressions of the clients' ability to relate may be useful screening variables, allowing TLT to be used in an optimally effective way without doing a disservice to clients needing TUT.

It is particularly noteworthy that variables predictive of good TLT outcome are not necessarily the same as those in TUT. When the counselor made an initial judgment that the client was willing to change, when the counselor had confidence that the client would profit from treatment, and/or when the counselor predicted enjoyment in working with the client, then that client was likely to have a positive outcome in TLT; but these factors had less predictive value for TUT outcome (Chapter 4). Such factors are probably more predictive in brief TLT because there is little time to work through initial resistance to change, while such time is available in the longer TUT. Unlike these variables, motivation for therapy, usually considered an important outcome predictor, was shown in Chapter 4 to be about equally predictive in TLT and TUT. Thus, it is important to be reasonably motivated in *any* type of counseling, but in brief TLT it may be more important to be high on readiness or willingness to change, even if the client is quite disturbed.

Some theorists (e.g., Lambert, 1979) have wondered whether the types of clients doing well with TLT are the very same as those who do well in any treatment; our evidence suggests that this is *not* the case, consistent with McNair's (1969) formulation. There do appear to be some quite distinctive client attributes that allow the client to begin quickly to change in TLT, while such attributes are not so relevant to progress in longer TUT. Such factors as a positive client-counselor relationship seem to be very helpful and even necessary in the early stages of TLT, but they might not be particularly important initially in TUT. We underscore the conclusion that factors of direct relevance to the treatment (e.g., willingness to change, client's awareness of pain, counselor's immediate reaction to working with the client) are of utmost importance in choosing appropriate TLT clients, rather than the more underlying factors such as client personality disturbance. TUT, in contrast, allows time to work on such treatment factors within the treatment, so such initial factors have less impact.

Counselor Moderators in TLT

Similarly to our exploration of client moderators of TLT effectiveness, we also examined a number of possible counselor moderators. Here we were questioning whether there are types of counselors that do generally better or worse TLT than do other types. While theoretically it would have been possible to have studied both intrinsic and counseling-related variables, as was done for clients, we chose to focus only on the counseling-related factors. There was no reason to hypothesize that intrinsic counselor variables (e.g., sex or personality type) would have a particular impact on TLT, since they seem to have no such effect on TUT (Parloff, Waskow, & Wolfe, 1978). Furthermore, we were more interested in describing changeable attitudes or background relevant to the counselor role, since findings in this area would lead to more practical implications for agencies turning to a counseling time limit. A limitation of this program of research, however, was that there has been no study linking counselor techniques to outcome; thus, while we summarize the findings about counselor variables vis-à-vis effective TLT, the perhaps crucial role of counselor in-session behaviors remains to be investigated.

Two of the four counselor variables concerned rather general counseling-related factors: theoretical orientation and experience. Using a standard measure of counselor theoretical orientation in two different studies, we examined the impact of professed beliefs and attitudes toward counseling practice in general on actual approaches to and effectiveness in TLT. Almost none of the standard subscales regarding counselor orientation had any relationship to TLT (or TUT) effectiveness (Chapter 4). While one finding did qualify this statement (and we must note that one significant finding out of so many could be due to chance), that finding was true for TUT but not TLT: client-rated outcome in TUT favored counselors able to admit to feelings of insecurity, discomfort, and nonunderstanding, who view counseling as involving close personal relationships. We suspect that the brevity of TLT may not always allow the degree of intimacy occurring in longer TUT, and thus that such openness in a counselor may be neither helpful nor harmful in TLT. In the Chapter 7 study on counselor goals and outcome expectancies, we investigated whether an active-directive approach led a counselor to be more optimistic and appropriate in approaching TLT. While this study was not concerned with outcome, the results have implications for outcome and are consistent with the Chapter 4 results: inventoried orientation had no effect on the goals and expectancies a counselor had for TLT. Similarly, it was found that counselor experience with TUT or with TLT (although here the range was admittedly small) was not related to TLT outcome, even though experience with TUT was moderately related to TUT outcome (Chapter 4).

Since global characteristics such as orientation and experience were nonpredictive of TLT results, we might suspect that factors more directly relevant to in-session (TLT) attitudes might be more accurate moderators. We studied two variables under this category: attitude toward TLT and comfort with TLT duration. Therapist attitudes toward TLT before beginning to do much TLT and the amount of learning about TLT since the beginning of the project were positively correlated with therapist-rated outcome in TLT but not client-rated outcome (Chapter 4). It seems that such factors may indicate a general favorability (or negativity) set in a therapist that spill over into that therapist's outcome ratings, but do not enter into the actual sessions enough to influence clients' reactions. A final null finding regarding counselor moderators comes from counselor comfort with TLT duration (Chapter 5). Clients' ability to make continued growth after TLT termination was not affected by counselor comfort with the length of the contact. Hence, even on specifically TLT-oriented counselor variables, we located no counselor factor that consistently helped or prevented a more positive outcome in TLT (at least as rated by clients).

Based on the weight of the above evidence, we might speculate that the aggregate data may mask the effect of attitudinal or behavioral characteristics. Thus, it might be expected that some individual counselors are better at doing TLT than at TUT, due either to attitudinal variables similar to the ones studied or to different techniques that were not studied. Apparently this is not the case: even looking at individual counselor as a moderator variable, we found no pattern of individual counselors being generally better at TLT than at TUT (Chapter 4). It is true that some counselors tend more frequently to rate their clients high or low in having changed, but this tendency does not occur with their clients' own ratings. Such data seem to indicate a response set rather than a difference in effectiveness visible to clients.

Our findings leave us with much more sophisticated knowledge about which counselor variables do *not* affect the results of TLT. After examining a number of possible counselor variables, we found that not even on an individual basis is one counselor consistently more effective than others at doing TLT versus TUT. It is clear, then, that it must be an interaction between client and counselor, and/or counselor characteristics as perceived by the individual client rather than those measured objectively that make the difference. Most of the variables we examined appear relevant to the counseling relationship but were actually one step removed; such variables are not necessarily manifested within the counseling sessions or with all clients. Apparently what works with one client does not necessarily work with another: TLT is no more uniform than any other therapy.

Indeed, major significant findings regarding TLT outcome included counselors' initial ratings of expected enjoyment of working with the client; if a client and counselor seemed to "click" well together from the beginning, a positive outcome could be predicted with more assurance than that based on any counselor factors (Chapter 4). Linking process or in-session counselor behavior, and its interaction with client variables, to TLT outcome may be the way to understand better how to do effective TLT. In this area, perhaps more than in the others, traditional empirical research may not be the best starting point. Hill (in press) has suggested a more clinical and subjective approach to process research that, at least at the beginning, may yield better hypotheses and richer information than the more detached methods of traditional process/outcome research. Since TLT effectiveness appears to be due to some individual patterns in the process between client and counselor, we need to use a research method that can study this individuality.

The Process of TLT

In the previous sections, we questioned the effectiveness of TLT, focusing on outcomes. When TLT and TUT were compared, we looked at the end results on clients, but had not yet inquired into the actual TLT process and the ways in which this process is particularly influenced by the existence of time limits in addition to brevity. Part Three studied the process and expectancies evoked by time limits; here we shall summarize and integrate those findings.

As noted previously, clients generally expected to receive far fewer than 12 sessions, regardless of whether they already knew about the time limit (Chapter 8). Perhaps because of these already-limited duration expectancies, students made relatively little discrimination in their role expectancies for TLT and TUT (Chapter 6). This finding was quite surprising, since much of the brief-therapy literature (summarized by Butcher and Koss, 1978) emphasizes the very active roles of both client and therapist in TLT, in contrast to less activity in TUT. We suspect that clients at the beginning of their counseling have little idea of how the process will occur and what their roles are; differentiation between roles in TLT and TUT at this stage is virtually nonexistent. However, the ever increasing presence of the end of counseling, along with an in-vivo education about how to participate as a client in counseling, probably causes the client to become more active as the counseling ensues. While such an evolution in roles may often occur very naturally and spontaneously for many clients, it seems possible that rather passive people may encounter some difficulties in the counselor's expectations that they take a highly active role in their treatment. In such cases, TLT may be a frustrating experience but, if helped by an able counselor, it may result in a quite positive encounter in learning to take a more active role in one's life.

Similarly, clients at the early stages of their counseling expected quite similar outcome for TLT and TUT (Chapter 6), with one exception. Students who perceived their presenting problem as chronic reacted more favorably in terms of outcome expectancies for TUT than for TLT. These reactions seem quite consistent with the realities; for most clients, the existence of a time limit made little difference, since they were not expecting counseling of long duration anyway. But for the more chronically troubled client, there is a greater feeling of entrenchment in problems (problems that, by definition, have been part of the client for a long time), and having a relatively brief limit set on counseling may fit all too readily the client's already-existent sense of pessimism about solving his or her difficulties. This pessimism and concommitant negative expectancies of TLT are important: the client may sense intuitively what we already know empirically and clinically, that TUT or at least a longer limit may be a better choice for this client. A client's subjective experience of his or her own adjustment is one of the major predictors of TLT effectiveness.

Counselors' expectancies, on the other hand, seem to be somewhat more pessimistic regarding TLT than warranted. While they attempt to achieve about the same numbers and types of goals in TLT as in TUT, with the exception of a lesser degree of personality reconstruction in TLT, they thought TLT would bring about fewer client changes of all types (Chapter 7). They also did not differentiate between TLT and TUT in terms of the amount of activity they expected themselves or their client to take (Chapter 7), similar to the lack of differentiation expected by clients (Chapter 6).

In clients' and counselors' initial approach to TLT, then, we see very little differentiation between TLT and TUT in terms of their expectancies for the ongoing process. The only initial impact of the time limits on the counseling participants appears to be in their projection of the results. Does the time limit later affect the process to a greater extent?

Two types of data address this question, one directly and one more indirectly. First, after doing TLT and TUT, counselors said they were more active and structured in TLT (Chapter 2). It may be that the counselors' inexperience in TLT caused their failure to anticipate such a role difference before counseling began (Chapter 7), but that the time limits stimulated more activity once the sessions actually ensued.

Second, our exploratory study of the TLT process (Chapter 9) gives us indirect evidence of the impact of time limits on content and behavior in counseling sessions. The first quarter of TLT tends to focus on the time limits and goals of the relationship, leading to resentment of the time limits and subsequent scheduling problems in the second fourth. These difficulties accepting the time limit are followed by client resistance during the third fourth, but are then resolved by acceptance and termination issues brought up in the final fourth of counseling. Interestingly, although the clients did appear to struggle with the time limits during sessions, counselors did not note any differences in expressed client satisfaction across the various fourths of the counseling sessions. At least as far as the counselors could detect, the struggles with time limits do not necessarily indicate client dissatisfaction with counseling. Indeed, such struggles appear to be a very normal and natural part of TLT, as Mann (1973) indicated. This point is important to keep in mind, as it may be these very struggles that lead counselors to feel discontent with doing TLT. Just as with most other conflicts that arise in counseling, the act of struggling with time limits may be productive and enhancing for the client. In contrast with other such conflicts, though, if a client expresses difficulties with time limits and the counselor already feels some dissatisfaction with doing TLT, the consequent battles may feel negative and draining for the counselor, leading to more exhaustion and frustration in doing TLT.

A major difference between the processes of TLT and TUT postulated by Mann (1973) is the explicit emphasis of TLT on termination. In fact, however, we found that an average of only 1.3 sessions were devoted to termination issues in TLT (Chapter 9). While this may seem to be a proportionately large number, it is much smaller than Mann's recommendation of the last three or so sessions focusing on termination. As noted in Chapter 9, it is not yet known whether Mann's method or these therapists' procedures yields better results, and whether the proportion of termination sessions is any different for TUT. Accordingly, the impact of this factor on the process and outcome of TLT awaits further investigation.

Summary Profiles of Effectiveness

If we integrate our research findings with clinical impressions and with the literature, what is the composite profile of a successful client and counselor in TLT? We are now able to sketch these profiles with some clarity, while bearing in mind that we are interpreting the data somewhat freely. While the composite picture may fit no individual perfectly, cohesive evidence from a variety of sources allows reasonable confidence in these profiles. (To avoid sexist language, we portray the client as male and the counselor as female; clearly, the profiles fit both sexes.)

The successful TLT client comes to an agency seeking help with certain problem behaviors or feelings that have been troubling him. He sees these difficulties as relatively recent in onset, so that they have not become an ego-syntonic part of his self-perception. While the presenting problems are experienced as directly and currently painful to him, his overall behavior does not appear very disturbed to others. Indeed, just as his hurt is more internally than externally apparent, he sees the control over making changes as residing within him; and the time for changing is ripe. His problems notwithstanding, his general concept of himself is good, and his ideal self is not vastly different from his real self. He is initially able to make good emotional contact with his counselor, and the two seem to "hit it off" quite well together from the very beginning. (This latter characteristic is perhaps most important of all, and is a major variable differentiating our good TLT client from a comparable TUT client.) He is willing and able to be active in the counseling sessions, taking much of the responsibility for making the venture a success. While our client is definitely not afraid of intimacy, he may have some unresolved dependency desires, in a developmental sense. He is able to see the psychological aspects of his problems, although he is not necessarily deeply insightful. Finally, he may not particularly like the time limit but is eventually able to see it as a necessary reality, and views the counseling as having started some new ways of thinking that he will extend and integrate himself after termination.

And his counselor? She has confidence that TLT can be an effective treatment. She restrains herself to goals less extensive than personality reconstruction, although she certainly sees the counseling as going beyond supportiveness and toward the actual effecting of client change. Her initial mention of the time limits stresses her belief that TLT will be effective for this client and also notes the agency necessity for such limits in order to better serve its clientele. She then goes on to use the limits within the counseling sessions as an in-vivo example of coping with the reality of limits. She may work towards insight on the presenting problem, but does not overemphasize the use of insight to the exclusion of behavior change. When her client expresses dissatisfaction with the time limit, she is able to see these feelings as independent of the actual value of the counseling for the client. Her goals are to help the client begin the change process by the end of TLT and to give the client tools to continue this change past termination. Finally, she takes good clinical care of herself by following up her clients after termination, since she knows that consolidation of changes may occur after she has stopped having sessions with the client; such follow-ups are gratifying to both her and her client.

In what type of agency does our successful TLT counselor work? Regardless of its setting, it is an agency that finds that the average counseling (TUT) duration was sufficiently long that a time limit would help reduce average duration. The actual time chosen is selected according to agency goals and typical TUT duration. The decision to implement a TLT policy involves the clinical staff to a great degree. Once the policy is implemented, counselors can still (and perhaps need to) have a certain percentage of their client load in TUT. Extensive in-service training of staff on TLT is done both before and throughout the first years of the TLT policy, and an important part of this training is work on goal-setting in TLT. The agency realizes that its clients and its funding sources want its help on changing disruptive feelings and behavior, and that the staff's interest in working toward major personality change is secondary to its service requirements. However, the agency remains very aware of the restrictions it is placing on its counselors, and implements some procedures (like follow-up by counselors) that acknowledge the often inherent unsatisfactoriness of working in TLT. Client are carefully screened for TLT, using a combination of clients' self-perceptions and counselors' initial reactions. In particular, since counselors' initial expectations of enjoyment in working with a client are quite predictive of TLT outcome, the agency may use the first session as a screening session, prior to actually beginning therapy. Our successful TLT agency, in other words, sees neither TLT nor TUT as a panacea, and flexibly responds to the needs of its clients and its counselors.

Future Research Directions

When endings are reached, summaries of knowledge are best intertwined with acknowledgments of unfinished business. In TLT, a typical termination involves discussion of both the completed and the incomplete work. Here, after sketching profiles of successful TLT clients, counselors, and agencies, what remains before a full portrait is possible? The focus here will be on raising some rather general additional research questions, since the more specific ones have been noted in the previous chapters.

Several unsettled questions about clients in TLT remain, some of which, indeed, have been stimulated by our attempts to answer other questions. How does a client's personality dynamics and pathology affect TLT? Are these characteristics more or less important than client goals? How does a TLT policy affect the potential client population's feelings about the agency?

We also wonder about counselors doing TLT. In what ways can they be stimulated to feel more content and optimistic about doing TLT? Are there other therapist factors not yet studied that differentiate those counselors good at TLT? What techniques are more effective in TLT versus TUT?

But as we settle more and more of the questions about clients and therapists separately, we raise even more questions about the dynamic interplay between the two, since such interaction seems more important than individual characteristics. What are appropriate goals for TLT, and how are they established? What factors affect the client and therapist's initial "hitting it off"? How much focus on the time limits is necessary? In what ways does the time limit make the process of TLT different from that of TUT? What is the optimal number and proportion of sessions to devote to "termination issues"?

Finally, there are agency issues warranting more investigation. Would flexible time limits work better than a fixed time limit? How effective is interrupted counseling (in which a client receives a brief period of counseling, followed by a planned period away from counseling, ending in a final brief stint in counseling)? What is the optimal time limit, or how does one select different clients for different time limits? And, ultimately, we need to know what types of agencies can best use TLT, and which should use other ways of coping with a waiting list.

With these questions, we leave the reader, hoping that our book will have stimulated both a broader understanding of TLT and an increased desire to continue the investigation process. TLT is clearly an effective and promising treatment approach, allowing increased accountability as long as we use this modality flexibly and rationally. Defining and exploring some of the parameters of such use has been the goal of our work; our exploration is but a foundation upon which increasingly sophisticated knowledge can be built.

REFERENCES

BLOOM, B. L. Focused single-session therapy: Initial development and evaluation. In S. H. Budman (Ed.), *Forms of brief therapy*. New York: Guilford Press, 1981.

BUDMAN, S. H., BENNETT, M. J., & WISNESKI, M. J. An adult developmental model of short-term group psychotherapy. In S. H. Budman (Ed.), *Forms of brief therapy*. New York: Guilford Press, 1981.

BUTCHER, J. N., & KOSS, M. P. Research on brief and crisis-oriented psychotherapies. In S. L. Garfield & A. E. Bergin (Eds.), *Handbook of psychotherapy and behavior change: An empirical analysis*. New York: Wiley, 1978.

GASS, M. Comparison of time-limited therapy and time-unlimited therapy related to self-concept change, adjustment change, problem resolution, and premature termination. (Doctoral dissertation, United States International University, 1975). *Dissertation Abstracts International*, 1975, *36*, (University Mocrofilms No. 75–20, 246).

GELSO, C. J. Research in counseling: Methodological and professional issues. *The Counseling Psychologist*, 1979, *8*, 7–36.

GURMAN, A. S. Integrative marital therapy: Toward the development of an interpersonal approach. In S. H. Budman (Ed.), *Forms of brief therapy*. New York: Guilford Press, 1981.

HENRY, W. E., & SHLIEN, J. M. Affective complexity and psychotherapy: Some comparisons of time-limited and unlimited treatment. *Journal of Projective Techniques*, 1958, *22*, 153–162.

HILL, C. Counseling process research: Philosophical and Methodological Dilemmas. *The Counseling Psychologist*, in press.

JOHNSON, D. H. & GELSO, C. J. The effectiveness of time limits in counseling and psychotherapy: A critical review. *The Counseling Psychologist*, 1980, *9*, 70–83.

LAMBERT, M. J. *The effects of psychotherapy (Volume 1)*. Montreal, Quebec: Eden Press, 1979.

MANN, J. *Time-limited psychotherapy*. Cambridge: Harvard University Press, 1973.

McNAIR, D. M. A season for brevity. *Seminars in Psychiatry*, 1969, *1*, 411–431.

MUENCH, G. A. An investigation of the efficacy of time-limited psychotherapy. *Journal of Counseling Psychology*. 1965, *12*, 294–299.

PARAD, H. J., & PARAD, L. G. A study of crisis-oriented planned short-term treatment: Part II. *Social Casework*, 1968, *49*, 418–426.

PARLOFF, M. B., WASKOW, I. E., & WOLFE, B. E. Research on therapist variables in relation to process and outcome. In S. L. Garfield & A. E. Bergin (Eds.), *Handbook of psychotherapy and behavior change: An empirical analysis*. New York: Wiley, 1978.

PAUL, G. L. Strategy of outcome research in psychotherapy. *Journal of Consulting Psychology*, 1967, *31*, 109–118.

PHILLIPS, E. L., & JOHNSTON, M. H. S. Theoretical and clinical aspects of short-term, parent-child psychotherapy. *Psychiatry*, 1954, *17*, 267–275.

REID, W. J., & SHYNE, A. W. *Brief and extended casework.* New York: Columbia University Press, 1969.

Shlien, J. M. Mosak, H. H., & Dreikurs, R. Effects of time limits: A comparison of two psychotherapies. *Journal of Counseling Psychology*, 1962, *9*, 31–34.

STRUPP, H. H. Toward the refinement of time-limited dynamic psychotherapy. In S. H. Budman (Ed.), *Forms of brief therapy.* New York: Guilford Press, 1981.

STRUPP, H. H., & HADLEY, S. W. A tripartite model of mental health and therapeutic outcomes. *American Psychologist*, 1977, *32*, 187–196.

WATTIE, B. Evaluating short term casework in a family agency. *Social Casework*, 1973, *54*, 609–616.

WILSON, G. T. Behavior therapy as a short-term therapeutic approach. In S. H. Budman (Ed.), *Forms of brief therapy.* New York: Guilford Press, 1981.

Appendices

Appendix A

Time-Limited Therapy Questionnaire

Name _____ Date _____

Years Post Doctoral Counseling Experience $\bar{X}$ for senior staff = 7.2, range 2–16.

Would you please partial out the following influences on your theoretical orientation to counseling (enter percentages so they should total to 100).

$\bar{X}$'s	Theory
18.3%	Behavioral
18.3%	Gestalt
31.5%	Phenomenological/Existential/Rogerian
25.1%	Psychoanalytic
5.3%	Other (please specify)_____

1. Had you any experience in setting time limits in therapy prior to the TLT Project?
   __9__ yes __6__ no

2. Relative to other therapists you know, rate the amount of experience you had prior to the TLT project in doing time limited work:

   a.   much more experience ___0___
   b.   more than average amount ___2___
   c.   about average amount ___8___ $\bar{X}$'s = senior staff – 3.0
   d.   less than average experience ___2___   interns – 4.0
   e.   much less experience ___2___

3. Did you have experience in structured, short-term therapy prior to the study?
   ___11___ yes ___4___ no

4. Relative to other therapists you know, rate the amount of prior experience you had in doing structured, short-term work:

   a.   much more experience ___0___
   b.   more than average amount ___7___
   c.   about average amount ___3___ $\bar{X}$'s = senior staff – 2.8
   d.   less than average amount ___3___   interns – 3.4
   e.   much less amount ___2___

5. In terms of duration, what is the kind of therapy that you personally feel most comfortable doing? (Senior staff in parenthesis following frequency)

   a.   very long-term work (over a year) ___3___ (3)
   b.   moderately long-term work (6 months to a year) ___6___ (5)
   c.   short-term work (2 to 6 months) ___5___ (1)
   d.   very short-term work (one session to 2 months or 8 sessions) ___1___ (0)

6. What was your attitude prior to the study toward the efficacy to TLT? (Senior staff frequency in parenthesis following frequency)

   a.   very positive ___0___ (0)
   b.   positive ___5___ (3)
   c.   somewhat positive ___7___ (5)
   d.   neutral ___1___ (0) $\bar{X}$'s = senior staff – 3.1
   e.   somewhat negative ___2___ (2)   interns – 2.8
   f.   negative ___0___ (0)
   g.   Very negative ___0___ (0)

7. What is your attitude toward the efficacy to TLT now that you have participated in the study? Selected from the alternatives in "6" above $\bar{X}$'s senior staff – 2.6
   interns – 2.4

8. In general, if you think of time limits in terms of number of sessions, what time limit would you most often apply to work with CC Clients (assume that you would set time limits for the purposes of the item)? _____ sessions.

   $\bar{X}$'s: senior staff – 13.1
      interns – 13.4

9. Since the beginning of the TLT study, have you done any reading related to time-limited work? __12__ yes __3__ no.

10. If you have done reading, would you specify one such reading which has been the most meaningful to you._____

11. Rate the amount of learning you have done about TLT since beginning in the study: (senior staff in parenthesis following frequency)

   a. much learning __1__ (1)
   b. a moderate amount __5__ (3)
   c. a slight amount __9__ (6)
   d. none __0__ (0)

12. Do you plan to do time-limited work after you have completed your counseling in the project __14__ yes __1__ no.

13. Would you be willing to participate in a project that entails time limits of 12 and 20 sessions (with similar participation as in the current study)? __14__ yes __1__ no.

14. What is the theoretical orientation of the person from whom you personally learned the most about counseling or therapy (a person with whom you had personal contact like a supervisor in your internship)?

15. What three famous therapist/counselors (living or dead) would you select to spend significant time with?
   1. _____
   2. _____
   3. _____

16. As you see it now, could you enumerate any conditions under which TLT (of up to 16 sessions) is most appropriate or is the treatment of choice at the CC?

17. Any additional comments about TLT or the project would be appreciated.

Appendix B

Correlations Between One-Month and Eighteen-Month Follow-Up

**Pearson Correlations Between Responses to Item on
One-Month and 18 Month Follow-up**

Item	Correlation Coefficient	p level
II a. I feel (due to counseling)	.54	.001
b. I relate to people (due to counseling)	.26	.018
c. I accomplish things I need to do (due to counseling)	.56	.001
d. I think (due to counseling)	.33	.003
e. Others act as though I have changed (due to counseling)	.61	.001
III. Satisfaction with results of counseling	.69	.001
IV. Do you feel counseling lasted long enough to help you in ways you wanted or need to be helped	.45	.001

V.	The extent to which you and/or your life have changed as a result of counseling	.72	.001
VI.	Rate counselor in terms of how well he/she did in helping you:		
	a. helping you understand your concerns	.57	.001
	b. helping you resolve your concerns	.71	.001
	c. Creating an atmosphere in which you felt safe in talking about your problems	.65	.001

Appendix C

Pre-Counseling Assessment Blank

COUNSELORS: PLEASE COMPLETE THIS FORM AFTER YOUR FIRST INTERVIEW WITH YOUR CLIENT. After filling it out, leave it in the client's folder and CJG will obtain it after treatment is terminated.

Client's name_____

Counselor's name_____

Duration of treatment (Circle)   8 session limit   16 session limit   unlimited

1. Rate the client's overall degree of disturbance or psychopathology (think in terms of pervasiveness of the pathology rather than the acuteness of the client's problem right now). (Circle)

1	2	3	4	5	6	7
mildly disturbed			moderately disturbed			severely disturbed

2. Rate the client's motivation for counseling.

1	2	3	4	5	6	7
poorly motivated			moderately motivated			highly motivated

3. Rate the client's willingness to change.

1	2	3	4	5	6	7
low willingness			moderate willingness			high willingness

4. Rate your own degree of confidence that this client will profit from the treatment which you are able to offer him/her.

1	2	3	4	5	6	7
little confidence			moderate confidence			much confidence

5. Predict the extent to which you will enjoy working with this client.

1	2	3	4	5	6	7
no enjoyment			moderate enjoyment			much enjoyment

Appendix D

Post-Counseling Assessment Blank

COUNSELORS: PLEASE FILL THIS OUT AFTER YOUR <u>LAST</u> SESSION WITH YOUR CLIENT. LEAVE IT IN YOUR FOLDER AND NOTIFY CJG THAT THE TREATMENT HAS ENDED.

Client's name_____

Counselor's name_____

Treatment group (Circle)   8 session limit   16 session limit   unlimited

Number of Actual Counseling Sessions _____

1. Please rate your <u>activity level</u> in this therapy in comparison to your activity level in the therapy you do in general. (Circle)

1	2	3	4	5	6	7

   much less active   about as active   much more
   in this therapy   as usual   active in this

2. Rate the extent to which you <u>structured</u> this therapy in comparison to your tendency to provide structure in the therapy you do in general.

1	2	3	4	5	6	7

much less
structuring
than usual

about as much
structuring as
usual

much more
structuring
than usual

3. Rate the extent to which you dealt with <u>historical material</u> in the client's life in this therapy as compared to your use of such material in the therapy you do in general.

1	2	3	4	5	6	7

much less
than usual

about the same
as usual

much more
than usual

4. Rate the degree of <u>overall personality change</u> this client has undergone as a consequence of treatment.

1	2	3	4	5	6	7

no personality
change

moderate personality
change

much personality
change

5. Rate the degree to which the client is <u>behaving more effectively</u> as a consequence of treatment.

1	2	3	4	5	6	7

no more
effectively

somewhat more
effectively

much more
effectively

6. Rate the degree to which client is <u>feeling better</u> (e.g., self-regard, optimistic) as a consequence of treatment.

1	2	3	4	5	6	7

no better

better

much better

7. Rate the extent to which you feel confident that the changes the client has undergone as a result of treatment will persist (be durable).

1	2	3	4	5	6	7

much doubt

moderate
confidence

much
confidence

Appendix E

Therapist Orientation Questionnaire (Form 1972)*

Indicate your AGREEMENT or DISAGREEMENT. CIRCLE one of the following:

5 Strongly agree   5
4 Agree   4
3 Undecided   3
2 Disagree   2
1 Strongly disagree   1

1. The therapist's personality is more important to the outcome of therapy than his professional training.   5 4 3 2 1

2. A good therapist will help his patients become aware of their bodily movements and postures, and help them explore their possible meanings.   5 4 3 2 1

3. It is sometimes all right to visit a patient socially in his home.   5 4 3 2 1

4. Understanding why one does things is *not* the major factor in correcting one's behavior.   5 4 3 2 1

*From D. M. Sundland, Therapist Orientation Questionnaire. Paper presented at the Third Annual Meeting of the Society for Psychotherapy Research, Nashville, June 1972. Reprinted by permission of the author.

5. Effective therapists vary their technique from patient to patient. 5 4 3 2 1

6. A therapist should never interrupt a patient while he is talking. 5 4 3 2 1

7. It is unnecessary for a patient to learn how early childhood experiences have left their mark on him. 5 4 3 2 1

8. A mature, mentally healthy person will necessarily move in the direction of society's goals. 5 4 3 2 1

9. A good therapist expresses to his patients a sense of personal involvement and concern. 5 4 3 2 1

10. Good psychotherapists encourage their patients to use meditative techniques. 5 4 3 2 1

11. Primary emphasis should be placed on the patient's manifest behavior. 5 4 3 2 1

12. It is very beneficial to use the "guided-daydream" technique. 5 4 3 2 1

13. Psychotherapists should join organized groups and attempt to influence state and federal legislation pertinent to psychotherapy. 5 4 3 2 1

14. People can be understood without recourse to the concept "unconscious determinants of behavior." 5 4 3 2 1

15. A patient can be very critical of me or very appreciative of me without any resulting change in my feeling toward him. 5 4 3 2 1

16. The patient's coming to experience his feelings more fully is *not* the most important therapeutic result. 5 4 3 2 1

17. It is important that a therapist show caring and concern for his patients. 5 4 3 2 1

18. Ideally, psychotherapy would be available free-of-charge for all who wanted it, just like public education. 5 4 3 2 1

19. Desensitization and re-conditioning are effective psychotherapeutic techniques. 5 4 3 2 1

20. I would not interrupt a patient during a therapy session as I might if we were having merely a social conversation.   5 4 3 2 1

21. It is very important for a therapist to conceptualize, think through how a patient is relating to him.   5 4 3 2 1

22. A therapist should have empathic understanding of his patients.   5 4 3 2 1

23. Rather than talk about another person, good therapists have their patients talk to an empty chair as if the person was sitting there.   5 4 3 2 1

24. The most beneficial outcome of therapy is for the patient to know the reasons for his behavior.   5 4 3 2 1

25. The social class of a patient should not affect the psychotherapy he receives.   5 4 3 2 1

26. It is a useful therapeutic technique for patients to shout, or beat pillows to express blocked feelings.   5 4 3 2 1

27. It is preferable for the therapist to feel impersonal in the therapy relationship.   5 4 3 2 1

28. It is never all right for a therapist to have physical contact with patients (except perhaps for occasional handshakes).   5 4 3 2 1

29. No matter how emotionally mature and sensitive a person is, he cannot be a good therapist without training in psychopathology.   5 4 3 2 1

30. With most patients I do analytic dream interpretation.   5 4 3 2 1

31. Most therapists are more effective with some patients than with others.   5 4 3 2 1

32. It is important for the therapist to confront the patient with his (the therapist's) feelings and thoughts.   5 4 3 2 1

33. Good therapists keep all aspects of their private life out of the therapy session.   5 4 3 2 1

34. Even a good therapist may find it difficult to cope with a patient's hostility.   5 4 3 2 1

35. A successful adjustment to the social environment is <u>not</u>
    an important goal of a therapy.   5 4 3 2 1

36. The therapist should not act as though he were personally or
    emotionally involved with the patient.   5 4 3 2 1

37. I instruct most patients to free associate.   5 4 3 2 1

38. It is desirable for the therapist to reinforce the patient's
    expressions of positive feelings about himself.   5 4 3 2 1

39. Hopefully the current fad of sensitivity training will
    soon disappear.   5 4 3 2 1

40. A good therapist constantly and deliberately uses his
    thorough knowledge of psychopathology and his training
    in psychotherapeutic techniques.   5 4 3 2 1

41. I am a fairly active, talkative therapist, compared to
    most therapists.   5 4 3 2 1

42. Inherent in human beings is a natural propensity toward
    health, physical, mental, and emotional.   5 4 3 2 1

43. Whatever the intensity or nature of the patient's emotional
    expression, the therapist is most effective when he feels
    detached, objective, and impersonal.   5 4 3 2 1

44. State licensing or certification of psychotherapists is necessary
    to protect the public.   5 4 3 2 1

45. For effective therapy, it is only necessary to concentrate on
    the here-and-now experiencing of the patient.   5 4 3 2 1

46. The most important results of therapy are the new feelings
    and emotions that the patient comes to experience.   5 4 3 2 1

47. In effective therapy, the patient learns mostly through the
    verbal and conceptual interchange between himself and
    the therapist.   5 4 3 2 1

48. It is <u>unwise</u> for a therapist's remarks and reactions to a patient
    to be unplanned, spontaneous, not thought-through.   5 4 3 2 1

49. Psychotherapy should be conducted by or supervised by
a psychiatrist.   5 4 3 2 1

50. It is never all right to accept a friend or relative
for psychotherapy.   5 4 3 2 1

51. The most beneficial outcome of therapy is the patient's
becoming more open to his feelings.   5 4 3 2 1

52. The patient should be directly confronted with evidence
of his irrational thought and behavior.   5 4 3 2 1

53. It is possible to make sense of a patient's behavior without
assuming motives of which he is unaware.   5 4 3 2 1

54. A good therapist is able to get the feeling and meaning
of his patient's communication.   5 4 3 2 1

55. Deliberately expressing approval of desirable patient
behavior is not a good therapeutic policy.   5 4 3 2 1

56. A warm, giving attitude is the most important characteristic
of a good therapist.   5 4 3 2 1

57. I interrupt a patient while he is talking.   5 4 3 2 1

58. A good therapist treats the patient as an equal.   5 4 3 2 1

59. Patients get better more because their therapists are the
kinds of persons they are, than because of their therapist's
professional training.   5 4 3 2 1

60. Release of pent-up bodily energies is important as part of
psychotherapy.   5 4 3 2 1

61. For a patient to improve his current way of life, he must
come to understand his early childhood relationships.   5 4 3 2 1

62. People do not have any inherent "drive toward health."   5 4 3 2 1

63. My own attitudes toward some of the things my patients
say or do stop me from really understanding them.   5 4 3 2 1

64. An effective change in the patient is <u>not</u> the major gain
from therapy.   5 4 3 2 1

65. A good therapist will almost never let silences build up
during the therapy hour.   5 4 3 2 1

66. The crucial learning process in therapy is a verbal and
conceptual process.   5 4 3 2 1

67. It is sometimes all right to take a walk with a patient
during
the therapy hour.   5 4 3 2 1

68. It is important to analyze the transference reactions of
the patient.   5 4 3 2 1

69. A treatment plan is <u>not</u> important for successful therapy.   5 4 3 2 1

70. Marathon psychotherapy groups are useful in helping a
patient progress in treatment.   5 4 3 2 1

71. I am fairly passive, silent therapist, compared to most
therapists.   5 4 3 2 1

72. The patient's coming to accept and experience his feelings
is <u>not</u> the primary gain he derives from therapy.   5 4 3 2 1

73. It is important for a patient to be helped to make a
social adjustment.   5 4 3 2 1

74. In working with dreams, effective therapists have
their patients role-play the characters and other elements of
their dreams.   5 4 3 2 1

75. It is important that the therapist model self-disclosing behavior
by talking about his own thoughts and feelings.   5 4 3 2 1

76. It is important for the therapist to feel a deep personal and
emotional involvement with his patients.   5 4 3 2 1

77. Encounter groups are a useful addition to the approaches to
mental health.   5 4 3 2 1

78. The more effective therapists do things during the therapy
hours for which they have no reasoned basis, merely a
feeling that it is right.   5 4 3 2 1

79. It is desirable for therapists to encourage experimental
     behavior on the part of patients in their attempts to
     overcome their problems.   5 4 3 2 1

80. For a patient to improve his current way of life, he
     does not necessarily have to come to understand his early
     childhood relationship.   5 4 3 2 1

81. It is important for the therapist to clearly structure the
     therapeutic relationship.   5 4 3 2 1

82. At times, I feel contempt for a patient.   5 4 3 2 1

83. Body movements and postures tell us a lot about the
     patient's psychopathology.   5 4 3 2 1

84. It is irrelevant whether a therapist "cares" for the people
     who come to him for help.   5 4 3 2 1

85. It is quite acceptable to interrupt a patient while he is talking. 5 4 3 2 1

86. In effective therapy, the patient learns mostly through the
     effective and unverbalized relationship between himself
     and the therapist.   5 4 3 2 1

87. Psychotherapy is much more an art than a science.   5 4 3 2 1

88. The patient should be given useful information to help
     him achieve his life goals.   5 4 3 2 1

89. There is not an innate tendency in human beings toward
     emotional health.   5 4 3 2 1

90. It is never all right to offer the patient a ride, or ask him
     for one.   5 4 3 2 1

91. Effective therapists almost always know what they are doing,
     and why, and where they are heading.   5 4 3 2 1

92. An effective therapist adheres closely to one major school
     of thought in conducting his therapy sessions.   5 4 3 2 1

93. To make sense of a patient's behavior, one must assume
     motives of which he is unaware.   5 4 3 2 1

94. Having the patient move in the direction of the goals of society is
not an important therapeutic aim.   5 4 3 2 1

95. A good therapist acts personally and emotionally involved and
concerned with his patient.   5 4 3 2 1

96. I am very secure and comfortable in my relationships with
my patients.   5 4 3 2 1

97. In all human beings there is a sort of "life force," a striving
for perfection.   5 4 3 2 1

98. A therapist should realize that his efforts may prove harmful
to patients.   5 4 3 2 1

99. A good therapist must guide the patient towards taking
responsibility for his own behavior and life situation.   5 4 3 2 1

100. I prefer to conduct intensive rather than goal-limited therapy.   5 4 3 2 1

101. It is sometimes all right for a patient and a therapist to embrace. 5 4 3 2 1

102. A good therapist occasionally makes a patient angry.   5 4 3 2 1

103. Good therapists do a lot of talking during the therapeutic hour.   5 4 3 2 1

104. The most important results of therapy are the new ideas
and new ways of thinking about himself that the
patient achieves.   5 4 3 2 1

Appendix F

Evaluations of Counselors One Month and Eighteen Months After Termination (Combined) by Initially High and Low Adjusted Clients

Means for the Two Counselor Evaluation Items on Which the Initial Adjustment by Treatment Group Interaction Attained Statistical Significance When Both Times of Testing (One- and 18 Month) Were Analyzed Together

		Treatment group		
Item	Initial adjustment category	8 session $\bar{X}$	16 session $\bar{X}$	TUT $\bar{X}$
1. How well counselor did in helping client understand his/her concerns (#6a of CCFQ); 1 = very well, 2 = well, 3 = fairly well, 4 = slightly, 5 = not at all; client-rated)	High	1.75	2.38	2.32
	Low	3.00	2.36	1.59
2. How well counselor did in creating safe atmosphere. (#6c of CCFQ; same scale as #6a; client-rated)	High	1.50	2.13	2.17
	Low	2.91	2.13	1.64

Appendix G

Relationship of Number of Sessions to Outcome

Product-Moment Correlations Between Number of Sessions and Clients' and Counselors' Evaluations of Counseling

Item	All clients		8 session TLT		16 session TLT		TUT	
	One mo.	18 mos.	One mo.	18 mos.	One mo.	18 mos.	One mo.	18 mos.
1. Overall personality change due to treatment (counselor rated)	.37**	—	.61**	—	.48**	—	.40	—
2. Client Behaving more effectively due to treatment (counselor rated)	.31**	—	.43*	—	.46*	—	.32	—
3. Client Feeling Better Due to Treatment (Counselor rated)	.21	—	.37	—	.34	—	.21	—
4. Counselor confidence that change will persist:	.28*	—	.09	—	.22	—	.49*	—
5. I feel: (due to counseling)	.27*	.35**	.33	.43*	.27	.04	.31	.44*
6. I relate to people: (due to counseling)	.19	.32**	.27	.23	.28	.19	.08	.30

231

7. I accomplish things I need to do: (due to counseling)	.10	.17	.06	.28	.23	.16	.02	.06
8. I think: (due to counseling)	.26*	.07	.07	.02	.03	.18	.32	.02
9. Others act as though I have changed: (due to counseling)	.11	.39**	.18	.31	.10	.00	.08	.49*
10. Client satisfaction with results as counseling:	.04	.28*	.26	.41	.14	.04	−.13	.34
11. Client feeling that counseling lasted long enough:	.02	.19	.16	.48*	.26	.19	−.04	.33
12. Overall change as a result of counseling:	.20	.28*	.21	.43*	.24	.21	.15	.29
13. Counselor helpfulness in getting client to understand problems:	.25*	.31**	.31	.59**	.37*	.23	.19	.35
14. Counselor helpfulness in getting client to resolve problems:	.15	.24*	.30	.43*	.27	.04	.04	.27
15. Counselor creation of a safe atmosphere:	.13	.35**	.47**	.65**	.30	.49*	.01	.34
16. Most noticeable change due to counseling (rated as positive, ambivalent, negative)	.14	.20	.37	.46*	.05	.06	.13	.19
17. Clients free comments: (rated as positive, ambivalent, negative)	.20	—	.06	—	.26	—	.26	—
18. What counseling experience meant to client (rated as positive, mostly positive, mostly negative, negative)	—	.33**	—	.49*	—	.09	—	.40

Notes: (a) All correlations given such that a positive relationship between number of sessions and favorable responses yields a positive sign.

(b) Items 1–4 are counselor rated; 5–18 are client rated.

(c) Counselor rated items were done upon termination. Thus the one and 18 month designations are not applicable to the counselor rated items.

(d) The magnitude of the r's required for significance varies among items and for the one vs 18 month follow-up because of differing sample sizes.

$* = p < .05$

$** = p < .01$

Appendix H

Client-Rated Counseling Outcome (Measure III)

Name_____

Instructions: We would like you to recall the counseling you had with Dr. _____ at the Counseling Center during the period of _____, 1978. To the best of your recall, please complete the following questions (circle the number that best reflects your response). Please leave no blanks.

COMPARED TO WHEN YOU CAME TO THE COUNSELING CENTER:

1. How did you feel at the end of counseling?

1	2	3	4	5	6	7
Much Worse	Moderately Worse	Slightly Worse	About the same	Slightly Improved	Moderately Improved	Much Improved

2. To what extent was there a change in your behavior at the end of the counseling?

1	2	3	4	5	6	7
Much Less Effective	Moderately Less Effective	Slightly Less Effective	No Change	Slightly More Effective	Moderately More Effective	Much More Effective

3. To what extent did you seem to understand yourself at the end of counseling?

1	2	3	4	5	6	7
Much Worse	Moderately Worse	Slightly Worse	About the same	Slightly Better	Moderately Better	Much Better

4. Rate your overall change in counseling?

1	2	3	4	5	6	7
Much Worse	Moderately Worse	Slightly Worse	About the same	Slightly Improved	Moderately Improved	Much Improved

For the following questions we would like you to compare yourself now with how you were feeling, acting, and thinking at the end of counseling.

COMPARED TO THE END OF COUNSELING

5. I now feel

1	2	3	4	5	6	7
Much Worse	Moderately Worse	Slightly Worse	About the same	Slightly Better	Moderately Better	Much Better

6. I see my behavior as now being

1	2	3	4	5	6	7
Much Less Effective	Moderately Less Effective	Slightly Less Effective	About the same	Slightly More Effective	Moderately More Effective	Much More Effective

7. I now understand myself.

1	2	3	4	5	6	7
Much Worse	Moderately Worse	Slightly Worse	About the same	Slightly Better	Moderately Better	Much Better

8. In looking to your own answers to the above questions, to what extent would you attribute these changes between the end of counseling and now to:

(Effect of each factor, check one)

	None	Low	Medium	High
a) the passage of time	___	___	___	___
b) the changes in life circumstances	___	___	___	___

(Effect of each factor, check one)

		None	Low	Medium	High
c)	the counseling you received at the Counseling Center	___	___	___	___
d)	further counseling or therapy	___	___	___	___
e)	self-awareness	___	___	___	___
f)	family	___	___	___	___
g)	friends	___	___	___	___
h)	religion	___	___	___	___
i)	Other _____	___	___	___	___

9. Comments:

Appendix I

Counseling Outcome Measure

Counseling Name_____

Instructions: We would like you to recall the time-limited counseling you did with _____
_____ during the period _____–_____,
1978.

To the best of your recall, please complete the following questions (circle the number that
best reflects your response).

COMPARED TO WHEN HE/SHE CAME TO THE COUNSELING CENTER:

1. How did this client seem to feel at the end of counseling?

1	2	3	4	5	6	7
Much	Moderately	Slightly	About	Slightly	Moderately	Much
Worse	Worse	Worse	the same	Improved	Improved	Improved

2. To what extent did this client seem to show change in behavior at the end of counseling?

1	2	3	4	5	6	7
Much	Moderately	Slightly	About	Slightly	Moderately	Much
Worse	Worse	Worse	the same	Improved	Improved	Improved

3. To what extent did this client seem to understand him/herself at the end of counseling?

1	2	3	4	5	6	7
Much Worse	Moderately Worse	Slightly Worse	About the same	Slightly Improved	Moderately Improved	Much Improved

4. Rate this client's overall change in counseling.

1	2	3	4	5	6	7
Much Worse	Moderately Worse	Slightly Worse	About the same	Slightly Improved	Moderately Improved	Much Improved

Comments:

Appendix J

The
Client Change
Inventory

Counselor_____

Instructions: We would like you to recall the time-limited counseling you did with _____
_____ during the period of _____–_____
1978.

To the best of your recall, please complete the following items. Indicate your degree of
agreement or disagreement with each of the following statements by putting a circle around
one answer for each item. There are seven possible answers for each item:

> 1. Strongly disagree
> 2. Moderately disagree
> 3. Slightly disagree
> 4. Neither disagree nor agree
> 5. Slightly agree
> 6. Moderately agree
> 7. Strongly agree

Please do not omit any item.

Life Adjustment

1. The client's initial symptoms failed to respond to treatment.

   Strongly disagree   1   2   3   4   5   6   7   Strongly agree

2. The client experienced satisfaction through work and/or school.

   Strongly disagree   1   2   3   4   5   6   7   Strongly agree

3. The client showed improvement in ability to function in life situations.

   Strongly disagree   1   2   3   4   5   6   7   Strongly agree

4. The client failed to improve in self-selected problem areas (i.e. failed to show some achievement of own goals).

   Strongly disagree   1   2   3   4   5   6   7   Strongly agree

Self Concept

5. Client viewed self unrealistically at the end of counseling/therapy.

   Strongly disagree   1   2   3   4   5   6   7   Strongly agree

6. The client seemed more comfortable with him/herself by the end of treatment.

   Strongly disagree   1   2   3   4   5   6   7   Strongly agree

7. Client was realistic in ability to effect change.

   Strongly disagree   1   2   3   4   5   6   7   Strongly agree

8. The client did not show improvement in the area of self-esteem.

   Strongly disagree   1   2   3   4   5   6   7   Strongly agree

Communication Skills

9. The client showed improvement in capacity to express own needs and feelings.

   Strongly disagree   1   2   3   4   5   6   7   Strongly agree

10. Client was rarely able to express emotions in session.

    Strongly disagree   1   2   3   4   5   6   7   Strongly agree

11. The client showed improvement in ability to understand others' points of view.

    Strongly disagree   1   2   3   4   5   6   7   Strongly agree

12. The client was unable to act appropriately assertive by the end of treatment.

    Strongly disagree   1   2   3   4   5   6   7   Strongly agree

Interpersonal Relationships

13. The client showed improved capacity for close relationships.

    Strongly disagree   1   2   3   4   5   6   7   Strongly agree

14. The maturity of the client's relationship with others seemed to improve.

    Strongly disagree   1   2   3   4   5   6   7   Strongly agree

15. The client's motivation to work to improve relationships seemed low.

    Strongly disagree   1   2   3   4   5   6   7   Strongly agree

Attitude toward Therapy

16. The client expressed negative evaluation of the outcome of counseling/therapy.

    Strongly disagree   1   2   3   4   5   6   7   Strongly agree

17. The client would probably be very reluctant to seek additional counseling/therapy (at the Counseling Center or elsewhere) even if it were indicated.

    Strongly disagree   1   2   3   4   5   6   7   Strongly agree

18. The client showed the capacity to carry on the therapeutic work by him/herself.

    Strongly disagree   1   2   3   4   5   6   7   Strongly agree

19. The client expressed positive attitudes toward the counseling/therapy.

    Strongly disagree   1   2   3   4   5   6   7   Strongly agree

Client-Therapist Relationship

20. The client and I had similar views of the nature of the client's problems.

    Strongly disagree   1   2   3   4   5   6   7   Strongly agree

21. The client and I had similar views of the nature of change occurring in counseling/therapy (how helpful it really was).

    Strongly disagree   1   2   3   4   5   6   7   Strongly agree

22. Counseling/therapy seemed relatively unimportant to this client.

    Strongly disagree   1   2   3   4   5   6   7   Strongly agree

23. The client seemed to avoid thinking about what was discussed in counseling/therapy sessions between the sessions.

    Strongly disagree   1   2   3   4   5   6   7   Strongly agree

Client Insight

24. The client was never quite able to understand the factors that contributed to his/her conflicts.

    Strongly disagree   1   2   3   4   5   6   7   Strongly agree

25. The client achieved some measure of "insight" in counseling/therapy.

    Strongly disagree   1   2   3   4   5   6   7   Strongly agree

26. The client failed to understand his/her part in current problems.

    Strongly disagree   1   2   3   4   5   6   7   Strongly agree

27. The client was better able to integrate feeling and intellect by the end of counseling/therapy.

    Strongly disagree   1   2   3   4   5   6   7   Strongly agree

Time-Limited therapy

28. The client seemed to feel comfortable with the time limits by the end of counseling/therapy.

    Strongly disagree   1   2   3   4   5   6   7   Strongly agree

29. The counselor seemed to feel comfortable with the time limits by the end of counseling/therapy.

    Strongly disagree   1   2   3   4   5   6   7   Strongly agree

30. A central focus was established early in treatment and maintained throughout treatment.

    Strongly disagree   1   2   3   4   5   6   7   Strongly agree

Note—Subscale titles were not given to respondents.

Appendix K

Semistructured Interview Questionnaire

INTERVIEW PROTOCOL

Client Name_____Date_____

Interviewer Names_____

1. How often do you think about what happened in counseling/therapy?

2. What are some of the things you have learned about yourself in counseling/therapy that seem especially important to you?

3. While you were coming to the Counseling Center, to what extent did you think about what had been discussed in your sessions between sessions?

4. In what ways, if any, have you changed since ending counseling/therapy?

5. How much of what was learned in counseling/therapy applies to your current life? (Elaborate)

6. To what extent can you open up and discuss your intimate feelings with people you are close to: (Is there any change in this from before counseling/therapy to end of counseling/therapy to now?)

7. Who are the people you are able to do that with? Has that changed?

8. Is there any change in the way you cope with problems now as compared to before you began counseling/therapy?

9. Do you feel there was "unfinished business" in counseling/therapy? (If yes, can you tell me some more about it).

   b) If so, to what extent have you attempted to continue those efforts?

10. Have you had any additional counseling or therapy sessions since completing your sessions with Dr. _____ at the Counseling Center? (specify frequency, nature, duration, and evaluation)

11. How do you feel about yourself now as compared to six months ago?

12. What accounts for that change? (or lack of change)

13. To what extent were you able to continue on your own the growth you may have experienced in counseling/therapy? Can you elaborate?

14. In your view, what happened in counseling/therapy that may have allowed you to continue working on your own. (If that did not occur, what might have prevented you from continuing on your own?)

15. Some people have theorized that one of the main advantages of TLT is that it sets a change process in motion in the student receiving it; that is, what it serves to do is build the kind of readiness in the student so that when he or she stops counseling he or she is ready to continue or even accelerate the growth that has occurred during counseling.

    For example, some students have reported that while only some change occurs during counseling, major changes occur afterwards, and these seem in some way tied to what the student learned during counseling.

    Has this occurred for you? If so, how?

Appendix L

Definitions of Factors in the Therapist Orientation Questionnaire*

TOQ Factors Labels and Definitions, from Sundland (1972)

I. *Social Criteria for Success and Deliberate Directiveness (5 items):* Taps the therapist's acceptance of the desirability of adjustment toward the goals of society and the therapist's directing his/her patients toward those goals.

II. *Affective Gains (5 items):* Focuses on therapist's belief that the most important element of therapeutic gain is a learning process that is affective, nonverbal and nonconceptual.

III. *Training, Planning, and Conceptualizing (9 items):* Assesses the therapist's reliance on knowledge of and training in psychopathology and therapeutic techniques and his/her belief in the development of an overall treatment strategy. Low scores reflect the therapist's reliance on his/her own personality and spontaneity.

*Therapist orientation scale factors, labels, and definitions from D. M. Sundland, Therapist Orientation Questionnaire, Up-to-Date, presented at the Third Annual Meeting of the Society for Psychotherapy Research, Nashville, June, 1972. Reprinted by permission of the author. Cluster labels and definitions from K. I. Howard, D. C. Orlinsky, and J. H. Trattner, Therapist orientation and patient experience in psychotherapy, *Journal of Counseling Psychology,* 1970, *17,* 263–270. Copyright 1970 by the American Psychological Association. Reprinted by permission of the author.

IV. *Verbal Learning and Cognitive Gains (6 items):* Taps the extent to which the therapist considers the client's cognitive understanding through a verbal, conceptual process to be the central aspect of therapeutic gain.

V. *Psychoanalytic Techniques (9 items):* Focuses on the therapist's belief in unconscious motivation and use of classical psychoanlaytic techniques.

VI. *Active, Involved Therapist (6 items):* Reflects the therapist's degree of emotional, personal involvement in therapeutic relationships (high scores), as opposed to an objective, impersonal approach.

VII. *Therapist Security (4 items):* Probes the degree to which the therapist does not admit to feelings of insecurity, discomfort, and/or nonunderstanding in some therapeutic relationships.

VIII. *Informal Behavior (6 items):* Indicates the extent to which the therapist is willing to deviate from his/her formal therapeutic stance with a patient, e.g., offer patient a ride, social visit at patient's home, physical touch.

IX. *Inherent Growth (4 items):* Focuses on the philosophical belief by the therapist in an innate tendency within people which moves them toward physical and mental health.

X. *Interruptive Activity (7 items):* Ascertains the therapist's approval of being, in general, an active talkative therapist.

TOQ Cluster Labels and Definitions, from Howard et al. (1970)

I. *Psychoanalytic Orientation (13 items):* This cluster reflects an approach to therapy in which the therapist maintains a careful, passive, impersonal, theoretically orthodox position with respect to the client, and employs free association and analytic dream interpretation to seek unconscious and infantile determinents of behavior.

II. *Impersonal Learning vs. Personal Relationship (8 items):* This is a bipolar cluster in which one pole (Impersonal Learning) emphasizes therapy as a verbal, conceptual learning process which is best facilitated by a controlled, nonevaluative, impersonal manner in the therapist. The other pole (Personal Relationship) stresses nonverbal, affective communication in the patient-therapist relationship as the basic therapeutic process which is best facilitated by a frank, spontaneous, personal manner in the therapist.

III. *Therapist Role Responsibility (2 items):* Cluster three seems undefinable to us. Howard et al. say that the cluster "represents the therapists taking the responsibility for "sensitivity and helpfulness toward the patient." High scores represent the belief that the therapist must be empathically understanding and constantly and deliberately use his/her thorough knowledge of psychopathology and his/her training in techniques to help patients.

IV. *Inner Experience (7 items):* This cluster assesses the therapist's attention to the client's inner experience as the prime target of therapy, as opposed to the client's manifest social behavior.

V. *Therapist Directiveness (5 items):* The final cluster taps the "tendency to prescribe an actively guiding, instructing, confronting therapeutic approach intended to improve the patient's social adjustment."

Appendix M

TOQ Active-Directiveness Subscale Items

+ 8. Primary emphasis should be placed on the patient's manifest behavior.

+ 9. People can be understood without recourse to the concept "unconscious determinants of behavior."

+11. The patient's coming to experience his feelings more fully is *not* the most important therapeutic result.

−20. With most patients I do analytic dream interpretation.

−23. I instruct most patients to free associate.

+25. I am a fairly active, talkative therapist, compared to most therapists.

+33. The patient should be directly confronted with evidence of his irrational thoughts and behavior.

---

*Items from D. M. Sundland, Therapist Orientation Questionnaire, Up-to-Date, paper presented at the Third Annual Meeting of the Society for Psychotherapy Research, Nashville, June, 1972. Adapted by permission of the author.

+34. It is possible to make sense of a patient's behavior without assuming motives of which he is unaware.

−39. For a patient to improve his current way of life, he must come to understand his early childhood relationships.

−45. It is important to analyze the transference reactions of the patient.

−47. I am a fairly passive, silent therapist, compared to most therapists.

−51. The more effective therapists do things during the therapeutic hour for which they have no reasoned basis, merely a feeling that it is right.

+52. For a patient to improve his current way of life, he does *not* necessarily have to come to understand his early childhood relationships.

+59. Effective therapists almost always know what they are doing, and why, and where they are heading.

Note. The minus sign preceding an item indicates a negatively loaded item; the plus sign, a positively loaded item.

Appendix N

Goal Statement Inventory*

Instructions: Please consider your knowledge of this client <u>at this time</u> and <u>the type of therapy structure</u> to which the client has been assigned. Indicate your expectation as to whether each of the following items <u>would</u> or <u>would not</u> describe a treatment goal for your work with this client in this type of treatment, by checking the appropriate line.

Would be a goal	Would NOT be a goal	
————	————	1. Understand relation between her physical symptoms and her emotional problems
————	————	2. Improve marital or family adjustment
————	————	3. Achieve specific reality goals (e.g., get a job, change residence, develop new interests)
————	————	4. Develop more effective controls over her behavior (e.g., reduce hostile outbursts, acting out)
————	————	5. Increase awareness of patterns of reacting to significant others
————	————	6. Improve occupational adjustment
————	————	7. Increase self-esteem, self-confidence, or self-assertiveness

*From D. M. McNair and M. Lorr. Three kinds of therapy goals, *Journal of Clinical Psychology,* 1964, *20,* 390–393. Copyright 1964 by the Clinical Psychology Publishing Co., Inc. Adapted by permission of the publisher.

_____ _____ 8. Develop or increase motivation for psychotherapy

_____ _____ 9. Understand relation of past experiences to present difficulties

_____ _____ 10. Stabilize and prevent worsening of present adjustment without major personality changes

_____ _____ 11. Reduce current manifest anxiety or tension

_____ _____ 12. Reduce or alleviate some currently disabling symptom

_____ _____ 13. Increase awareness of unconscious motives, conflicts and feelings underlying her problems

_____ _____ 14. Improve sexual adjustment

_____ _____ 15. Understand her responsibility for her problems and treatment of them

_____ _____ 16. Relate to others more easily and with less friction

_____ _____ 17. Loosen or reduce excessive defenses

_____ _____ 18. Realistically accept and deal with her present limitations

_____ _____ 19. Strengthen current defenses

_____ _____ 20. Handle a current crisis more effectively

_____ _____ 21. Experience corrective emotional experiences within therapeutic relationship

_____ _____ 22. Improve relations with authority figures

_____ _____ 23. Understand relation between current emotional life and current life situation

_____ _____ 24. "Work through" a specific pathological pattern (e.g., guilt reaction, blind spot)

_____ _____ 25. Release inhibited hostility or aggression

_____ _____ 26. Develop more effective reality testing

_____ _____ 27. Alleviate a specific concern by providing reassurance (e.g., she is not deranged, does not have VD)

_____ _____ 28. Accept and trust the therapist and see him/her as a person genuinely interested in her

_____ _____ 29. Satisfy her dependency needs within the therapeutic relationship

_____ _____ 30. Remain out of a neuro-psychiatric hospital

Appendix O

Items Comprising Goal Scales of the Goal Statement Inventory

Reconstructive Goals
9. Understand relation of past experiences to present difficulties
13. Increase awareness of unconscious motives, conflicts, and feelings underlying her problem
23. Understand relation between current emotional life and current life situation
24. "Work through" a specific pathological pattern (e.g., guilt reaction, blind spot)
17. Loosen or reduce excessive defenses
22. Improve relations with authority figures
5. Increase awareness of patterns of reacting to significant others
25. Release inhibited hostility or aggression
8. Develop or increase motivation for psychotherapy
21. Experience corrective emotional experiences within therapeutic relationship
15. Understand her responsibility for her problems and treatment of them
1. Understand relation between her physical symptoms and her emotional problems
7. Increase self-esteem, self-confidence, or self-assertiveness
14. Improve sexual adjustment

*From D. M. McNair and M. Lorr. Three kinds of therapy goals, *Journal of Clinical Psychology*, 1964, *20*, 390–393. Copyright 1964 by the Clinical Psychology Publishing Co., Inc. Reprinted by permission of the publisher.

Stabilization Goals

30. Remain out of a neuropsychiatric hospital
10. Stabilize and prevent worsening of present adjustment, without major personality changes
27. Alleviate a specific concern by providing reassurance (e.g., she is not deranged, does not have VD)
18. Realistically accept and deal with her present limitations
19. Strengthen current defenses
26. Develop more effective reality testing
29. Satisfy her dependency needs within the therapeutic relationship
28. Accept and trust the therapist and see him or her as a person genuinely interested in her

Situational Adjustment Goals

6. Improve occupational adjustment
3. Achieve specific reality goals (e.g., get a job, change residence, develop new interests)
4. Develop more effective controls over her behavior (e.g., reduce hostile outbursts, acting out)
16. Relate to others more easily and with less friction
20. Handle a current crisis more effectively

Goals with No Significant Factor Correlation

11. Reduce current manifest anxiety or tension
12. Reduce or alleviate some currently disabling symptoms
2. Improve marital or family adjustment

Appendix P

Therapy Process Questionnaire

Counselor's Name_____ Date_____

Client's Name_____ Session # _____ Week # _____

Which type of client is this?

A. Time-unlimited
B. Time-limited-12-session
C. Time-limited-other-than-12-session. Please specify the nature of the limit_____

_____

INSTRUCTIONS. Please check the items that occurred this session only, and answer the open-ended items as completely as possible. MANY THANKS!!

I. SCHEDULING
_____ The client called or stopped in to cancel this session.
_____ The client no-showed this session.
If you checked either of the above items, don't continue responding to this questionnaire. Thank you.

_____ The client was late for this session (5 minutes or more).

_____ The client left this session early.

_____ The client talked about leaving this session early, but stayed the entire session

_____ The client indicated that s/he would be unable to meet at the regular time for the next session, and s/he asked for a schedule change.

_____ There were one or more emergency contacts between this session and the last session. Please specify the nature of the contact.

_____

_____ The client asked for or made scheduling changes. Please specify._____

_____

II. MENTION OF TIME LIMITS   Omit this section if the client is time-unlimited.

_____ The client asked for more sessions.

_____ The client implied more time would be desirable.

_____ The client mentioned which session it is—as a reminder, complaint, etc., without the therapist bringing it up first.

_____ The client asked which session it is/how many sessions left.

_____ The client incorrectly remembered which session it is.

_____ The client dealt with the time limit in other ways. Please specify.

_____

III. COUNSELING GOALS   Omit this section if you and the client have not explicitly discussed and determined a central problem for counseling.

_____ The central problem was discussed and determined for the first time this session..

_____ The central problem was discussed and determined in an earlier session. If so, in which session? _____

_____ The client showed improvement in symptoms in the area of the central problem this session.

_____ The client showed re-appearance of symptoms in the area of the central problem this session.

_____ The client showed worsening of symptoms in the area of central problem this session.

_____ The client presented new issues, aside from the agreed-upon central problem during this session.

_____ The client dealt with the central problem in other ways. Please specify.

How *specific* do you and the client see your formulation of the central problem for counseling?

1	2	3	4	5	6	7	8	9
Highly								Highly
General								Circumscribed

What is the central problem for counseling?_____

_____

IV. SATISFACTION/DISSATISFACTION

How satisfied do you think the client was with *this* counseling session?

1	2	3	4	5	6	7	8	9
Very								Very
Dissatisfied								Satisfied

How do you know about the client's level of satisfaction with this session?

_____ The client expressed it directly.
_____ The client expressed it indirectly. How?_____
_____ The client didn't express it; I am assuming the level of satisfaction with this session.

How satisfied do you think the client was with the therapist this session?

1	2	3	4	5	6	7	8	9
Very								Very
Dissatisfied								Satisfied

How do you know about the client's level of satisfaction with the therapist this counseling session?

_____ The client expressed it directly.
_____ The client expressed it indirectly. How?_____
_____ The client didn't express it; I am assuming the level of satisfaction with the therapist this session.

V. RESISTANCE

How much resistance to therapy did the client show this session?

1	2	3	4	5	6	7	8	9
Little								Much
Resistance								Resistance

Did the client show any of the following behaviors?

_____ The client was unusually silent this session.

_____ The client was unusually withholding this session.

_____ The client asked personal questions about the therapist this session.

_____ The client was unusually chatty this session.

_____ The client discussed the physical surroundings of the room or Center this session.

_____ The client did an unusually large amount of "story telling" this session.

_____ The client did an unusually large amount of talking about others this session.

_____ The client avoided, to an unusual degree talking about him/herself this session.

_____ The client inappropriately praised, to an unusual degree, the therapy this session.

_____ The client inappropriately praised, to an unusual degree, the therapist this session.

_____ The client demeaned, to an unusual degree, the therapy this session.

_____ The client demeaned, to an unusual degree, the therapist this session.

_____ The client showed resistance to therapy in other ways. Please specify, and you may use examples from other sections in this response if they constitute resistance—i.e., if the client being late for a session was seen as resistance, please note.

_____

_____

_____

VI. TERMINATION

_____ The client terminated counseling prematurely this session (against the judgment of the therapist).

_____ The client terminated counseling this session by mutual therapist/client agreement.

_____ The client showed satisfaction about impending termination this session.

_____ The client showed dissatisfaction about impending termination this session.

_____ The client dealt with termination in other ways. Please specify.

_____

VII. OTHER

In what ways, if any, did the client deviate from his/her normal style of interaction in this session?

Index

261